MICHELLE OGUNDEHIN

HAPPY INSIDE

EBURY
PRESS

FOR DAD
(1942–2017)
I WISH I COULD HAVE PUT THIS ALL
INTO PLAY IN TIME TO HELP YOU

CONTENTS

AWAKENING

1

INTENTION

2

BALANCE

3

ENERGY

4

ACTION

'What day is it?' asked Pooh.
'It's today,' squeaked Piglet.
'My favourite day,' said Pooh.

A.A. MILNE
ENGLISH NOVELIST, POET AND PLAYWRIGHT
(1882-1956)

AWAKENING

'PEACE. IT DOES NOT MEAN TO BE IN A PLACE WHERE THERE IS NO NOISE, TROUBLE OR HARD WORK. IT MEANS TO BE IN THE MIDST OF THOSE THINGS AND STILL BE CALM IN YOUR HEART.'

ANONYMOUS

This book is your nine-chapter guide to a new way of thinking about your home. It is the path to a more empowered you, as well as something of a manifesto for self-responsibility. Because, the establishment of a happy home – one that makes you feel fantastic, not one that just looks good – can be the ultimate foundation for the life you dare to dream of having, and the nurturing relationships that you need to believe you deserve. From such a space you can achieve a sense of emotional balance that will assist you in finding your true purpose and fulfilling your potential. It can be the launch pad from which to achieve a sense of flow in your work, and most importantly, it will be your place of retreat and recovery when the winds of change and the inevitable curveballs of life attempt to knock you, or your loved ones, off course.

'The purpose of life – to be happy inside.
The purpose of home – to be happy inside.'

After all, home should be a place that restores, rejuvenates and replenishes, but so often it does not. Instead, it can sabotage heartfelt desires by dampening your emotions and causing undue stress and strife. Your home also acts as a mirror to the current state of your emotions, thus amplifying both nurturing or unwelcome states of being: whether you're happy or stressed, tired or relaxed, your home will reflect, and magnify, it all. So, if you want positive personal change of any sort, you must first address your environment. We all need homes that support, rather than undermine, our wellbeing.

But how do we define wellbeing? For the purposes of this book, I understand it to be a state of self whereby you feel ready to seize each day as it comes, whatever it may throw at you. In other words, that you operate from a solid foundation of balanced contentment – of happiness. And this is no wishy-washy conceit. Life today is increasingly unpredictable, hectic, fast and always 'on', and it shows no signs of slowing down. We are in the midst of what has been dubbed 'the Age of Anxiety', in which the superficial seems to reign supreme, infamy is more desirable than respect, consumerism is promoted at every turn and the

digital realm appears to have superseded reality. Against such a backdrop it is understandable to feel increasingly overwhelmed, and many in the West are struggling to cope with rising levels of poor mental health, obesity and chronic illness. And yet, while many supposed 'cures' treat the symptoms, they appear to do little to address what might lie behind such a growth in recorded disease. And this should be cause for great concern.

For all our advanced technology and supposed sophistication, we are at heart primal, emotional beings, which means that to feel centred, healthy and happy, we also need to feel safe, secure and protected. It is therefore increasingly essential that our homes support us, as nurturing, sensory, tactile retreats, not so much as insulation from contemporary life, but strengthening us, body and soul, to deal with it. Thankfully, whatever the size of your current home, whether it's rented or owned, and regardless of your present financial status, you have at your fingertips the most extraordinary potential. It simply needs to be awakened, and then harnessed in your favour. After all, according to decades of research, happy people live longer, exhibit fewer mental health issues, have more friends and do better at work, so it behoves us all to do everything possible to get with the *happy inside* programme. And happiness can be quantified, which means that there are measurable steps that can be taken towards its attainment. In the opinion of Martin Seligman, widely regarded as one of the founding fathers of the positive psychology movement, our individual states of happiness, or well-being, can be measured via five key contributing factors:

- OUR ABILITY TO ENGENDER POSITIVE EMOTIONS

- ENGAGEMENT IN ACTIVITIES THAT ALLOW US TO LOSE OURSELVES IN THE MOMENT

- THE NATURE OF OUR RELATIONSHIPS WITH OTHERS

- A SENSE OF BELONGING TO, AND SERVING, SOMETHING BIGGER THAN OURSELVES

- ACCOMPLISHMENT, WHERE ACHIEVEMENT IS PURSUED FOR ITS OWN SATISFACTION NOT EXTERIOR VALIDATION

To this I would also add the degree to which you feel in charge of your own destiny, and how much you consider that your very existence makes a difference to the world, at any level. Crucially, though, this is not about setting yourself up against ridiculous aesthetic standards – for example, by comparing your home with Instagram's constant, but highly curated, parade of interiors loveliness. Rather, the intention is to give you some ideas and recommendations, alongside the benefit of my hard-earned experience and a few tricks of the trade. This will help you to set up your home, and a way of living within it, to get you where you want to be at your own pace. There are no rules, per se, because there can be no absolutes or definitive answers when embarking on such a journey; it's ultimately up to you to make these suggestions your own. Besides, putting yourself under pressure 'to be happy' is more likely to derail any attempt than promote it. •

BUT WHO
IS YOUR HAPPY
HOME FOR?

Let me, though, now insert a brief pause for thought. Because, as the ancient Greek philosopher Aristotle said, 'Knowing thyself is the beginning of all wisdom'; so, do you know who you are? And more importantly, is this who you really want to be?

That might seem an odd question, but bear with me. I once took part in a 'life-coaching' exercise that at first sounded rather macabre. It was this: write your own eulogy. Shocked? Don't be. The point is to articulate how you would like to be remembered. And once you've done it, to ask yourself if you are that person today. After all, it's easy to look across the tracks and see successful people (however you might define 'success'), or those who appear to have found their purpose, or who radiate joy, and wonder what their secret is. We muse that perhaps they've only achieved it because they were born in the right place and at the right time or were just lucky. After all, it is much harder to think of our destiny or happiness as not only our own responsibility but also as something within our capacity to change, even if not to control.

Thus, as an exercise in self-reflection, contemplating your eulogy will show you who you truly aspire to be, and I'd encourage you to do it *before* you begin your home-health journey because it will in turn inspire a more holistic perspective on your *happy inside* goals. To put it another way, rather than asking yourself what do I want to achieve with my home, start with the question who do I want to be?

For example, you may already be thinking that you would like to be tidier, slimmer, fitter or better organised. But are these the qualities or characteristics that you'd want applauded at your funeral? Instead, might you wish to be remembered as someone who always had time for their friends? Someone who was a good listener? Someone who was seen to be calm in the face of adversity? A patient parent? Or an inspiring boss? These are the qualities of someone who is resilient, someone who can maintain their sense of self, integrity and ethical ambition, no matter what. These surely are the characteristics we should all aspire to? Not least because the pursuit of happiness is a multi-faceted endeavour, as we examined earlier, it can only benefit from being considered from all angles. Besides, if you set your sights on some of the above, you may well become tidier, slimmer, fitter and so forth along the way. But most crucially, and the core message of this book, is that you'll make everything a lot easier for yourself if you have your home on side to support you. •

SMOOTH SEAS DO NOT MAKE SKILFUL SAILORS

For myself, if I track back and recall all of the places that I have tried to make my own, it would tell you the story of my life. Each of these abodes taught me something about the link between the state of my environment and its impact on my life, from my relationships and finances to the state of my hormones and my feelings of self-worth – in other words, how much my emotional health and physical wellbeing were profoundly connected to, and affected by, the need for a grounded sense of home. This book represents the confluence of all those learnings and the summation of everything I believe so that you can have a smoother ride!

Of course, my early training as an architect sharpened my sensitivity to the way in which our bodies respond to, and our brains perceive, our surroundings; and my 13-year tenure as editor-in-chief of British *ELLE Decoration* also had an impact. In this role I witnessed the rise and demise of many a trend, and I saw hundreds of homes. The ones I chose to include in the magazine deliberately spanned a wide range of looks, styles, sizes and locations but they always had one thing in common: they were spaces that their owners showered with attention and affection, tangible expressions of the pleasure of being at home.

Other major influences include a fascination with many of the teachings of Buddhism as well as the traditional culture and mores of Japan. In each there is an underlying sensibility that speaks to me of quiet contemplation and considered living, and I have introduced elements of both throughout this book.

And so I encourage you to start immediately, while taking it step by step. Each stage is not hard in itself to achieve, but each requires genuine belief and commitment. My desire is for you to acquire new habits for the everyday rather than prompting a one-off burst of overzealous endeavour. And be patient. My rule of thumb is that you can only effect significant change in a minimum of 90 days. This process should therefore be understood as a continuous journey of evolution, just as we ourselves are constant works in progress when it comes to self-development. A desire to 'get the house done' within a set time frame helps no one, just as an attitude of getting personally 'fixed' is similarly flawed, if not unachievable. Certainly there will be a moment when particular rooms just feel right, and thus we feel good within them. This is what we're aiming for. Nevertheless, to repeat, it'll be at least three months before you really notice a difference. This isn't about racing to completion. In so many ways, the key to happiness is to focus on the process.

One caveat, though: if you have resolved to set off on this path to becoming *happy inside* (both inwardly and outwardly), be sure to be doing it for yourself. Don't half-heartedly shift around a few chairs and throw out some old cushions and then sit back and wait for it to happen. If you don't believe it will help, then it won't – the motivation behind any desire for change is as important as the intention to change in itself. Doing up a property to maximise profit on a sale is one thing, curating your individual corner of the world for the benefit of your own wellbeing is quite another. This book is devoted to the latter pursuit. So if you want to take the leap of faith that the state of your surroundings impacts every aspect of your life, then get the whole of your family, however you define it, on board for the exciting journey that is becoming *happy inside*. •

1

INTENTION

'THERE ARE ONLY TWO MISTAKES
ONE CAN MAKE ALONG THE ROAD
TO TRUTH; NOT GOING ALL THE WAY,
AND NOT STARTING.'

THE BUDDHA

The best homes begin with their inherent bone structure, whether glorious or flawed, and end with the careful placement of possessions. This book will help you to enhance, tweak and colour the former, and curate, choose and arrange the latter. You can read the chapters in any order, although as with many things in life, it's best to start at the beginning and work through to the end for optimum results. Essentially, chapters one to four are a sort of intensive foundation course, and chapters five to nine are how you put it all into practice. Therefore please think of this as your first module and one of the most important chapters in the book. Don't skip it; it underpins everything that follows.

CLEARING
THE WAY

The solution to a home that no longer seems to meet our needs is almost always thought to lie in an upgrade of some sort: more rooms, a larger garden, an extended kitchen. And while sometimes a few architectural interventions can indeed make a significant difference to the way you live, what if you don't own your own home or you can't afford to move or make extensive renovations? Besides, believing more is always the answer only reflects the pervasive conviction that a newer, bigger, faster, updated whatever must be better. This is nothing more than marketing, often based on a model of built-in obsolescence, which can blind us to the opportunities of the here and now. Instead, what would happen if we could lean into any nagging impulse to not settle where we are and with what we have? Answer: we become open to a more creative approach of acceptance.

From this perspective, acceptance is definitely *not* about passive resignation, but rather about seeing things as they really are, not clouded by emotion or prejudice. In this state of mind we do three things:

we seek solutions rather than complaining; we focus on finding beauty in the every-day; and we practise letting go, because we understand that resisting what 'is' is ultimately futile. In terms of the home, this spirit of acceptance enables us to actively work *with* what we have in order to maximise existing potential, rather than focusing on what we think we lack, bearing in mind that the most common issues tend to be a perceived scarcity of space or the desire for more light. •

'Believing more is always the answer reflects the pervasive conviction that a newer, bigger, faster, updated whatever must be better.'

IN PRAISE OF
WHAT YOU HAVE

You'll be cheered to know that creating more light can be approached in many inventive ways that do not involve knocking down walls, and we'll explore some of these in the following chapters. But in this chapter we shall resolve the seemingly perennial quest for more room. To set out my stall right from the off: it is my absolute belief that most people do *not* in fact need more space; they need less stuff, combined with a rethink of the space that they do have. And this starts with really questioning the draw of the new in pursuit of happiness – whether it be for a bigger home, a smarter car, the latest phone or the most fashionable clothes. After all, these accoutrements, and even the myth of the 'forever' home, will not protect you against fear, anxiety, disappointment or hurt.

In fact, these seductive flights of fancy create only what the Zen teacher Charlotte Joko Beck calls 'the substitute life': a parallel universe in which all things will be just so if only you acquire x, y or z. It is patently not true. Yet this escapist fiction is one that many buy into, compulsively heeding

the siren call of the constant upgrade, and putting themselves under undue financial pressure in the process – but at what emotional price? Are they actually able to stop working for long enough to enjoy any of those newly capacious rooms, eat out in their designer togs or use any of the fancy functions on that must-have tech?

You have to ask yourself, what's the point if all it's done is to shackle you either to debt that you can ill afford, or that you can but only if you keep on working at the pace you currently are, whether you enjoy your job or not? And if you have children, I absolutely guarantee that they'll be happier watching a movie squashed next to you on a saggy old sofa than having a nice big playroom all to themselves with a parent next door too exhausted to engage.

Thus, even if you feel that extra space is required to accommodate something that you ardently desire, such as an addition to the family, whether human or furry, or the pursuit of a new pastime or passion project, I'd like to propose that you work through the entirety of this chapter before taking another step in the home-expansion direction.

And most especially if you're reading this thinking, but I haven't got room to swing a cat, let alone own one – I promise you, you have more space than you think.

I'd also like you to entertain the possibly uncomfortable thought that perhaps your impulse to move or upgrade is driven not so much by heartfelt desire as self-aggrandisement – the perceived admiration of friends and neighbours, a sign to the outside world that you have 'made it'? After all, it's a truism that the larger the house, the more likely everyone's in the den – human beings *need* cosy corners, as much as they need room to move. And how often have I seen people invest in a massive rear extension only to have front rooms left completely empty. Sadly, this is often the result of pursuing what you intuitively think you need (more light and space), but going about it in completely the wrong way.

As touched upon in the 'Awakening' introduction, getting to the heart of *why* you're undertaking this journey is imperative. You do not need as much as you think to have a meaningful life. The path to peace is not lined with possessions. •

---

*'You do not need as much as you think to have a meaningful life.
The path to peace is not lined with possessions.'*

WHAT'S THE
POINT
OF IT ALL?

2
4

In America there is a growing movement called FIRE dedicated to precisely this (the acronym stands for Financial Independence, Retire Early). In short, it's about living deliberately *below* your means, simplifying and reclaiming your life by resisting the lure and associated pressure of consumerism. Its followers aim to work hard in their twenties and thirties while maximising savings and investments such that they can quit work in their forties, specifically once they have children, to have a life that's rich in leisure time if poor in supposed luxuries. It even has its own lingo: there are those who practise 'lean FIRE' (extreme frugality), 'fat FIRE' (maintaining a more typical standard of living while saving and investing) and 'barista FIRE' (working part time in a coffee chain after retiring, in order to be eligible for the company health insurance). Without a doubt I feel this movement will spread, especially when we link such personal initiative with the knock-on benefits to the environment: buying less but better is a win-win all round. Perhaps not for those

CHAPTER ONE

manufacturers who seek to lure us with the unsustainable and the unnecessary, but voting with your wallet is a sure step towards the wider change we need to see.

It reminds me too of David Fincher's film of Chuck Palahniuk's 1996 novel *Fight Club*, in which Brad Pitt plays Tyler Durden, the alter ego of Edward Norton's unnamed lead character. Tyler is the embodiment of everything Norton, a white-collar worker in an insurance company, fears he is not. In the opening scenes, Norton intones that like many others he has 'become a slave to the IKEA nesting instinct'. Perusing catalogues and asking himself 'what kind of dining set defines me as a person?' Shortly afterwards, his entire apartment and all of his possessions are lost in an explosion. Norton's response: 'I was close to being complete and now it's all gone.' And yet Tyler, later revealed in the film to have been the perpetrator of this act of arson, reflects a different perspective: 'We are consumers. We are by-products of the lifestyle obsession. Martha Stewart is

polishing the brass on the *Titanic*! It's all going down. I say *never* be complete. Stop being perfect. Let's evolve, let the chips fall where they may.'

'You're right, it's just stuff,' sighs Norton.

'Correct,' snaps back the fired-up Durden. 'The things you own end up owning you. You are *not* your job. You are *not* how much money you have in the bank. You are *not* the car you drive.'

While I'm certainly not advocating destroying all of your things in a wanton act of explosive destruction, I love this film for its brutal lampooning of today's consumerist culture. It compels you to take a moment to consider, 'What *is* my self-worth tied up in – the size of my home, my job title? The fact that I own an original Charles Eames lounge chair? And is this who I really want to be? Do my things complete me, or could I be perfect in my imperfection already?'

As a final example, let's consider the American multi-billionaire Warren Buffett, globally renowned as one of the most successful investors of all time in his capacity as chairman and CEO of Berkshire Hathaway, and accordingly cited as the third wealthiest person in the world (number one is the man behind Amazon, Jeff Bezos, and number two Buffett's long-time friend and fellow philanthropist, Microsoft founder Bill Gates). Buffett famously lives in the same modestly sized, 6,570 square-foot (610 square-metre), five-bedroom house that he bought in Omaha, Nebraska, for $31,500 in 1958 (worth about $650,000 today; less than 0.001 per cent of his net worth), and has been known to take his own lunch of a McDonald's quarter-pounder and fries to his annual general meetings.

Arguably he could afford any McMansion he likes within immense private grounds, and he could dine at his pick of restaurants, or at the very least get his burger delivered. But he does not, and his choices speak not of miserliness but of immense confidence and strength of character. They say that he has nothing to prove to anyone but himself. He knows what he likes and, more crucially, he knows what he needs. As he puts it when speaking about his home, 'I'm happy there. I'd move if I thought I'd be happier someplace else.' And yet many a website and newspaper column inch has been devoted to this perceived madness. Why on earth, the journalists squeak, would he not buy something bigger? Answer: because he doesn't have to. It's Tyler Durden all over again. Or, to quote the Greek philosopher Socrates, 'The truly free individual is free only to the extent of his own self-mastery, while those who will not govern themselves are condemned to find masters to govern over them.' So, do you wish to be governed by your stuff? •

IT'S ALL
ABOUT
CONSIDERED
LIVING

How, then, if we're going to stay put, do we make homes that enable us to be at our authentic best while also facilitating all of the activities that can make us happy and keep us healthy? How do we create a sense of space (physical and emotional) *between* ourselves and the world at large? For it's surely only in this gap that the opportunity for happiness resides.

Well, let's shout this loud and clear, with no room whatsoever for doubt: the first step is the wholehearted banishment of clutter! Clutter is the arch-enemy of the restful home. It is the interiors equivalent of a to-do list that never gets completed, undermining any attempt at relaxation. Physical clutter equates to emotional debris, stifling energy and dampening enthusiasm. But before you think, 'Oh, clutter-clearing – been there, done that,' I encourage you to approach this chapter with what the Japanese call *shoshin*, a word from Zen Buddhism that translates as 'beginner's mind'.

It is an important principle that invites you to adopt an attitude of openness and the willingness to forgo preconceptions. Cast aside any notions about what you *think* this section on clutter-clearing might entail, and allow yourself to revisit these ideas with a 'beginner's mind'. After all, in order to make lasting change, we sometimes need to return to certain teachings again and again for them to truly sink in.

And when I refer to clutter-clearing, I do not mean just the physical act of disposing of excess belongings, but also the setting of a clear intention to continually commit to reducing the amount that you buy, and therefore own, by truly understanding why this process is so incredibly important. The ultimate goal is consistent considered curation – limiting the distractions that surround you while increasing what supports you, so that you can focus fully on living a purposeful life. It is not, however, about a home devoid of all possessions. •

' The ultimate goal is consistent considered curation – limiting the distractions that surround you while increasing what supports you, so that you can focus fully on living a purposeful life.'

LET'S DEBUNK SOME
CLUTTER-CLEARING MYTHS

IT'S ALL ABOUT STORAGE

Installing extra closets, buying lots of natty little baskets in which to subdivide everything, fitting extra drawers under shelves or into stair risers, or any of those other bonkers tricks that magazines love to suggest (and yes, I've published those features in the past too), just invites the filling of them. Neatly dividing what you already have and stealthily distributing it around your home is to miss the point. You need to actively get rid of stuff, not just reorganise and tidy it.

IT'S ALL ABOUT MINIMALISM

In my opinion, minimalism is a physical manifestation of an emotional state, one that seeks to negate every aspect of the self and to erase one's personal story. I think it only ever springs from a position of profound discontent. That said, for some people this is necessary: it is the embodiment of a clean slate, which can be a very brave move indeed towards a new

beginning, so I hold no judgement. However, this is not what I'm recommending. Clutter-clearing for me is not so much about aesthetics as efficiency.

YES, BUT EVEN IF IT'S NOT ALL ABOUT MINIMALISM, IT'S ABOUT GETTING RID OF LOADS OF YOUR THINGS

Nope. Your *things* should be seen, as the evidence of the narrative of your life (single or shared), of the hard-won toil of your evolution, with all its glorious ups and downs, twists and turns. Such objects are absolutely wonderful and they should be treasured accordingly, even if they have little material value. But then value is never about cost, it's about stories – where something came from, who you were (or were with) when you bought it, what was happening in your life at that time. Your *things* are your talismans, and they should be celebrated. Note: disliked things belonging to a partner are still their things; do not discard them without their permission! However, 'stuff' is different. 'Stuff' keeps you tethered to the ground when you're aiming to take wing and soar. 'Stuff' you can live without. So if you can't be bothered to dust it, clean it, polish, oil or otherwise look after it, then you need to think deeply about whether to keep it. And I have listed in detail the items that this might include in the next section.

YOU ONLY NEED TO DO IT ONCE

For sure there is often one huge burst of activity at the very beginning of this journey, but then it is a case of constant maintenance. Things will come in all the time, from birthday gifts to weekend newspapers. The goal is to have created such a perfectly curated space that, on the one hand, you do not buy unnecessary items on impulse, whether ceramic pots or black cashmere jumpers, and, on the other, that you get into the mindset of consciously questioning future purchases along the lines of 'Where will this go? Is this the best version that I can afford of what I need?' And then, 'Why do I want it in the first place, and do I *really* need it?' After all, it is perfectly possible to admire something in a shop, to love it deeply and appreciate its craftsmanship, but ultimately to leave it behind because you simply do not require it. Try to start thinking of shops as galleries where it's perfectly okay to be 'just looking'. No matter how gorgeous something is, as the author Richard R. Powell puts it in his book *Wabi Sabi Simple*, a meditation on the Japanese notion of the beauty in imperfection, 'If it enters your life only to become part of the general background chaos, better to leave it on the store shelf.' However, if you spot something and, regardless of any of the above, it sparks veritable fireworks of love 'n' lust, then purchase away, but know that inevitably something else will have to be displaced to make room for it. I find this latter lesson a good one to teach children too, as in, 'Yes, you may have that new toy, but what will you give away to make space for it?'

YOU DO IT AFTER YOU'VE SORTED OUT ROOM LAYOUTS AND ARCHITECTURE

No. No. Definitely no! It is simply not possible to plan a truly, holistically supportive space around things that you already own without sorting thoroughly through them first. Before you pick up a single paint brush, prior to losing yourself in wallpaper lookbooks or coveting a single stick of new furniture, you must declutter. And as I intimated at the beginning of this chapter, do not even think of moving house before you've completely worked through this section either. •

TIME TO
LET GO

And so it begins. As you start to reassess your belongings, determining which are your *things* versus what is just *stuff*, I'd like you to make a list, room by room, of every single item you own. Yes. Every. Single. Item. At this stage you can group together things like kitchen utensils, knives, forks, etc., and also multiples of the same type of thing, from trousers to dresses, duvet covers to throws, tumblers to plates, but add the quantity for each and divide books into hardbacks, paperbacks and picture/reference books and list the total of these for the whole house, not by room. Everything else gets a line of its own. Don't forget all of your accessories, pots and planters, curtains, floor coverings, artworks and removable shelving. Basically, anything that does not constitute the fixed architecture of your home. I also need you to put an approximation of the original purchase price next to each item (a total price for grouped items will suffice at this stage).

It'll take you ages, and at times you will surely lose the will to live, but that's the point. Without doing this, you will never truly acknowledge the mass of perfectly serviceable 'stuff' that you have accumulated and that you do not need but which nonetheless lives on in the background of your consciousness. This is beyond the old biros and clogged-up tins of paint for rooms that have long since changed their colour (all of which you can chuck out as you go, by the way); I'm talking about the excess stuff we tend to overlook: the surplus pillow cases and sheets, the novels you'll never read again, kitchen appliances you'll never use, and definitely clothing. One exception: I firmly maintain that you can *never* have too many cushions! (See Chapter 6.)

The thing is, the average home contains 300,000 items, and yet you will probably make regular use of less than a third of them. The same goes for your wardrobe; we habitually wear one-third of the clothes we own. Your mission is to assess the other two-thirds of everything.

For example, it may seem like sacrilege to propose getting rid of books, but there will doubtlessly be some on your shelves that you didn't particularly enjoy, or never finished and never will, so pass them on. I used to collect fancy (and expensive) hardback, slipcased editions of the classics, Charles Dickens et al. I rather imagined myself as someone who would one day read them all, having somehow managed to skip the majority at school. However, in undertaking my own clearing mission I recognised that in truth I had no interest whatsoever in reading these books, which is why I never did in the first place, and thus I probably never would. So why was I holding on to them? Most had not even been removed from their original cellophane wrappings. Just bought and filed for some fantasy future or, my last excuse, acquired because I thought my children might like to read them one day. Eventually I sold them all on eBay, made some money back, and struck them off my insurance list, which brings me smartly on to my next point.

A secondary benefit of a full possessions inventory (the first of course being you on your way to a newly streamlined home) is that you can ensure that you are adequately insured. Far too many people significantly underinsure themselves thinking they're making a canny saving on their annual premiums. This is the worst kind of false economy because what many don't realise until it's too late is that, in the event of a disaster, most insurers will pay only the corresponding percentage of the claim, *even if that value falls well below the total sum covered*. In other words, if you've valued your contents at £50,000, but they are actually worth £100,000, in the event of a claim for £25,000, you might get as little as half that sum back because you're effectively 50 per cent underinsured. The key omissions for most people are the true value of the contents of their wardrobe, the cost to replace carpets, blinds and curtains (although in some policies this is covered under buildings insurance, so check the small print), ornaments, children's toys, and artworks.

And if you're thinking I've strayed off on something of a dull tangent by mentioning insurance, it's deliberate. A true desire for change comes from a meeting of the head and heart: the confluence of the emotional and the practical; the want-to-do balanced by the why-should-I-do-it. So, clutter-clear because you wish to give yourself a sense of freedom to really live your life, but also do it so that you don't pay under, or over, the odds for insurance. And if the worst should happen, you have the comfort of knowing that you can instantly quantify every single thing that you'd like replaced: ergo, pragmatic *and* purposeful motivation! •

I HAVE
MY LIST – NOW
WHAT?

Now that you have your painfully constructed list, the really in-depth sorting
begins. What to keep and what to let go.
And while the Japanese tidying goddess
Marie Kondo is absolutely on the right
track with her mantra of keeping only those
things which spark joy, it's also about keeping things that trigger memories and record
significant moments, happy *and* sad. They
may well be one and the same in some in-
stances, but in others they are very different.

If I were to draw an emotional parallel,
I'd say it's like understanding that when you
acknowledge that you have been hurt it can
fortify, rather than diminish you, leaving
you knowing yourself that much better
and thus able to move on with purpose in
search of new love – in effect, you become,
to paraphrase Ernest Hemingway, stronger
in the broken places. No need to surround
yourself with photographs of a former partner to remind you of the lessons learned,
but that little trinket you self-gifted when
you were feeling miserable, absolutely yes.
Being wrapped in the comfort blanket of

'You must keep only that which is truly useful, fit for purpose, and the best that you can afford.'

memory is not the same as wallowing; the former respects where you've come from, the latter is getting stuck there.

Additionally, you must keep only that which is truly useful, fit for purpose and the best that you can afford. After all, I'm not sure that my kitchen spatulas exactly inspire crescendos of emotion of any sort, but they are certainly simple, durable, made of wood, and not chipped, broken or burnt, so they get respect, and they get to stay. But all those old magazines? Slightly dodgy flea-market knick-knacks? Mismatched bowls and plates? Easy to let go. After all, your cast-offs may well be someone else's treasure. Let them go so they can have a chance to be loved again. But spare anythings, extra some-things, items that were gifts? Not so easy. Here, then, are your sorting criteria for all the harder-to-clear stuff. (Note: as we move through chapters 5 to 8, which tackle indi-vidual home zones, I'll cover specific items to treasure or trash pertinent to kitchens, bedrooms and so on. This chapter is about the big picture.)

BROKEN THINGS THAT YOU'LL MEND ONE DAY

If it can't be done right this minute with a needle and thread or a tube of Super Glue, recycle or throw it away. Especially if you have children. I say this because as a very sage friend once said to me on spying my neatly stacked 'to-do-later' pile shortly be-fore I was due to give birth to my son, unless I tackled it straight away, it'd still be sitting there when he turned 18. I think I finally jettisoned the last of it when he was four.

MULTIPLES

It's okay to keep extras of things such as printer cartridges, plain paper, pens and paper clips, and essential to keep spare toi-let rolls, cleaning solutions, kitchen towels, batteries, bulbs and matches. But do you really need four sets of salad servers? Or two for the price of one of almost anything? They may seem like great savings in the moment, but where will you put all those extras? Unless you have some lovely empty shelving in a garage or basement expressly for the purpose of stockpiling basic items, only buy according to the space you have available. I even take issue with the old adage regarding bedlinen: one on the bed, one in the wash and one in the cupboard. Nope. You need one set on each bed and one spare per bed (the only exception being small children's beds to accommodate potential 'accidents'). Also, clearly this doesn't apply to crockery and cutlery, nor plants and my beloved cushions. However, even with crockery, do you really need 12 of everything if you're a family of three and never actually host dinner parties? (More on this in Chapter 7.)

ANYTHING YOU ARE INDIFFERENT TO

For example, if you dropped that fruit bowl and it broke, would you care? These are things you can definitely live without. Pass them on to someone who might genuinely appreciate them. This category also applies to things that no longer hold any fondness or relevance to you today: coin collections, stamp albums, old school exercise books. Although be careful here: sometimes it's

better to consolidate these items; rather than keeping the whole lot, you pull out a few favourites and honour them accordingly, in a frame or a new smaller album, because at some point they meant something to you, and this is your history. But you'll know when it's just rubbish: endless cuttings and tear sheets that smell damp because they've been kept unread in a box forever. Likewise magazines – will you really revisit them all? Or could you keep a few special editions rather than the whole set?

THE PRACTICAL BUT SELDOM USED

An item bought because you felt you ought to, but which you either don't use regularly enough to justify its existence or have lost the manual so you haven't a clue how to operate it now anyway. Here things often fall into the but-I-might-need-it-one-day camp. To which I say, okay, then hang on to it for another year and if you still haven't used it, get rid of it. After all, if it really came to it, you could probably borrow one through the ever-expanding sharing economy, or buy a new one (and then sell it on), as newer models will inevitably exist by the time you might actually need said very specific item, and they'll undoubtedly be far superior to whatever you have mouldering away in storage.

ANYTHING THAT ANNOYS YOU

That jug which always dribbles. A cup that's hard to hold because the handle is too small. Placemats that can only be hand-washed because otherwise the colour runs, so they're tricky to dry too. That figurine from a distant relative who hasn't yet real-ised that you're no longer six and not that madly into collecting china cats any more. We usually keep this stuff because it's not broken and therefore we feel we cannot in good conscience discard it. You can. It an-noys you. And you don't need that in your life. Trust me, someone else will love it.

ANYTHING THAT EMBARRASSES YOU

An adjunct to all of the above that's subtly different: that beloved but tatty dressing gown that you'd cringe if the postman actu-ally saw you wearing it; towels with holes in them; favourite but supremely ragged train-ers; permanently stained anythings. This is the sort of stuff we become immune to see-ing until it gets inadvertently pulled out in public and we find ourselves embarrassed, muttering excuses about having forgotten this or that was in such a state.

THINGS YOU HAVEN'T USED IN A YEAR

Self-explanatory, but also those things that we seem incapable of throwing away because, although there's nothing actually wrong with them, they don't appear to fit into any of the aforementioned categories: for example, old phones, kitchen gadgets, oversized serving dishes or outdated electrical appliances.

GIFTS

Sometimes when gifts have been received we feel obliged to keep them because they've been beautifully crafted, we love the designer or we appreciate the sentiment. But would you have gone out and spent your own cold hard cash on them? And, to be blunt, do you now want to pay the insurance premium on them? If not, perhaps they need to be reconsidered. Let's also take a moment to reassess the need for birthday presents in the first place. If there is something you truly desire and friends or family are happy to contribute towards or purchase it for you, then great, as long as it accords with our earlier criteria (acutely needed, best in class, fit for purpose, with emotional significance, etc.). But if there's nothing you really want, or need, why not suggest a shared experience instead? Our most precious commodity these days is time, so maybe a supper together, an evening spent putting those old photos into albums, or a long phone call might have infinitely more value than a random acquisition. This especially applies at Christmas (primarily for adults, that is). Stop perpetuating the stress of aimless consumerism by buying random tat nobody needs. Spend your money, and time, more meaningfully. After all, how would you feel if your purchases were immediately regifted or recycled?

'Our most precious commodity these days is time, so a supper together, or a long phone call might have infinitely more value than a random acquisition.'

37

JUST-IN-CASE ITEMS

You cannot live your life based on a wholly unquantifiable expectation of the future. It doesn't exist yet, and when it comes, have faith that whatever happens, you'll have everything you need to deal with it. In the meantime, perhaps you really could let go of the various just-in-case bits and bobs no doubt listed as 'miscellaneous' or 'other' on your inventory. Certainly you'll be a

'Never give things up in a spirit of self-sacrifice, nor must you throw out things that belong to someone else. Things disposed of in this manner will cause resentment, whether overtly or subliminally, and this is a sure-fire path to domestic disharmony.'

lot more prepared to deal with anything that might crop up if you've cleared your home to the point where you are able to be relaxed and happy inside it. And for those who say, 'Oh, but what always happens is that I throw something away and the very next day I need it!' Well, indeed that would be mildly annoying, but it is mere coincidence, not an excuse to not declutter. In addition, I think it's often the case that while the thing you threw away might well have been perfect for whatever it is that now needs fixing, it probably actually isn't, or you have something else that will do the job just as well, but it's easier for our minds to tap into regret for the thing lost. Let go the remorse. Let go of the stuff. And do it cheerfully as you revel in all the extra space you've created and all those lovely clear shelves and drawers.

A NOTE ON 'NOT SURE' ITEMS

First ask yourself, do you love them enough to pay the premium required to insure them? Yes? Keep. If they're not that valuable, go back to the top of this list and be sure they don't fall into any of the earlier categories. If you still can't quite bring yourself to part with whatever it is, then if you were to move house tomorrow, would you pay someone to wrap and box it for you? Tentative yes? Still keep. Basically, if you're wobbling, I suggest you leave it precisely where it is. Forget that whole stick-it-in-a-box-and-put-it-to-one-side-for-six-months thing – you'll just have an extra box in your way, for an unnecessary amount of time, assuming you even have a spare box conveniently to hand in the first place! Just leave whatever it is precisely where you found it.

Every time you see it from now on, you will consciously re-evaluate it. And one day you might realise you can live without it, or not.

More important is that you never give things up in a spirit of self-sacrifice, nor must you throw out things that belong to someone else. Things disposed of in this manner will cause resentment, whether overtly or subliminally, and this is a sure-fire path to domestic disharmony.

COLLECTIONS OF THINGS

Pay special attention to these. Are they evidence of a real passion or an unhealthy obsession? Is the root of your collecting a desire to have multiples of something adored or a need to have one of everything of something? Clearly the former should be treasured, if not potentially thinned out a little, or more carefully catalogued, or otherwise appreciatively contained (and we'll cover ways to do this in Chapter 9), but the latter? Unless there is an emotional attachment to the items, you may find that you can bin/give away/eBay the lot. Distinguish between the two and, again, you'll know what to do. What's key is to really delve into *why* you collected stamps or football cards in the first place, and what it means to you today. Have you kept them all this time because they evoke cherished memories? Or have they basically been stashed in a box, forgotten, for want of anything better to do with them? After all, we tend to forget only that which we do not care about.

THINGS KEPT IN LOFTS

If you have one, when did you last go up there? If you're an annual skier, and this is where you keep your kit, then fine, but anything else – old files, paperwork, ancient baby toys? Pull it all down, and be ruthless in your sorting. Be honest with yourself: if you haven't been up there in a year, none of this stuff adds value to your life. What I hope may occur, though, is that you unearth a few forgotten gems – perhaps a vintage tea set from your parents or a funny drawing you, or your child, did at school. If such things are found and they prompt fond memories, then consider them for use or display, don't leave them unappreciated. Crucially, having clear space above your head, rather than the dead weight of forgotten possessions, will bring an incredibly powerful yet subconscious lightness to your being. Conversely, things in basements get a teeny bit more of a free pass. You still need to sort and be ruthless, but having dead weight tethering you to the ground is moderately preferable to having it sit over your head. Likewise things in garages. Such convenient storage space can be a marvellous way to keep bulkier items like prams, cots awaiting a next baby, sports stuff, etc., out of your home. But they are not an out-of-sight excuse to hoard.

OTHER PEOPLE'S THINGS

Your home is not a free storage locker for other people's clutter either; even if it's not yours, it will dampen the soul of any space in which it resides. The only energy allowed to circulate in your home should be that which you have knowingly welcomed in, and we'll cover this in depth in Chapter 3. As such, have them come collect whatever it is as a matter of some urgency. Often things are 'stored' for friends, or for our children because the original owner needs to do a

clutter-clear for themselves. So we're not helping them by offering a transitional harbour. The reality is that if, for instance, a friend has abandoned a fixed domicile to go on a dream world tour, it will be more beneficial for them in the long term if they did their own thorough clear-out *before* they go (and then hired an actual storage container for the hopefully much-reduced remainder), otherwise they will simply return to find themselves as they were before.

On holding things for our children – truthfully, are you clinging to the past for yourself? All those baby clothes? School projects and old Lego? Will they ever really want them? Again, invite them over to sort through it with you. Decide together what is significant, and determine who shall continue to hold it as a considered plan of action. The only choice is between consciously retaining things for personal display, passing them on or letting them go.

And if whomever won't come to collect or sort them, point out that clearly then they don't need, or want, whatever it is, so you will be doing them a favour by disposing of it all accordingly. And give them the date that it'll all go to the dump; that way, they'll still have the option to intervene beforehand. Obviously exceptions must be made if the people concerned are abroad, but nevertheless at some point presumably they will come to visit, so address the situation then, by having it all ready to be looked at together. Nine times out of ten if someone is far afield, they will have forgotten that you were ever holding on to anything for them in the first place, so after consultation you may bin with abandon and their blessing. •

WHERE TO
DISPOSE OF STUFF

DONATION BOXES

While I don't buy into the keeping-a-box-to-stash-things-you-can't-decide-what-to-do-with approach, I do wholeheartedly condone a charity box or bag. Not so big that you couldn't carry it yourself to your local shop but big enough that once it's full you'll want it out of the house pronto. Choose a cause that means something to you, and all those probably smaller items that are perfectly serviceable but you simply don't have the feels for any more can go off to do some good. And if you have a lot of items, or even furniture, many charities will come and collect. But ring them first to see what they will and won't take.

ELECTRICAL ITEMS

Unfortunately, many charity shops don't take these as they don't have the facility to test that everything's in working order before offering them for resale. However, some larger branches will, so again, call ahead to find out. A quick internet search should also prove helpful in finding local centres. Alternatively, there are now an

41

4
2

increasing number of recycling points for electrical and electronic goods, and even batteries can often be dropped off at dedicated collecting points in most large supermarkets. Please don't throw them in the bin: every time you recycle even a single button battery, it conserves resources, helps the environment and reduces unnecessary landfill. Such a little thing to do, yet it would make a big difference if we all did it.

'It's often the case that things in sales are there because nobody wanted them in the first place. So why are you buying them?'

STUFF FOR THE BIN

So, you've successfully filled several bin liners with things that are neither repairable or recyclable; take them to the bin or dump immediately! Many a clutter-clearer has gone astray at the final furlong by exhausting themselves with the clearing and then the bags sit in the hall, garage or basement for an age. This stuff is now deadweight, literally sucking the energy out of you and your home. Jettison the lot promptly and feel the immediate uplift. Plus it'll nip in the bud any temptation to 'just have another quick peek inside the bags' before you throw everything away. •

A FEW FINAL NOTES

THE FALSE
SEDUCTION OF SALES

It's often the case that things in sales are there because nobody wanted them in the first place. So why are you buying them? The only way to benefit from a sale is if you are able to acquire something you genuinely need or desire at a lower price than usual. Otherwise, give them a miss as it's a strong person indeed who can consistently resist the allure of slickly marketed apparent bargains. An exception might be a visit to a very favourite store in pursuit of a considered treat – a reward to self for a personal achievement, a course finished or a goal attained. This is always acceptable. Nevertheless, it's still worth asking yourself if an experience, rather than a purchase, might be a more enjoyable reward, and a better use of your money, too – a trip to the cinema, a weekend away?

SHARED SPACES

Sharing with a significant other can be a source of great joy but also extreme frustration. Often I find this occurs when the possessions or collecting habits of one partner threaten to overwhelm the other, or where one person moves into a space already owned or inhabited by the other. Tension naturally arises because the whole point of a shared life is to share, not for the one to fold into the other! What is paramount is that both parties be equally involved in the creation and decoration of the shared home – whether existing or actually new – alongside the dedication of a specific zone for the display of each person's individual 'treasures'. It could be as small as a single shelving unit in the living room, or as grandiose as an entire private room, but it needs to be done: this is free space for each person to see themselves as an individual within the healthily interdependent comfort of their shared life. And interdependent is the key word here, the alternatives being co-dependent or dependent. When you can hold on to who you are within a relationship, it will be that much stronger for it. A shared home can be an opportunity to celebrate the values that brought you together in the first place, as well as providing visual recognition of the characteristics that make you different. If you cannot bear to accommodate your partner's things (note that I say 'things' here, not 'stuff' – that *has* to go, whoever's it is!), then there are probably deeper questions you need to ask yourself about the nature of your compatibility.

CHILDREN'S ROOMS

These must be the exception to most of the above as I firmly believe that children be allowed to fully express themselves emotionally. Their stories are still unfurling. Let their rooms be the absolute expression of this developing narrative. Let them choose the wall colours (often bright). Pin all their pictures up however they want (often wonky), and be sure to display all of the things that are important to them, celebrating *their* innate creativity. The contents may still be efficiently arranged to make the best use of space, but nothing makes me sadder than seeing pristine children's bedrooms decorated in the same style as the rest of the adult home – it's as if the children are not really allowed to exist. Your children are not mini-yous. They are their own people. Our role as parents is to enable them to be

just that. Guiding, prompting, encouraging but never subsuming. And it can start with their own little corner of the home, by allowing it to become their fully inhabited private space. Let go of any need for absolute order here; there are more important things to worry about than tidy kids' rooms. *Cleaning* their bedrooms is a different matter, though; the need for a regular vacuum can be the best prompt for a major clear-up as otherwise it's remarkable what can get sucked into a hoover's belly!

A WORD ABOUT PLAYROOMS

If children's individual bedrooms are quite small, then there can be an argument for the creation of a play area elsewhere, but if you have kids, then really the whole of your home should be considered a playroom, with the implication that nowhere is out of bounds, and everywhere is allowed to get messy. Rather than confining playthings to 'elsewhere', allow the toys to spread, but factor in storage that is both easy to use and aesthetically acceptable for collecting everything up at the end of the day (I use a pair of large, lidded rattan baskets that slide unobtrusively under a console). Make it portable, too, so that as children grow, it

'Nothing makes me sadder than seeing pristine children's bedrooms decorated in the same style as the rest of the adult home – it's as if the children are not really allowed to exist.'

can be put to a different use or removed altogether. Separating our offspring from our 'grown-up' spaces seems to smack slightly of denying their very vitality and rightful place at the heart of the family. Besides, is it not their home too? And are your children not your very inspiration for living well in the first place? Instead, why not professionally frame some of their artwork and mount it pride of place next to the TV, and incorporate other drawings and models into your display shelves? The boost your children will feel in being honoured in this way will reap rewards on many levels.

As for yourself, what would happen if a currently dedicated playroom was re-commandeered? Could a dividing wall come down and give you all one much larger living room, or facilitate a cinema room that the whole family might use together? And if you remain adamant that the kids' stuff should be contained and that at least one room in your home be kept permanently child-free, then in the self-growth spirit of this book, it's perhaps worth spending a moment to consider what might lie behind this desire – what does it mean to you to be a parent, and why do you need a space to forget this? •

SUMMARY

If there was a fire, what would you grab? If you can answer this, beyond the obvious of anything with a pulse, then you already know your true material priorities. Channel your inner Tyler Durden and remember this when sorting. And besides, you're fully insured now, aren't you, so you really do have nothing to lose. Additionally, learning from Warren Buffett, if not the FIRE movement, we can see that the true cost of any item is the value of the money that you might have made had you invested the purchase price rather than spent it on something that will inevitably depreciate. So, unless you *really* love something – that is, you believe that you will keep it forever, and/or pass it on to future generations – it could be a lot more than just that initial outlay down the drain. Shop more mindfully; shop for life. Resist the temptation to give in to a feeling of lack and embrace instead a new perception of what you are gaining – time, space and money for living.

But take your time. There is no need to do all of this in one go or to be unnecessarily brutal with yourself. Sometimes it's important to sit with things for a while. You don't need to proffer excuses, simply accept a little indecision in yourself and move on.

What you'll find is that the constant evaluation of your possessions will gradually become a habit. From now on every time you open a cupboard, closet or drawer, you'll find yourself actively contemplating the true value, to you, of the contents. And little by little, you will let more and more go until you are convinced that every single thing that surrounds you is a part of the story that you wish to tell.

And if this feels impossible right now, I promise you it's not. Attend to the little things and know that even small changes *will* prove significant. Do it drawer by drawer, closet by closet, room by room. There's no mystery to it. But you must start. Conquer ambivalence, doubt or whatever else holds you back, and get cracking! Know too that, as the motivational author Steven Pressfield puts it in his book *The War of Art*, 'the more important a call or action is to our soul's evolution, the more resistance we will feel toward pursuing it', so if you're feeling the fear, that's good, because it means you know you need to do this. And before you know it, you'll be ready for the next stage – ensuring that the envelope which surrounds all of your now lovingly curated possessions is worthy of them. •

'Little by little, you will let more and more go until you are convinced that every single thing that surrounds you is a part of the story that you wish to tell.'

2

BALANCE

'HAPPINESS IS NOT A MATTER OF INTENSITY BUT OF BALANCE, ORDER, RHYTHM AND HARMONY.'

THOMAS MERTON
AMERICAN TRAPPIST MONK, MYSTIC AND POET
(1915–1968)

You've now edited your belongings down to the things you truly love, the things you need, the things that work well, and are the best you can afford. But before you buy *anything* new, you must turn your attention to the treatment to give to every wall, floor and ceiling – the envelope of your home – as well as the fabrics and finishes to be used for any furniture or fittings. I shall refer to this as 'defining your palette'. Because, while reducing your possessions will certainly give you a sense of order and control over what you own, this simply creates a neatly organised and tidy home, not necessarily a happy one, an essential beginning but nowhere near the end.

CREATING
THE PERFECT
PALETTE

Make no mistake, *the path to the creation of a happy inside home is all about the palette.* However I do not mean not the shape, provenance or form of any objects within it, I mean the quality and precise specification of every single material, finish and colour that you choose to surround yourself with. In this way we break away from the misguided approach that I so often see of trying to build an interior around a key possession. Starting with a specific *thing*, whether a glorious lamp or a marvellous rug, is equivalent to searching for an entire outfit to match a piece of jewellery – not impossible, but significantly harder than if you began with something like a favourite colour.

However, choose too many colours and components for your palette and the overall decorative effect will be chaotic and uncoordinated, choose too few and it'll be bland. This chapter is about how to get that balance right – what to choose and how to use it. •

HOW TO
DEFINE YOUR
PALETTE

Developing a personal home palette is, much like the process of curating your belongings, another considered step towards a habit of becoming more mindful of the sensory impact of your surroundings. It's important to take the time to discover the materials that resonate with you, to permit yourself to dream a little, but not overthink it – try to respond from the heart not the head. You don't want to include materials that you're drawn to only because they're on-trend or purely practical. Rather you must delve into the very soul of your choices, not just their surface appearance. What do they remind you of? Do they recall a particular place or happy holiday, perhaps? Thus, as you build your palette, because it comes from within, it will be intrinsically emblematic of you – this is what will give it its power. And if you live with a significant other, then it must be a representation of what you *both* love. This might be difficult for some, but as indicated in Chapter 1, true partnership

happens at the point where two people meet, rather than being a fight for supremacy. Look for the overlaps and focus on the tastes you share.

What's important is that your choices are broad enough to give you the scope to play a different tune in each room but narrow enough to ensure that there is an underlying sense of clear cohesion, that it's all composed in the same key, if we are to pursue the musical analogy. In other words, *you cannot begin to decorate your home without an overall sense of the finished composition.* Note by note, everything must work together. And by defining the boundaries within which you will now operate, your palette will also prevent impulse purchases of items that may look spectacular in the shop or showroom but, when brought home, are clearly out of place, as well as providing a secondary framework (the first being the clutter-clearing accomplished in Chapter 1) within which to further edit or update retained possessions.

And if your home is rented, or it came ready-furnished, this is not a block to this exercise. Defining your palette is as much about the creation of a long-term wish list as it is something to put into action straight away. Neither does it imply that whole swathes of your existing furnishings must be jettisoned or floors ripped up. Sometimes a judicious use of re-upholstery, wood stain or furniture paint is all that it takes to bring things into line.

By way of illustration, let's say you've rented a flat that came complete with an ugly brown faux-leather sofa, and pale pink is your favourite colour. While the dream scenario might be a rose-toned, linen-covered three-seater with petite turned-wooden legs, you needn't feel defeated by circumstance or compelled to move. Instead you might treat yourself to a dreamy powder-pink knitted throw, or if funds won't stretch that far, you could purchase a length of the right-coloured fabric to drape over it or even dye a linen bedsheet to use as a cover. The point is, you've done the work of identifying the colours you love, and this will stop you buying, say, a turquoise throw because it's going cheap in a sale and you're desperate to cover that sofa. For sure, this bright new throw will work in the practical sense of concealing the brown, but it won't add to the overall sense of cohesion that sticking to your palette will create. It's also highly unlikely to be something that you'll take with you into any subsequent home.

So, use the questions that follow to get you started, jotting down all and any thoughts as they arise, but again, don't overthink it. For example, if spring is your favourite season, is it because it evokes optimism, greenery and freshness? Note everything that comes to mind, as all these thoughts will gradually take on a meaning as materials or finishes. Or, if you ultimately intend to delegate any elements of sourcing, they will help you to create a brief for whatever you wish to achieve. •

'Defining your palette is as much about the creation of a long-term wish list as it is something to put into action straight away.'

ON COLOURS

Which are the colours around
which you think you feel happiest?
Or the most confident? Most relaxed?

Which is your favourite season
of the year? And why?

Given the choice between a beach
or mountains, where would you
prefer to go? Why?

Do you consider yourself a town
or country person? Again, why?

Do you generally prefer bright
or light hues around you?

How do you feel about warm
versus cool colours?

Or deep or dark colours? Are they
comforting? Or too moody?

What's your instinctive response
to the idea of neutrals?

What about an all-white space?
Clean and calm? Or boring?

ON MATERIALS

Which materials make you
want to reach out and touch them?

How do your feel about natural
wood? Marble? Lacquer?

For any of the above materials,
do you prefer light or dark?
A lot or a little?

Do you like smooth, shiny surfaces?
Or lumpy, bumpy, more natural ones?

Which fabrics do you like your
clothes to be made from?

How do you feel about patina?
Does it connote a sense of history
or just look worn out?

What about vintage things or
second-hand items?

What do you think makes you feel
good: a sense of light and space?
Or warmer, cosy comfort?

GENERAL MUSING

When do you feel happiest?
And where, if anywhere, do you
feel this in your current home?

Is there a particular design era
that you love?

Is there a style specific to certain
countries that you appreciate?

What would your dream home
look and feel like?

Is there anywhere that you've visited
that's made you feel particularly
grounded, or charged with energy?

If you've been on holiday and
felt particularly inspired, what were
the colours and materials that
surrounded you then?

THE 28 NOTES
OF THE PERFECT
PALETTE

Hopefully your head is now starting to fizz with ideas. But we must streamline and focus that inspiration for the perfect palette has only 28 finishes! Not to limit you in any way, nor impose a blanket look in every room; this is simply the precise number of rich and varied notes required to compose *different but cohesive* looks across your entire home – your interior symphony! The 28 notes are broken down as below, with more detailed explanations of each category to follow:

6 core colours
  (of which one must be white)
2 accent colours
2 metallics
2 woods
3 signature finishes
2 humble textures
6 fabric textures
2 natural stones (or other composite
  stone-type materials)
3 ceramic tiles

DEEP DIVING
INTO THE DETAIL

To note, at this stage do not concern your-self with the exact specification of each material or colour. For example, if you're tempted to list patterned wallpaper as one of your signature finishes, you don't need to find the right one immediately; it's suffi-cient to put 'floral print wallpaper' on your list, knowing that you like flowers. Likewise fret not about colour coordination, as al-most any combination can be made to work together; it's nothing more than a case of adjusting their precise tones, and we'll cover the details of that later.

However, an absolute of the *happy inside* philosophy is that you be primarily surrounded by elemental materials – mar-ble, granite, wood, glass, cotton and wool, etc. – as these will only ever contribute to your wellbeing. But as well as being natu-ral in origin, these materials also need to be tactile. As physical, sensory beings, we have a primal need to surround ourselves with surfaces that stimulate our fingertips or thrill our toes – ideally a mix of the rough and smooth, textured and silky. In this way the things that we touch every day can add real emotional value to our homes, as well as tangible health benefits – did you know that tactile stimulation triggers oxytocin, the love hormone, lowering cortisol levels and reducing anxiety and stress? – especially important in this digital age, when our working days are so often spent umbilically connected to the super-smooth screens of our phones, tablets or laptops.

On the flip side, materials that are banned include plastics, vinyls, melamine or synthetics of any sort, from nylon carpets and polyester fabrics to formaldehyde-exuding MDF. These all contain large quan-tities of chemicals and you do not want these in your happy, therefore shortly to be non-toxic, home (more on this in Chapter 3). Bring as little of it inside as possible. •

COLOUR

More than anything else, the colours that you choose for your home set its mood music. Colour directly impacts your energy levels, and its associated psychology is a subject that has already filled many a tome. In very simple terms, though, colour *is* emotion. Certain colours can make you feel happy, on edge, calm, quiet, excited or flat and every nuance in between. Clearly they affect different people in different ways, but very broadly speaking we can think of colour in terms of warm versus cool; light versus dark; bright versus dirty.

A balanced palette combines aspects of all three of these divisions and the best way to start is by imagining the feeling you wish to create in each room. It will be different according to which room you're thinking about, and in some cases, for example bathrooms, it might even vary according to the time of day – the contrast between speedy morning teeth-cleaning versus a leisurely evening bubble bath. Just keep jotting down the words or feelings as they strike you – relaxed, energetic, warm, soft – and gradually these will lead you towards certain sections of the colour spectrum. To help, I've listed overleaf some of the moods that you might wish to conjure and paired them with colours that I associate with each. Use it as a starting point, but feel free to combine categories too.

And while it's often suggested that you turn to your wardrobe for inspiration, I disagree. What governs our sartorial colour choices can be fundamentally different from what works for us at home, and it's confusing to mix the two. Just because you love stripy jumpers doesn't mean you want your lounge to be decorated the same way.

Finally, a quick note on accent colours, tones and undertones, as these are frequently used terms. Accent colours are shades that you wouldn't necessarily paint a whole room in, but you still adore. It's fun to use these for painting the inside of closets or for accessories like ceramics and cushions. Regarding tones: if you took 'sky blue' as an example, and picture the sky as it appears to you, it will be deeper or paler according to where you live. If this was a paint, the differing blues would be achieved by adding progressively more white, black or grey: white

would make it paler, black deeper, and grey what I call 'dirty'. We could also add the primary colours of yellow, red or blue to any base colour to make it either sun-kissed, rosy or cool. When we talk of undertones, then, it is the delicate hint of another such shade that sits just beneath the base colour, gently nudging it towards warmth or coolness, brightness or something more muted. The adjustment may be subtle but it's important because undertones affect mood and if they differ widely across a palette, colours will not sit happily together. A green with an undertone of yellow, for example, is unlikely to work well with a blue-based grey, just as a white with an undertone of blue will make an already cool, north-facing room, feel colder. All materials will have an undertone to some extent too, from wood to metallics, but it's obviously easiest to manipulate in paint, which is why playing with undertones can help pull any palette together. Plus, paint is like make-up – easy to apply, easy to change and capable of completely altering the underlying canvas. So don't be afraid to use it with abandon.

COOL

This connotes laid-back spaces, ones that form a backdrop to life. They do not shout, but whisper. Surfaces are smooth, superbly finished and likely to be glossy; bare wood is not part of this vocabulary. Likely to be predominantly white with accents of pale blue or grey but with an undertone of red to offset coldness.

CALM

A softer, more accommodating look. Good for spaces that are intended to cosset and wrap around their owners. Natural textures start to creep in, and surfaces range from matt to metallics. Baby blue or pink tones take the edge off cool to give you a feeling of relaxation.

PALE

Gently warmer than cool or calm, and with a greater range of materials, from natural wood to high-gloss lacquers. Here almost any colour goes but only in their pastel iterations rather than the fully saturated originals. Think ice-cream hues: lemon, pistachio or even vanilla mixed with strawberry.

PRETTY

This doesn't have to mean pink, but it often does because no other colour radiates such a gentle appeal. The key to using it well, though, is to combine it with complementary yet contrasting colours – think denim blue to add 'edge' or sage green to add chic. The pink itself can be dirtied with grey to achieve a gender-neutral effect.

EASY

Suggestive of an environment that soothes and relaxes. As such, associated colours spring from the softer sides of the green and blue families. However, touches of grey and powder pink will prevent the look from becoming too languid, and a dash of turquoise or even chartreuse also works. Consider navy as your undertone.

EARTHY

Warm, enveloping and all about comfort, this conjures up the natural tones of elemental materials, in particular wood, balanced by touches of the more delicate shades of nature, sky blues and leafy greens, underpinned by terracotta, burnt umber, leather brown and pale yellow.

DEEP

Good for spaces that require concentration and focus. Think crimson, purple and the rich shades of plum, cherry and other berries. Keep it contemporary with smudges of dark grey and contrasting complementary colours to balance it out. But use blue or grey as an undertone if you want to give it weight.

DARK

Dreamy and mysterious, very dark colours can be dynamic not depressing. But the way to make it work is to keep it super-textural. Mix all materials and finishes with abandon. And pick undertones with care. Green can be more unusual and striking, blue more inky. Consider warm charcoal grey and navy too.

DIRTY

Similar to pale but instead of being diluted by white, the colours are toned down with grey so they lack hard edges. If you play with the saturation filter on a camera phone, you'll get the idea. These colours are intrinsically soothing to the soul.

WATERY

Cool and calming yet also capable of being warm and enveloping, a tricky double act to pull off. Think deep blues and emerald greens through to duck-egg blue and jade. The key is a green undertone here, not grey, as otherwise it'll become too cold.

WARM

Think cosy rather than strident brights, like pale pink, amber and umber, as the fast track to warm without becoming muggy. The use of a wealth of shades from the red end of the spectrum, blushing roses to ruby reds, differentiate it from the earthier look.

HAPPY

Imagine Crayola colours: bright unadulterated primary shades, unapologetic and straightforward. From Mediterranean sky blue to Mr Happy yellow, these are not for the faint-hearted, but neither are they only for children's rooms.

HOT

Vivid and vivacious, these are the colours of passion. Red might be the cornerstone but it works best in small doses alongside deep magenta pink, hazy ochre yellow, persimmon, ginger red and orange.

63

WHY YOU
MUST INCLUDE WHITE

Everyone should employ white in their home to some extent as a core colour, as much as an accent colour, because it heightens any other shade chosen and can be used to enhance a feeling of lightness.

Specifically, on the purchase of a new home, *always* paint all walls entirely in white before you contemplate any level of new decoration. It is the only way to see how the light moves through different spaces and to identify the natural areas of sun and shade, which will ultimately determine other decorative finishes as well as the placement of furniture (more about this in Chapter 3). Do not buy an expensive paint (albeit one that is VOC-free, see Chapter 3 for more about this), and certainly don't get caught up in the many shades of warm, hot, cool or otherwise tinted whites currently on the market. A standard Brilliant White

is what you need here: cheap and cheerful, slap it up, do it quickly, do it straight away, and preferably before you move any furniture inside or change any flooring. Rest assured, as you progress through each room, every wall and surface will receive proper dedicated attention in due course, and that will be the time to ensure good coverage and neat edgings. Before then is a waste of energy. That said, washing every surface down with a good sugar soap solution to remove entrenched grease and dirt before starting is always recommended, particularly if a property has not been redecorated for a while.

If you're already installed and feeling on the brink of a revamp, then back to white is imperative for you too, whether it's just a couple of rooms or the whole house – you'll just need to be a little more diligent in masking carpets and covering furniture. Nevertheless, wherever possible blank everything out as best you can, from skirtings to ceilings and everything in between. A white base coat will serve as a good undercoat for any new paint, albeit good decorating protocol demands the sanding down of gloss paint beforehand. Alternatively, use a quality white primer to cover it first, otherwise further coats of paint won't stick.

And if you rent, well I've never yet met a landlord who objected to tenants giving a property a fresh coat of white paint! And it's important that you can do this – so always ask up front if it's possible; it's not only a way of psychologically taking ownership of a space, literally marking it as your territory, but it also provides you with a clean, neutral backdrop against which to set your possessions. •

WOOD

Such a huge variety of wooden finishes is available that it can be overwhelming to know where to start. Use the following series of prompts to consolidate your thinking. And if you absolutely can't abide wood – though I'd push you hard to reconsider, as this is one of nature's most versatile offerings – then a possible option is to increase one in *each* of the following categories instead: signature finishes, humble textures, natural stone.

● **Do you feel drawn towards light or dark wood?** If light, is it the white/grey tones or warmer yellow tones you prefer? If dark, do you prefer black-toned or more brown?

● **If you like the white/grey or yellow tones**, is it naturally occurring white/grey, such as birch or ash, or a lime-washed finish that you like? If yellow, do you prefer warm, like light oak, or cooler, like sycamore?

● **If you like more black or brown tones,** is it the dark tones of exotic woods like ebony or charred finishes that you like? If brown, do you prefer deep shades, like teak or walnut, or brighter with red tones, like cedar or cherry wood? Note: I'd always champion a good wood stain to get more exotic dark finishes rather than the actual wood, for reasons of sustainability.

● **When considering furniture or flooring.** For furniture, do you like the wood grain showing or do you prefer it to be polished smooth or even lacquered? For flooring, precision-cut engineered boards or a more natural look?

● **Pursuing the flooring options,** if engineered boards are your thing, then wide boards or narrow? If natural, new or reclaimed?

And so it goes on. Inevitably the answer to some of these might be 'yes' to both options. And that's fine. Just keep digging away at what you think you like. Once it feels as if you're homing in on a favourite, go forth and seek samples! Almost all reputable manufacturers will be more than happy to mail offcuts of their wares, sometimes for free, sometimes for a small charge to offset postage. Make the most of this service because it's essential to feel and touch wood in order to understand its qualities and to narrow down the feel you're after. Samples will also help you when you come to choosing colours to complement them. Bear in mind, though, that all batches of any natural material will vary, so a single piece can never truly indicate how it will look on a larger scale unless you have selected a customised stain or lacquer for a guaranteed consistent finish. ●

METALLICS

These ebb and flow in fashion more than any other finish; one minute copper is riding high in the charts, then it's all about blackened steel. You need to resist the lure of trends. Every metallic finish has a different intrinsic quality, so focus on choosing those that truly inspire you and forgo the rest. If you find this difficult, look to your favourite pieces of jewellery as this might provide a hint of what you're drawn to.

Try, though, to choose one from the inherently warm camp (as defined in the list opposite), alongside one from the cool category, as this will help the overall balance of your palette as well as giving you more flexibility. It's like the principle of yin and yang, in that hot and cold *can* sit hand in hand, one complementing the other.

If you really feel you cannot mix it up, that's okay, but be mindful that the balance will need to be adjusted elsewhere. In other words, if you go all cool in this category, then another must veer completely towards the warm to compensate. That said, silver can be used alongside stainless steel *plus* another metallic from the warm camp, just as brass could be mixed with bronze alongside something additional from the cool side. This is because these specific pairs – silver/ stainless steel and bronze/brass – share such similar looks and emotional properties.

However, because metallics are invariably quite broadly distributed around your home, be wary of introducing more than two with very contrasting attributes, such as brass *and* copper with stainless steel, thinking it won't make much difference. It will. And the inevitable ripple effect will be that the interloping items will have to be swapped out or even discarded to restore the balance. Instead, consider varying the finishes of your original choices, using matt with polished surfaces, for instance, or antiqued, brushed or hammered looks. This will acceptably up your options without unduly tipping the aesthetic scales. •

WARM FINISHES

COOL FINISHES

BRASS
An alloy of copper and zinc.
Radiant. Timeless. Multi-functional.

BRONZE
An alloy of copper and tin.
Usually duller in tone than brass.
Heavier. Equally timeless.

COPPER
The base to many other metals.
Naturally antibacterial. Bright.
Red-based. Upbeat.

GOLD
More yellow than brass.
Lustrous. Reflective. Exclusive.

ROSE GOLD
A mixture of copper and gold.
Pink-toned. Light. Unusual.

WHITE GOLD
Very pale yellow-toned.
Gorgeous but rarely used in
homes in its pure form!

ALUMINIUM
Bright. Silvery white. Best when shiny.
Lightweight.

BLACKENED STEEL
Strong and corrosion-resistant.
Finer than iron. Blue-grey to black.

IRON
Used to make steel. Dark grey. Solid.
Dependable. Can be more rustic.

LEAD
Grey. Matt. Malleable.
Generally for exterior use only.

PLATINUM
Silver-white to grey-white in colour.
Precious. Mixes well with gold.

SILVER
Cool. Timeless. Warmer in
the hand than stainless steel.
Ages beautifully.

STAINLESS STEEL
Sharp. Utilitarian. Clinical.
Must be kept clean.

STONES AND CERAMICS

The strength of natural stone is that even when stained, cracked or pitted, it is still beautiful. And yet, in many contemporary homes it only seems to get a look-in as an option for kitchen countertops or outdoor patios. This is to miss a tremendous decorative opportunity, and a huge array of extraordinary finishes. Tiles too can add a rhythmic textural charm to any surface, and should never be relegated to the bathroom alone. They're easy to care for, and when you combine stone in a tile format, installation becomes that much easier – plus tiles are usually cheaper than slabs. Moreover, advances in technology have enabled certain ceramic tiles to be embossed or digitally printed to look like anything from travertine to exotic types of marble. The benefit of this being primarily cost,

but also weight as they are considerably lighter than natural stone and so can be employed more widely where a heavier load could otherwise be an issue. In some cases, they are more durable and stain resistant too, not to forget sustainable.

Nevertheless, make your choice based on love not practicality alone. If you intend to use a large amount of a local stone, then visit the originating quarry to inspect samples wherever possible. There will always be one slab that captures your imagination more than the others – wait until you feel this thunderbolt! The same applies if checking out pieces in a showroom. Go with your gut. Then see what you can afford. But don't forget to factor in the costs of installation. Ask lots of questions. Fully consider all options. And hold tight to your dream. And if your heart is set on something you've seen, but costs seem prohibitive, could you be canny and mix a marble countertop with a less expensive ceramic tile on the floor? Could you use cheaper offcuts and patchwork the pieces together for a truly bespoke effect? Alternatively, do one wall now and save up for the rest? Finally, never make a choice just by looking on the internet. As with wood, you need to touch and see stone before you buy it. With tiles you can be a little more flexible as any glazes and finishes may be naturally varied and this should be accepted as part of the look. The notes overleaf will help you understand the key characteristics of the most common types of stone, ceramics and composites available for domestic purposes.

AN ADDITIONAL
NOTE ON TILES

As stated previously, the perfect number of tile types to include in your palette is three. These can be any texture or size you like, but when it comes to walls, do not mix different shapes together, such as squares with rectangles. I have always preferred rectangular-shaped tiles as they lend a note of 'difference' without going too far, particularly if vertically aligned rather than the traditional interlocking pattern of a brick wall. Of course, many other shapes of tile are now available, from hexagons to diamonds, so if you wish to add something more unusual like this to your list, pop it into 'signature finishes', as one of the three permitted in that category. •

BRICK

Often forgotten as an interior building material, or routinely painted over, which is a shame as bricks are full of texture and inherent warmth. Also available in many different colours, from traditional terracotta to creamy yellow, rough-faced London stock bricks or sharp-edged blue engineering bricks, with a whole wealth of more unusual types also available.

COMPOSITES

Extremely durable solid surfacing materials made of natural stone or marble dust combined with resin. Capable of being moulded seamlessly into almost any shape, and useful if you want an entirely consistent look. Available in myriad colours and super-smooth finishes, including ones that approximate real marble. Great for kitchen countertops with integrated sinks and splash-backs.

CONCRETE

Composed of sand or gravel mixed with cement, concrete can be wonderfully workable and varied in texture – rough, smooth, polished or raw – and it can also be tinted different colours. Commonly associated with a more industrial look but also capable of being warm and luxurious. Most interesting when used unexpectedly, such as for worktops or interior walls. Great in combination with underfloor heating.

FLAGSTONE

Perhaps more familiar as paving slabs, this is also a type of quarried rock, usually sandstone-based but made up of other materials as well, such as silica or iron oxide, which give the stone its colour. Think castle floors! Typical shades range from grey-blue to brown and buff. Ideal for kitchen and conservatory floors, or for use outdoors. Like concrete, best combined with underfloor heating to keep it cosy underfoot.

GRANITE

Formed from solidified molten lava, granite is one of the oldest, strongest and hardest types of stone available. Often with a speckled or swirled look due to its granular, crystalline structure and varying considerably in colour, from pink to black. Luxurious yet affordable. Easy care and practically indestructible. Great for worktops.

LIMESTONE

Generally earth-toned in colour, and more muted than granite. Easy to work with and available in many finishes and textures. Best for flooring and walls.

MARBLE
A true miracle of nature. An elegant natural stone formed from limestone. Richly veined and flecked with different minerals, it's found in an extraordinary array of colours, from pure white right through to mottled black, and can be used almost anywhere. The only downside is its porous nature thus susceptibility to staining, even if sealed.

PORCELAIN
More durable and hard-wearing than traditional crockery ceramic, porcelain tiles are resistant to abrasion, frost and chemical damage as well as being virtually waterproof. Perfect for indoor/outdoor spaces and hallways.

QUARTZITE
Formed from quartz-rich sandstone, it can look very similar to lighter-toned marble, though it's generally cheaper. It also benefits from superior resistance to etching by household acids, from cleaning agents to alcohol and lemon juice, which makes it perfect for worktops.

SANDSTONE
Rustic, authentic, durable and easy to work. Available in pinks, reds, yellows and browns through to the classic light greys and creamy whites. Very versatile.

SLATE
An earthy, textured, usually grey-blue stone often used in tile or slab formats. Sturdy and durable, exuding dark warmth. Prone to scratching and chipping, but highly resistant to acids. Best for flooring.

TERRACOTTA
Translated literally as 'baked earth', the word 'terracotta' instantly conjures up images of worn 'n' wobbly flooring, rural farmhouses and earthenware pots. Inherently honest as a material, it's also a relatively inexpensive way to add an incredibly durable and characterful warmth to any home. Best for hallway and kitchen floors.

TRAVERTINE
A form of limestone originally formed near mineral-rich springs such that the gas bubbles became trapped, giving it its characteristically pitted surface (usually filled with an epoxy resin to provide a more polished durable finish as a building material). Delicate and supremely classy. Gloriously stylish for walls and floors.

EVERYTHING

ELSE

SIGNATURE FINISHES

These are those icing-on-the-cake touches that make your home unique. So if glitter or leopard print is your thing (or your partner's – don't forget them here!), write it down. A more sedate preference for terracotta, Moroccan zellige tiles or antique patchwork quilts – anything goes if it's what you love. And remember that even if you can't achieve the finish of your dreams today, you can still enjoy the sourcing, knowing that one day you might realise it. Sometimes the search may even lead you to something that you might love even more.

HUMBLE TEXTURES

Deliberately differentiated from other materials because they fulfil a different purpose: that of encouraging the introduction of coarser textures – think rattan, sisal and coir, or plywood, cork and hemp. These are materials that might be considered too lowly to be deemed beautiful, so they often get overlooked. And yet their inherent authenticity and tactility, not to mention affordability, are the very reasons for their inclusion. They are essential to the *happy inside* home, grounding you through an overt connection, both visual and physical, to the natural world.

FABRICS

It's a given that you now stick to natural materials at every turn, but even so, why select an identical set of cotton cushion covers when you could combine wool bouclé with silk, embroidered linen with velvet or sheepskin? Mix and match fabrics to your heart's content. And the same goes for patterns: polka dots and flowers with chinoiserie? Absolutely, as long as the colour tones are the same and it clicks with your overall colour palette. This is where you get to really indulge yourself.

AND IF YOU'RE LUCKY ENOUGH TO BE BUILDING A HOUSE FROM SCRATCH

Too often 'architecture' is considered separately from 'interiors' and yet they are but two halves of the same thing, the envelope of your home. Thus for maximum coherence, they *must* be considered together and your palette should therefore include all of your external materials as well as interior finishes to ensure a seamless flow from inside to out. In this case, add at least one to each of the following categories – metallics, wood, natural stone and ceramic tiles – bringing your palette total up to 32 different colours, textures and materials. •

73

'Mix and match fabrics to your heart's content. And the same goes for patterns: polka dots and flowers with chinoiserie? Absolutely.'

THE FOUR
'MOVEMENTS'
OF HOME

Now that you are well on your way to re-fining your palette down to the requisite 28 notes, it's time to introduce the idea of home as a sequence of just four interrelated zones – and this stands regardless of the size of your home or whether the layout is open-plan, more traditionally subdivided into separate rooms, multi-level or single-storey. Think of it as like the four interrelated movements of a classical symphony, each with its own mood, which in terms of the home will dictate the proportion of the pal-ette to be used to 'compose' it. The main ad-vantage of this method, is that it frees you to concentrate on one zone at a time without fear of an uncoordinated muddle at the end.

ZONE ONE:
HALLWAYS AND
ENTRANCES

The story of your home begins in these spac-es of welcome. This is also the most public zone, and the one with the highest level of traffic, as well as being the conduit to the comfort and calm we desire further inside. Chapter 5 covers the wider significance of this area, so here you need only ask yourself:

'What atmosphere do I wish to convey as the first impression of my home? And how do *I* want to feel when I step over my threshold?' Is your hallway an open book offering a taster of the delights within? Or more closed, withholding a little because the inner sanctum of your home is sacrosanct?

In considering which parts of your palette to use, if you could only pick one key material and one colour, which would they be? Start from these and then aim to select another 4–6 notes – just under a quarter of your entire palette. And if you suddenly find yourself thinking that there's nothing that works, don't panic! It's inevitable that your palette will need some tweaking as you work through this section. So take the time now to get it right, as it's vital that it works through all four of these zones.

ZONE TWO:
LIVING, DINING AND
RECEPTION ROOMS

These are the areas of your home in which all occupants gather, you receive visitors or host guests. They are often directly off entry spaces and the first rooms seen as your secondary public areas, hence in their decor it's logical that they make a nod to your entryway yet build on it in a very deliberate manner. However, this zone is also the space in which you will relax and wind down when children are in bed, guests have gone and night beckons. It must therefore achieve a degree of harmony between the hustle and bustle of the day, and the quiet required for letting go.

We will dwell on this in more detail in Chapter 6, so again, focus here on the general mood you would like to create. For example, do you see these main social spaces of your home as stimulating, noisy and full of extended family and friends? And would you want to echo this in your choice of decor? Or would you prefer a quieter scheme, for a more calming, relaxing backdrop? In terms of the palette, because this zone acts as a bridge between your public and private selves, you will employ the greatest number of notes from your palette here, about 15–18 of them, over half the total. Take a lead from those you have already selected for your hallway, but ramp it up a notch. Introduce your signature finishes in

'The main advantage of this method, is that it frees you to concentrate on one zone at a time without fear of an uncoordinated muddle at the end.'

order to increase the overall texture, richness and variety; and don't forget that you will inevitably be accommodating window treatments, alongside upholstery, so take the opportunity to deploy the full range of your fabric choices here too.

ZONE THREE:
KITCHENS, STUDIES AND
HOME OFFICES

These are the spaces of gratitude, for giving thanks for the abundance of our lives, whether we are creating it (home offices), inspiring it (studies) or celebrating it (kitchens). This zone is also one step towards the private as some rooms may never be seen by a casual visitor; accordingly, they offer an opportunity to have a little 'fun' with your decorative choices, to crank up the pace and avoid predictability.

However, because such rooms tend to be the focus of specific activities that take place in them on a regular basis (dis-

cussed more fully in Chapter 7), *consider less how they may feel and be led more by how you need to use them*. Be wary, though, of lurching into fantasy rather than the reality of your family and its habits; for example, if there are no hyper-keen cooks, are professional-standard appliances really required in the kitchen? Will a home office or study be a private escape pod for contemplative musing, or somewhere more open and playful with a sofa for anyone to hang out on?

Practically speaking, scoop up anything thus far unused on your palette and aim to employ no more than 10–14 notes across any one room. Toy with what you've chosen and consider more idiosyncratic and unconventional combinations – an entire wall in an accent colour or a splash-back made by layering all the various tiles used elsewhere. Could you wallpaper the kitchen? Add panelling to a study, or paint the ceiling an unexpected shade? If you have a downstairs loo, this would also be incorporated into this zone, often a space in which people already intuitively give themselves a freer decorative rein.

ZONE FOUR:
BEDROOMS AND BATHROOMS

Although this zone covers the private areas of your home, your spaces of sleep and retreat, in their decor they should reference Zone One because on arrival home you are always presented with the option to either engage or withdraw. To come into your main public spaces or disappear into a bedroom. Your hallway, then, whether via stairs or direct access, serves visually as the introduction to both. However, because we are now moving into the inner sanctum of our homes, we must visually denote a change of pace by turning to the more soothing elements of our palette: softer underfoot and using colours that evoke a feeling of calm, whatever that might mean for you – for some this will be lighter

hues, for others moodier, deeper tones. Chapter 8 addresses the specifics of this zone, so here is the moment to step back and reassess your palette as a whole. Have you factored in enough soft elements? Do you need to switch a few things around? Let's also return to the idea of colour tones. For example, if one of your chosen colours is green and another is grey, it will always work well within your scheme to combine these shades. Throw in your mandatory white and suddenly you have access to pale greenish greys for ceilings or smoky fir greens for fabrics, and every tone in between! The process of defining your palette absolutely isn't about selecting a specific hue and sticking to it stubbornly throughout. And your bedroom spaces will almost certainly require this level of dilution – literally toning down potentially stronger elements from elsewhere to adapt them for the spaces in which we want our bodies to slow down too. •

'Looking at a plain wall is akin to staring blankly into space. We have a fundamental *need* for visual nourishment and stimulation in our homes, for our eyes to dance lightly over surfaces and not find them wanting.'

HOW TO PULL
IT ALL TOGETHER

Once you understand the concept of your home as these four interconnected zones, and have completed your palette division and mood making accordingly, you are finally ready to start pulling it all together as a series of four 'looks', one for each zone. But, before you get the paint brushes out, I advise a little more patience, for we must build up our room schemes *plane by plane*, a cornerstone of the *happy inside* approach. And only once we have done this may we begin to think about actually starting to decorate!

But what do I mean by 'plane'? A plane is each single expanse of continuous wall, from corner to corner, whether that includes windows and doors, covings and mouldings, or is just plain with no other features. A ceiling can be another plane, as can the floor. And the idea behind working in planes is to break a room down into manageable chunks, so that you can respond directly to what's in front of you without being overwhelmed by the whole.

It's important to work like this because too often rooms are painted in the same colour throughout with coordinating skirtings, and that's it. What a waste! Your walls are your biggest surfaces to play with. They can easily be so much more. Besides, looking at a plain wall is akin to staring blankly into space. We have a fundamental *need* for visual nourishment and stimulation in our homes, for our eyes to dance lightly over surfaces and not find them wanting. Certainly the art of mindfulness – a mainstay of feeling calm and centred – entails staying with the present moment and revelling in what's happening right here in front of you, but think how much easier this would be if you gave yourself something wonderfully life-enhancing to look at! In addition, working on one wall at a time encourages a more conscious appreciation of the intrinsic bone structure of a room. It allows you to question whether existing features work. Perhaps a room has been unduly closed off, making natural circulation – of air as well as people – difficult, or if an area has been opened up by walls being removed, has it created a single space that now straddles two zones? In the latter case, you may need to consider the planes of each half separately. And don't worry: you'll always be aware of the entire room, because of the previous mood-setting exercise. •

THE SEVEN PRINCIPLES OF *HAPPY INSIDE* DECORATING

As such, from now on you are to think of each plane of a room as a composition in waiting and a canvas on which to create, with the ultimate aim of being able to stand in the middle of any room, no matter how large or small, and look at each wall in turn and feel that an overall sense of balance, alignment and consideration for its composition is reflected in *every detail*. This is essential to creating a holistic sense of calm, because our brains will always subliminally pick up on anything discordant, the sense that something is a bit off, and the body responds by not being able to fully relax, even if the rational mind cannot instantly identify what's wrong. The challenge is to achieve a balance between these two seemingly opposing forces – enough to look at but with nothing out of place. Here are seven key principles to guide you smoothly along that path.

1. ALWAYS START WITH YOUR FLOORING

Whether you want your home to be relaxing, calm or invigorating, always start with your floor, then follow with the colours for your walls and know that everything will flow from there. This is because floors are often overlooked, or left until last, whereas they should be one of the very first things you think about, as they will be in your eyeline from all viewpoints, underpinning everything in your home both visually and quite literally. Plus, if you own your own home, it'll be one of your biggest investments, so better to get this sorted before you buy anything else, on the premise that you can sit on a cardboard box on a wonderful floor and it will look magnificent, but anything on a cheap floor will be instantly, and permanently, compromised.

Of course that's a dilemma if you can't afford to install a new floor, or if you rent and have a hideous carpet or faux laminate in situ to contend with. But all is not lost. The answer is rugs! Not necessarily a coveted contemporary design or classic woollen Berber or any other more luxurious options; these I consider to be finishing touches whereas here the need is one of basic coverage. Also, new rugs can be fantastically expensive, especially if you want one large enough to conceal a whole room. So top budget tip: a carpet remnant (always choose 100 per cent wool), cut to fit and professionally bound around the edges (most good carpet retailers will offer

this service at a reasonable cost, but check independent shops too for the best quote). Ensure it's as large as possible (essentially wall to wall but orthogonal; no fancy shapes, please) and absolutely toned with your palette, and this will be a very satisfactory stop gap. The most important point is to have the edges properly sealed – DIY kits tend to *stick* over the raw edges whereas having them professionally sewn is much more durable, and smarter, for only a little extra outlay. It'll also ensure the edges are dead straight and the rug won't unravel or fray. Besides, cut carpet edges can be sharp because of the mesh the fibres are adhered to. Costs permitting, it's also fun to play around with the different edging techniques available, such as serging – a continuous wrap of thread giving a hand-stitched look – or bindings in contrasting colours, and of course you could even add a fringe! Natural fibres such as sisal and hemp are also good to experiment with for a long-lasting offcut rug. In fact, a poor floor could inspire the creation of a wonderfully personalised rug that you'll keep forever, even if it has to be cut to fit again when the dream parquet finally gets laid.

KNOW YOUR FOUNDATIONS

Whatever flooring you start with, it's always worth peeling up an unobtrusive corner to see what lies beneath. If there are floorboards, then congratulations, it's probably a solid base, but it may also be hardboard (possibly overlaying original wooden floorboards), concrete or just another layer of grot. Regardless, it's always better to know what you're working with.

START WITH A CLEAN SLATE

If this is a property that you own, then rip out any offending covering right away so you can start afresh, quite aside from the fact that old carpet is likely to be full of years of dirt. And if you rent, always check with the landlord before tampering with any existing fittings.

OR CALL IN THE PROFESSIONAL CLEANERS

However, if an in-situ carpet is relatively new and a colour that you actually like and is on your palette, then invest in a professional deep clean before you move in, but make sure the cleaning company uses certified all-natural eco-friendly agents for their cleaning, rather than anything chemical-based (see Chapter 3).

WHEN REMOVING AN OLD FLOOR COVERING, DON'T TOUCH THE SKIRTINGS!

These *should* go right down to the original floor base as their purpose is to conceal any gap between it and the wall surface. If your walls are old, removing the skirting boards may pull away a significant amount of plaster, so you'll end up needing to redo the walls as well as the floor. Any cracks or missing portions in a skirting can easily be replaced and it's a veritable wonder what wood filler can achieve in the hands of a trained tradesperson.

HOWEVER . . .

The only exception to the above is if you plan to significantly change the existing floor levels, such as by installing underfloor heating on top of existing boards, as then the skirtings might end up looking unduly short.

ARE YOU SURE ABOUT BARE BOARDS?

Unless a property is a modern development, bear in mind that floorboards were only intended as a basic covering for joists and beams over which a 'finer' finish would be laid. It's something of a modern anomaly to have them exposed, as there are often sizeable gaps between each plank which makes them very draughty. If you're determined to go back to bare, these gaps will all need to be meticulously filled. That said, sanded, sealed and varnished old boards on a ground floor can look wonderful.

BE MINDFUL OF NEIGHBOURS

If you live on the upper floors of a multi-occupancy building, then sound-proofing regulations usually restrict bare wooden floors because of the resultant noise for downstairs neighbours, so stripping back can rarely be the final finish.

BIGGER IS BEST FOR RUGS

While several rugs can be layered together if they are flat enough, the total area must at a minimum be able to underlap all the key pieces of furniture in a single room – for example, from the front feet of a sofa to underneath any associated armchairs. Rug islands under a solitary coffee table are forbidden!

IT'S ALL ABOUT FLOW

In small or medium-sized homes, the ideal is to use the same flooring finish throughout the entire ground floor as this can make it seem more spacious – no delineations between different rooms equals no visual borders, so your eye automatically 'sees' more space. In a flat, aim to keep the same flooring flowing from the hallway straight through to utility areas such as the kitchen and bathroom at the very least, only differentiating the bedrooms and possibly the living rooms, depending on the floorplan. (We will cover the essence of 'flow', the art of a good floorplan, in Chapter 3!)

LIMIT FLOORING OPTIONS

But vary finish by floor level. A different finish can be used on each subsequent floor of any size of property, changing from harder (or more textural) finishes in the more public areas to softer in the more private rooms. Generally speaking, the larger the home, the more floor finishes it can accommodate.

Applied decorative trims are obviously great for physically adding a line of alignment to work from. They are time-honoured ways to break up blank expanses of plaster, and they're used a lot because they're tremendously effective in bringing rooms together and giving the eye something to rest on. Listed from top to bottom, these might include cornicing, picture rails, dados, wooden panelling (wainscotting) and skirtings. And they certainly shouldn't be regarded as suitable only for older properties or a more traditional look. Any white box of a room can be completely transformed with the addition of a simple, but perhaps taller-than-average, skirting board, a plaster ceiling mould to accent a pendant light, or even something as simple as an extra length of decorative casing wrapped around an otherwise plain window to give it more oomph. Textured wallpaper in particular – the sort that you paint yourself after hanging, in any colour to match your scheme – is a subtle (and economical) way of gently lifting any surface and giving your eyes something extra to enjoy, without the full-on distraction of vibrantly patterned wallpaper. It comes in all manner of patterns and thicknesses, so even remarkably realistic faux dado panelling can be yours on a roll. Combined with trims, layered either above or below them and finished in one colour or more, all surfaces quickly come to life, even before the final touch of any artwork or other decorative accessories.

PICTURE RAILS

While originally used for attaching hooks from which to hang pictures, by default they also set a line above which pictures could not be placed, thus preserving the integrity of the ceiling plane. If adding such a rail to your walls, then a minimum of about 30cm (1 foot) from the ceiling will work well as long as your ceiling height exceeds 2.1 metres (just under 7 feet). Below this, do not use them. Consider instead either a dado rail or a discreet cornice trim.

DADO RAILS

Historically a trim to protect the part of the wall most likely to be bumped by the back of a chair, a dado rail can also be a smart way of visually dividing a wall into two. Such devices also help to contain wall-hung furniture, i.e. it can either go entirely above or below the dado. Set trims at approximately hip height (regardless of a room's ceiling height) and if including panelling, then this would be fixed directly below it. And if carried through each of a set of main front rooms, they also encourage an automatic sense of visual flow.

PANELLING

Easily created by fixing vertical wooden beading directly to the wall immediately below dado trims, and down to skirtings. Leave the wall plain in between or, a favourite trick, infill the panels with a textured wallpaper.

SKIRTINGS

Traditionally used to mask the join between wall and floor, and to block any gaps or draughts. Today, in modern homes with hopefully superior building techniques, there should be no floor-level breezes and instead the size of skirtings can be varied at whim, or dispensed with entirely to create different effects. A challenging device for any plasterer is the shadow gap, a deliberate inset all around the bottom edge of a room designed to create the illusion of a very narrow gap. While terribly chic and minimal, this can also be an awful dust-trap, and the bottom edge of delicate plaster is no longer protected from scuffs and scrapes – the other primary purpose of a skirting.

CORNICES

Basically a more decorative version of a skirting that's fixed around the top edge of a wall adjacent to the ceiling. A cornice is less commonly inserted into newer properties as ceiling heights are usually too low. It's also important to allow enough distance between it and a picture rail (or even a dado), so you may need to opt for one or the other. In tall narrow spaces which are otherwise plain, such as an upper landing, an oversized cornice can be a wonderful way to add an unexpected and intriguing detail to catch the eye at a high level.

3. ALIGNMENT IS EVERYTHING

But before you consider adding trims, it's essential to pick a line from which *consistent* positioning decisions can be made, as considered alignment inspires an instant feeling of cohesion and harmony. Anything placed on a wall, or around the periphery of a room, becomes a component in the composition of each plane, with a dynamic tension between it and the position of *all other elements* in the room, from doors and artwork, to the drop of curtains and blocks of applied colour or pattern. We do not want a very regimented sense of alignment, but we need to avoid everything appearing to jiggle up and down with no sense at all of an underlying rationale. Large, high-level items (artworks to wall-hung TVs) should have a coherence, as should anything placed at a lower level, such as dados or wall-hung sideboards. That said, it's not terribly helpful to have absolutely fixed rules as to the initial positioning of such a line, because the proportions of every home are different, only that once you've settled on one, you stick to it, and ideally use it from room to room too. A good way to start, though, is to stand in the middle of each newly whited-out room (preferably emptied of furniture, but if this is not possible, then pile it compactly into the middle so you can see the full perimeter of the floor) and try to see if there's any inherent sense of order. What details are there in situ that might be taken as a guide – perhaps original trims, if you're lucky, or the casings of windows? Are there any openings, recesses, alcoves or fireplaces? Any of these can be a mark from which to begin in an attempt to introduce a regular visual rhythm to a room.

But remember, we're trying to work *with* what we have in order to refine and align, not to obliterate a room's given bone structure. And if a room completely lacks any existing features of merit, don't worry. The top line of internal door frames can often be taken as a starting point because they are a standard size based on the average proportions of the human body, and if there is more than one door in a room, hopefully they will be set at the same height. See opposite for how best to hang everything together.

PICTURE HANGING

Use a single high-level key line (such as that provided via door frames) to align the tops of any very large pictures, or key wall-hung items such as TVs, around a room, regardless of how far away they are from each other. Although if you have picture rails, use this as your guide instead and hang all large artworks such that their frames sit a minimum of an inch or two below them. Hang any smaller pictures in a way that your eyeline is roughly level with one-third down from their tops. If by chance this puts them exactly on a level with a larger picture, experiment with moving the smaller ones up or down a little to avoid a strict line (more on this in Chapter 9).

BUT HIP HEIGHT IS A GOOD RULE OF THUMB FOR WALL-HUNG STORAGE AND SIDEBOARDS.

If the upper surface is intended for display, that is. If you have dado rails, then attach sideboards immediately beneath these, never cutting into them, unless they are significantly below hip height, in which case you may need to look into removing and replacing them. And to note: gender is not particularly an issue when I refer to hip height as a guide, as all adult hips are in fact at roughly the same level; height differences are usually related to torso length!

AND LARGER, HIGHER UNITS?

The top of these, whether open shelving or closed cupboards, should follow the line picked for the tops of any large paintings. Ideally also fitting neatly in between any existing, or newly applied, picture and dado rails.

SET ALL CURTAIN TOPS AT THE SAME HEIGHT

As you flow from room to room, this is a subtle but very effective way to create cohesion. Often this is predetermined by the window casings themselves, but if you have wonky windows, this can also be a way of making them appear level, because with a little stealthy carpentry (adding an additional wooden batten above existing casings for rails to be secured to) windows can be duly 'straightened' with the curtains.

ALWAYS OPT FOR FLOOR-LENGTH CURTAINS THAT JUST SKIM THE FLOOR

Never ever have curtains that fall in pools of fabric, or that stop just above radiators. The former is really dated and unnecessary, and the latter is actually quite inefficient for insulation – warmed air will always rise above curtains and radiators were originally introduced directly under windows only as the most efficient way to offset incoming cold air, rather than to heat the room itself.

4. DON'T BE A SLAVE TO CENTRING AND SYMMETRY

There is always a moment when everything has been placed in such a way that it feels balanced. And while a consistent horizontal line around a room will help to pull a look together, perfect centring and symmetry often do not as the brain assumes it has the measure of them in a single glance, and the eye tends to gloss over them. For example, if we consider even the most beautiful of faces, while the eyes and mouth will invariably be aligned, the face itself is seldom symmetrical around a vertical axis; instead it will be the small quirks on one side, the single mole or a slight uplift to a brow, that adds beauty. Applying this to the home, such as a wall with a centrally placed window, clearly in most cases it will make sense to give the same treatment to the walls on either side. But a *happy inside* touch of 'otherness' would be to suspend a hanging basket in front of the window, or to hang a beautifully framed picture on one side with nothing on the other. These act as visual nudges – we want our gaze to deliberately linger and be entranced. After all, if you picture a room that has a water stain in one corner, for all the potential beauty of its furnishings and fittings, your eye will repeatedly dart to the damp patch. We want to instil that same sense of being drawn to look more closely, but at something beautiful, not something that needs fixing!

5. MAKE ROOM FOR A VIEW

Regardless of the textural virtuosity of your walls, views outside are incredibly important. They allow the eye to travel beyond the physical borders of a room, implying freedom from constriction which makes any space feel bigger, and increases the sense of calm. Consider how the opposite of this works: how cosy a space feels when you deliberately block off such stimuli by drawing curtains or closing shutters. Or if we take this to the extreme: how oppressive a room becomes with no recourse to an external view at all, in the manner of a prison cell. So for some pointers on how to enhance a feeling of openness, check out the list opposite.

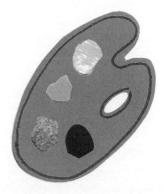

KEEP WINDOWS CLEAR
Windows are the eyes of your home; do not allow them to be cluttered by heavy or unnecessary window treatments.

GO WIDE WITH CURTAIN RAILS
Always fit curtain rails so that they're wide enough to allow open drapes to stand completely clear of the glass. This maximises the view as well as the amount of incoming daylight. You will have to allow for more fabric as a result, and if you are having curtains made with someone coming in to measure up for you, make sure you request this as it is not standard practice.

CHOOSE BLINDS AND NEVER NET CURTAINS
A more flexible, not to mention modern alternative to net curtains is a fine-gauge cotton blind that can be pulled down as privacy requires, for example in a bedroom while dressing, then rolled right up when screening is not a priority. Alternatively, use thin linen or hemp gauzes and have them properly hung, close to the glass, as secondary curtains that can be pulled back and forth as required.

SAY NO TO VENETIAN BLINDS!
Redolent of offices only, they are horrible dust-traps as well as being hard to the touch and often very annoying to operate.

CONSIDER SHUTTERS OR USE STICKY-BACK TRANSLUCENT WINDOW FILM
Both of these can be effective at screening lower window panes while allowing the upper panes to be left clear for the penetration of the maximum amount of daylight.

USE WHITE AS A BACKDROP
White is often the best backdrop for window walls as it encourages the focus to be on the view rather than what surrounds it. This is particularly important in small rooms, when window frames should always be finished in white gloss, too, to further blur any division between wall, window frame and the view being framed.

6. LEARN TO LOVE BUILT-IN STORAGE AND SHELVING

With no legs or brackets to distract the eye and with the full expanse of the floor uninterrupted by furniture, wall-hung shelving and built-in storage units are another way to make any room feel more spacious, and thus clutter-free. Even lifting storage units a few centimetres off the floor will make a huge difference. As for shelving, wherever possible opt for floating shelves (see below) with no visible supports to allow the focus to be on whatever is being displayed.

• **Ready-made versus custom-fitted?** With metal brackets that bolt to the wall and a shelf casing that slips over the top, floating shelves can be bought ready-made, but obviously these only come in set sizes and there may be limits on the load they can support. Custom-made floating shelves work particularly well within alcoves as this enables them to be fixed to the wall along three sides rather than just across the back and any competent carpenter should easily be able to construct some for you.

• **Get the look for less.** Standard kitchen units are an economical way of getting the floating-storage look for less, as these are designed to be wall hung and capable of carrying a decent amount of weight. They also have the added advantage of being modular, so you can join several together if required, and they often come with a wide range of off-the-shelf colour options and finishes for the fronts.

7. VIEWS FROM ROOM TO ROOM

As well as being able to stand in the centre of any room and not have your eye led astray by things that are out of line or by strident colour clashes, it's important to consider the view from one room to another, as something missed from one angle might be picked up with the benefit of a different vantage point. It's similar to how an artist might cross-check the composition of a painting by looking at it in a mirror: the transposed image reflected in the glass creates an alternative perspective.

Looking from room to room also helps us understand home decoration as a series of interconnected zones. After all, homes are always experienced in motion, with one 'stage set' continually being played out in front of another. This is why a seemingly ideal scheme on paper, doesn't necessarily translate into something that works in practice. In many ways this is the biggest challenge of designing an interior; unless you are spectacularly gifted, or very experienced, you can never really tell what it's going to *feel* like until the end. Regardless, this is another key benefit of the plane-by-plane approach: physically building up a scheme layer by carefully considered layer practically guarantees a better, more satisfying, result. And when you stand in one completed room, gazing happily across to another, you'll know it was worthwhile to be so patient. •

SUMMARY

To return to our musical analogy, the over-arching concept of this chapter is to set your key from the start (your palette) and then to play out different versions of it according to the moods you wish to create within each of the four defined home zones so that they all work harmoniously together.

However, 'Think first, decorate later' must be your battle cry. Resist the temptation to leap into action before taking the time to ask yourself, '*Why* am I choosing this?' throughout every part of this process. Really immerse yourself in remaking your home to support you, from the whiting out of walls to the application of colour and texture. This is imperative to its capacity to have a restorative effect. And as much as you have now let go of possessions that do not serve you, let go of any perceived decorative 'should-dos'. The only limit to what is possible is what you're prepared to try and what you can afford to do.

Give yourself the freedom to allow your palette to evolve too. Aim to keep the core elements consistent, but if and when an ache for change arises, accept that it represents something that needs to be articulated, so embrace it and enjoy finding the solution. *Not* that this is permission to veer completely off piste: for example, do not buy a purple lacquered console if this colour and finish is not already included within your picks. By all means experiment and play but stay within the prescribed total number of 28 palette notes and be consistent in their reapplication from zone to zone. Otherwise, the balance of your home will be thrown, and the overall effect will rapidly become too busy – the antithesis of the *happy inside* way. •

A PALETTE IN ACTION

The following album shows you how a palette might work in practice. They are images of my own home, so the choice of colours, materials and finishes is of course entirely particular to me, inspired variously by my love of Italy, Chinoiserie and a need for calm. To be clear though, the point of showing them is not to infer that this is in any way a 'perfect' palette, rather, it is to give examples of how materials might be mixed and used across the various zones of a home. It also demonstrates how flexible a palette can be in pursuit of flow – for example, antiqued mirror is listed as one of my signature finishes, inspired by two real vintage mirrors that are prized possessions, but I've also applied it as a wallpaper. And although I refer to green as a core colour, it has been put into play both as a dark bottle green downstairs and a much lighter minty shade upstairs. My use of pink however, is almost entirely confined to the same powder pale hue. The photographs also highlight the little things that really contribute to a sense of cohesion, such as unifying the

mount colours of framed artwork; having recurring motifs (for me textured wallpaper, marble and tiles); and sticking to the two shades of wood only rule! These, then, are the 28 notes of my personal palette:

6 x CORE COLOURS: *lavender, green, blue, grey, pink and white*

2 x ACCENT COLOURS: *blood red and mustard yellow*

2 x METALLICS: *stainless steel and brass*

2 x WOODS: *natural oak and dark-stained oak*

2 x SIGNATURE FINISHES: *antiqued mirror, textured wallpaper and glossy black lacquer*

2 x HUMBLE TEXTURES: *hemp and rattan*

6 x FABRIC TEXTURES: *velvet, cotton, linen, wool, sheepskin and embroidered silk*

2 x STONES: *Corian® and marble*

3 x CERAMIC TILES: *white, grey and lavender – all rectangular*

STUDY From the black lacquer and dark wood used for picture frames, to the antiqued mirror wallpaper, a touch of brass, marble, and the Victorian tiles (seen trimming the top, and at the foot of each shelf), these materials and colour swatches form the recurring textures and features of my palette. Likewise, the two shades of lavender, used in different ways throughout the whole ground floor (note the co-ordinating mounts in the picture frames too). And the simplicity of the floating shelves, neatly fitted between two wall-hung storage units.

LOUNGE Wall-hung cupboards topped with the same marble used in the kitchen and bathrooms have doors inscribed with a discrete scalloped pattern — a love for unexpected texture that's echoed in the embossed paper on the wall behind. The toning colours tie it all together while the darker dado rail physically links both sides of my living space even though wall treatments vary. The TV (hung on the left) blends in seamlessly thanks to its ability to display an artwork of choice when not in use, but also because I coordinated adjacent picture frames.

DINING END OF LOUNGE Adding instant texture and intrigue to an otherwise plain wall, applied panelling wraps around the whole of the front of my home, visually linking the living room on the right to my study on the left. The mirrored wallpaper repeats too, used for a whole wall in the study, and behind shelving (see picture on page 93), as do the full-drop lavender velvet curtains. The vintage Ercol dining chairs were dipped to remove their shiny yellowed 1950s varnish and re-stained, with a satin finish, to match the floors.

LIVING AREA While floating shelves enable you to focus on the display, rather than any supports, don't neglect the backdrop! Here I've used one of my tile picks to add interest. The picture frames too reflect my wider palette choices (brass, gloss white, natural and dark-stained oak), and the skinny painted strip, in my accent colour mustard, underneath the shelves is one of my favourite details — something you can only see when you're sat down. See too, above the picture rail, the pale grey gloss used for all downstairs ceilings.

KITCHEN   A sofa in the kitchen? Indeed yes, what a treat. Albeit usually with a little more room to sit than shown here! Nevertheless, it demonstrates the wealth of textural opportunity provided by fabric. My sofas, originally dark brown leather, were re-upholstered in a luscious pale pink velvet, another velvet coverlet is draped over the seats for extra squish and cushions dip into every corner of my colour palette. The wall behind is pale pink, and above, the ceiling has been painted mustard, for an extra hit of sunshine.

SPARE BEDROOM   A wall composed of marble offcuts, over-sized white tiles and the grey tiles used in an adjacent bathroom, currently serves as a wonderful bedhead. But, as requirements change, it could equally become an eminently practical backdrop to a desk. And because black lacquer is a consistent part of my palette, the side table, presently used by the bedside, can easily be relocated elsewhere. The pale grey on the wall is the same as that used on the downstairs ceilings. Upstairs, ceilings are all gloss white.

KITCHEN   Even in the simplest of spaces there's much scope for experimentation and fun. Here I've layered marble and tiles seen elsewhere above pale grey Corian® countertops with integrated upstands, and topped the lot with a row of shallow wall-hung units (housing the extractor fan and everyday kitchenalia) finished with the same scallop-detailed fronts on black carcasses as used in the living area opposite. Lower units, which accommodate appliances, all have glossy plain dark grey doors, reflecting their more utilitarian purpose.

MAIN BEDROOM   Upstairs, softly contrasting patterns, diluted colours and the introduction of a new shade on the walls (reflected in the duvet cover), gives my palette a softer spin. The fabrics too are lighter linens and cottons, however there's still a touch of velvet via one of the cushions. My beloved tiles pop up on the headboard/shelf, and the wall behind the bedhead is also textured, albeit using a smaller version of the larger tile design used downstairs. The black pendants echo black lacquered bedside cabinets.

HALLWAY   This is the only place such a dark green has been used on the walls. However, picture mounts and frames mirror other favoured finishes; the lamp coordinates with nearby fixtures, and the marble top is simply a darker colourway of that used elsewhere (used as such for other units upstairs too). Interestingly, this wall has seen the most changes of any in my home, and as I write, I'm considering taking it, and the cupboard fronts, to navy! Sometimes it just takes a while to get it right.

3

ENERGY

'BETTER KEEP YOURSELF CLEAN
AND BRIGHT. YOU ARE THE WINDOW
THROUGH WHICH YOU MUST SEE
THE WORLD.'

GEORGE BERNARD SHAW
IRISH PLAYWRIGHT
(1856-1950)

When we understand the home as a holistic organic
entity that both reflects and responds to those living
inside it, it becomes obvious that we need to avoid
energetic stagnancy at all costs – a state in which the
home feels gloomy and we feel sluggish. To achieve an
energetically supportive environment, natural daylight
is a must and air needs to be able to flow unimpeded
through every room. We also need to recognise that
every single thing within the home has an energy level
of its own, and thus everything must make a positive
contribution to the whole. So, in this chapter we
will explore the energy boosters to bring inside, and
highlight the energy sappers that need to go.

CHAPTER THREE

UNDERSTANDING ZONING AND FLOW

In pursuit of harmony, abundance and well-being, the Chinese have long expounded the virtues of feng shui, a set of guidelines for the best positioning of everything from walls to windows within a home. While I have a lot of time for such study, I've often found it unduly complicated to follow. And when starting with a house that's fully built, or a rental with restrictions on what you can do, it's usually impossible, or plain silly, to contemplate moving stairs or realigning doors. Of course many of the diktats of feng shui do not involve structural alterations, and much of it can be read as common sense with no requirement for complex Chinese algorithms or knowledge of the precise orientation of your abode. Its goal is simply the free flow of positive energy or *qi* (pronounced 'chi' and regarded as the circulating life force that constitutes the basis of much Chinese philosophy and Chinese medicine), as well as the clearing away of anything that might block that flow. •

ENERGY GOES WHERE ATTENTION FLOWS

But before we can address flow or furniture placement, whether with the aid of feng shui or not, we need to start with the very air that you breathe indoors. Why is this important? Let's go back a step and imagine you've decided to take a trip to the seaside. It's a little windy but as you stride along the beach, the blood rushes to your cheeks, your conversation is upbeat and animated, and your appetite at lunchtime keener, with every mouthful tasting delicious. That night, on returning home, you sleep soundly.

What's happening reflects your body's response to the abundance of negative ions in the air by the sea. And don't be put off by the name: negative ions are wholly beneficial. Ions are particles of air – either molecules or atoms – some of which are positively charged (lacking one or more negative electrons) and others negatively charged (oxygen atoms with extra electrons). There are always an abundance of negative ions in nature, near the sea, after a

storm, by waterfalls (even in a shower!), and the benefits include their ability to clear the air we breathe of free radicals (molecules that can damage our bodies), revitalise our cells, enhance immune function, purify the blood and balance the nervous system.

Contrast this with more obviously polluted environments, such as inner cities with high levels of traffic or hermetically sealed and artificially ventilated offices, which have precisely the opposite effect. But then, perhaps shockingly, also the inside of our homes. A growing body of scientific research has concluded that the average home is more polluted than a busy street corner because of the build-up of toxins that linger there, a situation that's exacerbated in winter when the heating gets cranked up and windows are rarely opened. What's worse is that these are not necessarily pollutants that smell bad, therefore alerting us to get rid of them. Indeed, the passive inhalation of contaminated indoor air has been linked to the rise in incidence

of allergies and other ailments, particularly in children. Combine this with research in 2001 funded by the US Environmental Protection Agency (EPA) which indicated that many people spend up to 90 per cent of their time indoors, and the risks to health become clear.

The World Health Organization (WHO) has stated that indoor air should have no more than 25 micrograms of fine particulates per cubic metre, or 50 micrograms of coarser particles. While that might not mean much on its own, consider this: the average toaster emits 300–400 micrograms of particles per cubic metre when browning bread to a golden finish. Should you prefer your toast a little crisper, burnt toast propels those emissions up to a heady 3,000–4,000 micrograms per cubic metre! This is more than 150 times the WHO limits. No wonder we might start to feel a little lethargic if we stay indoors too much, and all we've done so far is make breakfast.

Other common indoor air pollutants (covered in detail in the next section) include fumes from freshly dry-cleaned clothes and volatile organic compounds (or VOCs – carbon-based solvents that evaporate at room temperature) released by some household paint as it dries, as well as medium-density fibreboard (MDF), new carpets (or the adhesives used to fix them) and some upholstery. Let's not forget airborne allergens such as pollen, as well as mould spores, bacteria and viruses, alongside general household dust, cigarette smoke and pet dander. Throw in electromagnetic radiation from your TV, computers, Wi-Fi router et al., common domestic cleaning sprays, air fresheners (ironically), wood-burning stoves, the nitrogen dioxide given off by gas hobs or the particles emitted by scented candles made from paraffin wax, and you have something of a highly toxic cocktail. One that the Royal College of Physicians in London has estimated contributes to some 99,000 deaths per year in Europe alone.

So how do we combat this? It helps to again draw a very simplistic parallel with the human body. In a healthy person, the heart pumps night and day, cheerfully pushing our blood around to nourish our cells and organs and keep us alive. If the main arteries to the heart get blocked for any reason, we're well aware of the consequences, so it behoves us to do what we can to keep all pathways clear (maintain low cholesterol, exercise regularly, give up smoking, etc.).

'A growing body of scientific research has concluded that the average home is more polluted than a busy street corner because of the build-up of toxins that linger there.'

In terms of the home, this is like regularly opening windows to let fresh air blow through your home (assuming you do not live next to a busy road), routine vacuuming and not knowingly introducing any obvious pollutants. In other words, straightforward actions with easily quantifiable results.

But also circulating around the body is lymph, a fluid that contains our all-important infection-fighting white blood cells. Rather than travelling via the blood vessels, this fluid has its own network, our lymphatic system, with which it attempts to zip around the body, cleaning as it goes. It helps the immune system by gobbling up waste, dead blood cells, toxins and nascent cancer cells before any of them can do us any harm. However, the lymphatic system doesn't have a pump like the heart to stimulate it. It depends on our physical movement to do its job. We move, it moves. Medics refer to the lymphatic system as cooperative, as it relies on things external to itself to make it work. If we extend this bodily analogy to the home, in order to introduce the domestic equivalent of white blood cells, we must adopt a more proactive plan of action, an approach that may be summed up in four words – clear, cleanse, combat and continue. So let's examine these in more detail. •

CLEAR: WHAT TO GET RID OF

YOUR TOASTER

Do you have a grill element in your oven? Then you don't even need a toxic toaster, so that's some reclaimed space on your countertop as a bonus. However, the reason a toaster is so inherently polluting is not just the particles being emitted during the browning process, but the fact that it is full of crumbs, each being charred anew at incredible heat, every time you switch it on. So use your oven, with the grill on half power, and put the bread on the bottom shelf, furthest away from the element. It will take a touch longer to crisp, and use a little more electricity, but really, it might be killing you not to wait. Plus always go for golden, never brown.

OVEN DIRT

Toxic dirt can also apply to your oven, thus one of the best investments you will ever make is to buy one with a self-cleaning function. This works by super-heating the whole of the inside of the oven to effectively char off any residual dirt. While that's happening, which is admittedly not all that savoury, fling open the windows for the hour or so it takes, and bear in mind that this is about getting it back to as clean as the day you bought it, after which it's more a question of regular wipe-down

maintenance. Even with a self-cleaning oven, though, all trays and racks must be removed before cleaning can begin. As with the toaster, baking trays and wire grilles can become layered with baked-on deposits that we quickly become oblivious to, seeing instead a well-used accessory. These need to be made pristine again too, but not by using any of the commonly available oven cleaners on the market. Just one glance at the corrosive 'Danger!' symbol on the side of the bottle should be enough to put you off. Instead, the deep-cleaning potential (with no nasty odours) of a thick paste of baking soda and water, left for a couple of hours, has to be seen to be believed. If you have a nice big sink, better yet to leave them to soak overnight, with a generous slosh of basic white vinegar added to the water. After an enthusiastic scour in the morning, they will be as good as new. But even if a few stubborn deposits remain, don't make it into a horrible penance for yourself to get them scrubbed clean; just do a little more each time you use them, and before you know it, they'll be as good as new, and it'll be a matter of pride to keep them that way.

YOUR MICROWAVE

While they are not thought to be intrinsically dangerous, no one needs food that fast. Slow down! Get rid of it and clear even more space on your worktop. If you're really that hungry, boil some pasta. And if you're using a microwave because you think you're saving on your electricity bill, think again. Any savings would be negligible, and you'd be better off looking at the way you heat, cool and light (swap to energy-saving light bulbs) your home instead.

TOXIC CLEANING PRODUCTS

As per oven cleaners, throw out immediately anything that warrants a toxic warning flag – you don't want these in your home. Certainly baking soda and vinegar are fantastic for cleaning oven trays, and a good all-purpose spray can be made from one part vinegar to nine parts water plus a dash of washing-up liquid, with a few drops of an essential oil (lavender, lemon or tea tree) to mask the vinegar smell. However, if this doesn't appeal, then there are many ready-made ecological products on the market with wonderful natural scents. And as a suggestion, rather than trying to batter bacteria into submission with ever-stronger counter-agents promising destruction of 99 per cent of all known germs (which may well be giving rise to the antibiotic-resistant superbugs we hear about in the news), use biodegradable disposable paper towels for day-to-day surface wiping and hand-drying in the kitchen. Damp dish cloths and cotton tea towels rapidly become veritable bacteria breeding grounds if not boil-washed every day, which in itself would be very wasteful. Microfibre cloths made from bamboo (being highly sustainable to grow) are good longer-term alternatives for things such as furniture polishing and glass cleaning. And a steam mop is another worthwhile investment.

BLEACH

It'd be easy to think that bleach is pretty anodyne, being inexpensive and readily available at any supermarket. But although it derives from natural components (salt and water), the process for making it splits the salt and water atoms to create chlorine and lye (caustic soda), which are extremely dangerous to both humans and the environment. If you've ever coughed when pouring bleach down the loo to disinfect the bowl, that's probably because bleach mixes with ammonia (found in urine) to create chlorine gas, the inhalation of which is known to cause lung problems, exacerbate asthma and allergy symptoms, as well as creating dioxins – one of the dirty dozen of persistent environmental pollutants – which have been linked to cancer, miscarriage, immune disorders and more. This certainly adds another perspective to the time-honoured advice when swimming in chlorinated municipal pools: don't wee in the water!

When we consider how many freely available household cleaners and disinfectant wipes contain bleach, and that most people routinely forget to don rubber gloves every time they use them, it's sobering to think how regularly such noxious chemicals are coming into direct contact with your skin, let alone being inhaled. Happily, there are alternatives. White vinegar and baking soda again top the list. (For the loo, coat the bowl with a sprinkling of baking soda and leave for 30 minutes, then spray with the all-purpose cleaner mentioned previously and scrub. If all else fails, then neat vinegar should do the trick.) But despite it sounding pretty hardcore, you could also add 3 per cent hydrogen peroxide solution to your shopping list for cleaning glass, getting rid of tougher stains, whitening laundry (roughly one cup into the soap dispenser drawer), controlling mould (see below) and as a general disinfectant. It works because it's an oxidising agent, releasing oxygen in contact with living cells, whether bacteria or dirt, which converts the peroxide back into harmless water and contaminant-busting oxygen.

OTHER CHEMICAL NASTIES

Other chemicals to watch out for are: triclosan, an antibacterial agent banned in soaps in the US, but still used in the UK (and even included in some toothpastes!); butoxyethanol, found in some window-cleaning products, and thought to be harmful if inhaled; and quaternary ammonium salts, another common antibacterial agent used in many home-cleaning products, and even in hair conditioners and shampoos, despite being a known irritant.

HIGH-VOC PAINT

Paint manufacturers are legally obliged to indicate clearly on every tin of paint the level of VOCs (volatile organic compounds) contained. In the past, the higher the VOC level, the better a paint would dry, adhere and last, and these compounds were thought to rapidly evaporate, whereas low-VOC or zero-VOC paint was believed to be less durable. But since the realisation that paint actually 'off-gasses' (gives off low lev-

els of chemicals) over time, not just during application or while drying, the race has been on to create an effective, long-lasting yet healthily VOC-free paint, and thankfully today such products are freely available for interior as well as exterior use. Search them out, and while you may baulk at the slightly higher prices, just bear in mind that it's a small amount to pay for your good health.

OTHER BUILDING NASTIES

If you're building a house, adding an extension, undertaking general renovation or installing indoor cabinetry, then make sure that any wood you use has been treated with formaldehyde-free natural preservatives, otherwise, just like VOC-containing paints, it could be unhealthily off-gassing for some time after installation. Walls can be constructed using products such as Fermacell®, which is made from recycled paper, water and gypsum (a naturally occurring mineral used to make plaster and cement) and proven to be practically emission-free as it's made without additional glues. Another clean, green building material is Geocell®, a form of high-quality gravel made from 100 per cent recycled glass that's lightweight yet load-bearing, insulating and fire resistant, and can be used for building foundations and landscaping. VOC-free adhesives are also available for tiling, floors and window sealants.

MOULD

If you have mould anywhere in your home, you must get rid of it and tackle the cause as a matter of urgency. Mould gives off airborne spores that you definitely do not want to be inhaling. Hydrogen peroxide solution (as mentioned previously) is good for removing it, but the source of most mould problems is usually a humid atmosphere combined with inadequate ventilation, or water getting caught between building layers, so an external inspection for cracks may be required. Remember, too, that water loves to travel, so the site of any internal damp may be far removed from the actual point of water ingress.

DRY CLEANING

According to the EPA, the main health risk of dry cleaning is not through wearing clothes that have been dry-cleaned but direct exposure to the chemicals required to clean it, most notoriously something called perchloroethylene (also known as tetrachloroethylene) or PERC for short. While its usage was being phased out by some cleaners after it was declared 'probably carcinogenic to humans' in 2012 by the International Agency for Research on Cancer (IARC), this has by no means been mandatory. General guidance therefore seems to indicate that if you live near, or work in, a dry cleaners, long-term exposure

to PERC could be unhealthy. But if your exposure is limited to having a few shirts dry-cleaned each month, then a good policy would be to take them out of any plastic wrappings immediately on collection to give them a chance to air on the way home, and certainly before stashing them away in your wardrobe.

Better yet, try to track down an eco-friendly dry cleaner who uses alternative solvents. It can be hard to know who's really green and who isn't, so always ask for detailed information, knowing that reputable agents will be entirely upfront about what they use. Finally, bear in mind that many 'dry-clean only' garments are marked as such by the manufacturer as a precaution to avoid being held responsible for any shrinking and fading. Many delicate garments, from silk shirts to cashmere jumpers, can be safely washed with a gentle detergent in cool water without any problems at all. It may take a little more time, but again, what price for good health? Plus top tip for removing oil stains from silk: dust with a fine plain face powder. The powder absorbs the oil and the stain will be gone!

'Many scented candles
are manufactured using
paraffin wax, synthetic
dyes and fragrances,
You are what you breathe:
pay more and stay safe.'

PARAFFIN WAX-BASED CANDLES

When paraffin wax burns, it can give off a fine soot that contains known irritants such as toluene and benzene, the same pollutants found in diesel exhaust. Paraffin is, after all, a by-product of the fuel industry, and breathing in its fumes is allegedly as bad for you as second-hand cigarette smoke, worse if you suffer from asthma or have any sort of respiratory weakness. In addition, many scented candles are manufactured using synthetic dyes and fragrances, so as they burn, they're releasing a whole host of these artificially-based chemicals as well. Choose candles that specifically state they have cotton or paper wicks (keep the wicks nice and short too, to limit the amount of smoke) and are made from non-paraffin waxes such as beeswax, GM-free soy wax, coconut, sustainable palm or other plant-based sources, and are scented using only pure natural essential oils for a clean burn. If it doesn't say this loud and proud on the packaging, assume the worst. And it's the same for small tealights too – those bumper budget bags of a hundred lights for a couple of pounds? You are what you breathe: pay more and stay safe.

We are all now well aware of the disaster single-use plastics have been to the environment and our oceans, but are you up to speed on their effect on your personal health too? The main issue is that some of the chemicals used to create plastic are known to leach directly into food or water. Polycarbonate (used for water bottles and food-storage containers) and PVC (used to make bottles, cling film and the inner linings of some tin cans) contain Bisphenol A (BPA) and phthalates respectively, both known endocrine disruptors that adversely affect the production and levels of our hormones, as well as being associated with all manner of other health issues including asthma, cancer, obesity and autism. Regrettably, we are probably all exposed to some level of them on a daily basis. And while BPA and phthalates are the substances in the spotlight at the moment, given that plastic is a wholly synthetic product (derived from petroleum), who knows what else it may contain that might contaminate us? As such, it's a little unnerving how much of it surrounds us – it's the bags that our food is routinely packaged in, what the fresh produce drawers in our fridges are made from, and it's used for components of many of the things we touch every day. Yet while it's important not to get unduly alarmist about it, this should go hand in hand with choosing natural materials over man-made wherever possible, most especially with respect to the storage of food, and around children whose brains and nervous systems are still developing. Decant and discard is the way forward.

SWAP TO GLASS OR STAINLESS STEEL
Perfect for reusable water bottles and lunch boxes.

TRY BAMBOO OR SILICONE
Great for cooking and serving utensils, as well as children's crockery and cutlery.

USE SCREW-TOP GLASS JARS FOR FOOD STORAGE
Especially dried foods and baking ingredients. I love the Le Parfait Familia Wiss range.

DITCH CLING FILM
Use unbleached baking paper and bags to wrap food or sandwiches. And just pop a plate over a bowl of leftovers when storing food in the fridge or use old jam jars.

CHECK LABELS
Make sure your rubber gloves really are made of natural rubber! Synthetic rubber, like plastic, is made from petroleum, a non-renewable resource.

NEVER LET CHILDREN CHEW PLASTIC TOYS
And forget about plastic teethers!

NEVER HEAT OR FREEZE FOOD IN PLASTIC CONTAINERS
This accelerates the leaching process. Likewise, never wash plastic in hot water, drink hot drinks from plastic cups or heat oven-cooked ready-meals in their plastic or tin-foil containers.

CHECK THE TINNED FOOD AND DRINK YOU CONSUME
Because of the possible plastic linings inside tins.

DECANT COOKING OILS
Pour oil from plastic bottles into glass ones. I use rubber-sealed Kilner bottles.

REMOVE FOOD FROM PLASTIC WRAPPINGS
Do it as soon as you store food, or buy loose fruit and vegetables.

CHECK YOUR SHOWER CURTAIN. IS IT PVC-FREE?
Try hemp instead, as it's naturally resistant to mould and bacteria.

CHECK AT LEAST FOR BPA-FREE
If using some plastic is unavoidable, at the very least check that it's BPA-free. No sticker saying that it is? Then it's probably not.

NON-STICK COOKWARE

There is a lot of debate about the potential toxicity of non-stick cookware. If you're using it at lower temperatures, the surface is completely intact and not flaking, then one school of thought says its easy-clean convenience, combined with the fact that you'll potentially use less oil or butter to cook with in the first place, outweighs any concerns. I think it's a minor hardship to jettison a few non-stick pans in addition to the plastic, especially when there are alternatives. Just the chemical name of the coating – polytetrafluoroethylene (PTFE) also known as Teflon, a synthetic chemical made up of carbon and fluorine atoms – is enough to make me wary. That said, since 2013 all Teflon-coated products have been manufactured without a substance called perfluorooctanoic acid (PFOA), which was the prime suspect linked to a number of health conditions including kidney and liver disease. If you have a pan manufactured before that date, then good to know is that apparently exposure to PFOA only occurs if the pan is heated to more than 300°C (570°F); as a rough guide, top heat on a standard gas hob might reach about 190°C (375°F), but on an induction hob it could easily top 260°C (500°F) without even employing the boost function.

- **Never preheat empty pans.**
  They can very quickly reach high temperatures.

- **Always cook on the lowest heat possible.**
  But note that even the lowest heat will steadily increase the temperature of any pan over time.

- **Never use metal utensils or metal scourers on non-stick pans.**
  This can lead to scuffs and scratches that will jeopardise the integrity of the coating.

- **Replace cookware as soon as it shows any signs of wear or flaking.**
  Or simply switch to something safer. Such as stainless steel, cast-iron (which if seasoned correctly, as per the manufacturer's instructions, is naturally non-stick), ceramic-coated or stoneware pots and pans (I love the Venice Pro range by GreenPan), and use a silicone baking tray and silicone bakeware for making cakes, or line existing trays with unbleached baking paper.

ELECTROMAGNETIC RADIATION
Our mobile phones, computers, laptops, Wi-Fi routers, radio alarm clocks, and any other device that uses Bluetooth, GPS or other wireless modes of communication, all emit radio-frequency electromagnetic radiation (EMR). Add to this our potential proximity to mobile-phone masts and electricity pylons, together with the possibility of geopathic stress (a relatively new concept that suggests resonant energy from the earth may have an impact on health and wellbeing), and this amounts to another potentially harmful load on the body. And with over 5 billion mobile phones in use today worldwide, according to Professor Olle Johansson, a neuroscientist at the Karolinska Institute in Sweden, we are currently living in an environment estimated to contain more than 10 billion times more radio-frequency EMR than in the 1960s. Meanwhile, as heated debate rages over the precise impact this proliferation may be having on the human body, industry pushes ahead with the roll-out (no doubt very lucrative for some) of ever-faster, more powerful and widespread 5G coverage and plans to Wi-Fi-enable the whole world! Certainly a significant number of articles published in scientific and medical journals highlight the need for greater caution and more investigation; IARC has classified radio-frequency radiation as a Group 2B carcinogen, which means it's considered a possible cause of cancer in humans; and a 2008 Swedish study found a fivefold increase in the incidence of glioma (a form of brain cancer now recognised by the WHO as being linked to mobile phone usage) for those who started using mobiles when they were under 20 years old, suggesting that the age at first use is highly relevant.

In the face of this, and considering how complex and sensitive a biological system the human body is, it's hard to dismiss the idea that EMR cannot have any effect, especially on our children whose thinner skulls and the higher water content of their bodies make them especially vulnerable. That said, in discussing this issue with medical friends and other colleagues, opinions are sharply divided. But from my personal experience, when I used to have an active Wi-Fi router in my home, I can attest to significantly more disturbed sleep if I forgot to switch it off at night. I've subsequently ditched the router completely and disabled the Bluetooth function on my watch, ironically used to track my fitness levels! In my view, better safe than sorry. And I now sleep like a baby. As such, overleaf you'll find more ways to limit your EMR exposure.

COUNTER-ATTACK

Devices known as EMR blockers claim to neutralise the negative frequency of such electromagnetic fields by emitting positive frequencies. It's supposedly the same sort of 'destructive interference' used in noise-cancelling headphones, in which sound waves created by the headphone speaker cancel out those from an external source. So while such technology doesn't offer physical blocking or a reduction in radiation, they purportedly 'neutralise and harmonise' the emissions in a way that renders them harmless or, at least, less potentially bothersome for the body.

RECONSIDER CABLES

More direct (and quantifiable) action would be to ditch your Wi-Fi router, and go back to accessing the internet via an ethernet cable. Most routers should have the correct cable socket on the back already. However, it does mean that it needs to be close enough to your computer to be able to reach it; and you still need to go online to deactivate the router's automatic Wi-Fi capacity, otherwise when you switch it on to enable the ethernet connection it'll still be radiating. At the very least, always completely switch off your router at night before you go to sleep.

DITCH CORDLESS LANDLINE PHONES

Likewise swap these for a fixed phone as cordless phones continuously emit radiation, whether they're in use or not.

HEALTHY MOBILE USE

Get into the habit of utilising airplane mode more often. In addition, never carry a phone close to your body, invest in a EMR-blocking phone case – these enable you to use your phone as normal but block the radiation through the front to shield your brain – and regardless, always use a hands-free device rather than holding a phone to your head to take or make calls.

RECONSIDER ANY BLUETOOTH OR WI-FI-ENABLED TRACKING DEVICES

When you think that these are usually strapped directly to the body at vulnerable pulse points and yet they constantly emit radiation as they search for the nearest network to back up your exercise data, you might want to reconsider. However, many models actually allow you to turn-off the Wi-Fi and Bluetooth capacity while you're wearing them. Then it's easy enough to briefly switch it back on when you've removed it at night, and sync the day's data in one go. Besides, you should absolutely never wear such a device while you sleep (more in Chapter 8 on this).

PROTECT YOUR CHILDREN

Public health guidelines already state that children under 16 should not be using mobile phones except in an emergency, not that this information is easy to find despite being an official recommendation! However once you start to dig, you'll discover many a piece of research calling into question whether schools should be fully Wi-Fi-enabled – a five-year-old absorbs as much as 60 per cent more radiation than an adult. In fact, in France since 2015, Wi-Fi and wireless devices have been legally banned in any nursery for the under-threes, and their use has been kept to a strict minimum in schools for children up to 11 years old. And in Sweden – where, since 2003, medical conditions related to EMR have been officially recognised as a disability – the government funds the application of anti-radiation paint in the homes of people diagnosed as hyper-sensitive, and in schools, if even one child is deemed to be affected by Wi-Fi, the system is removed and the classroom shielded.

BUY AN EMF METER

If you are concerned, you can buy a meter for detecting the levels of EMR in your home. However, those that are sensitive enough to be effective are expensive, and without clear industry guidelines on what constitutes a 'safe' level, I'm not sure how beneficial such data might be beyond showing you that EMR exists.

ADDITIONAL SHIELDING

In addition to combating EMR within the home, if you really wanted to go to town, then there are all sorts of extras available to purportedly deflect, neutralise or otherwise shield you from external EMR. Advocates of such measures focus on the bedroom as the primary room to protect, in recognition of the importance of good sleep. Special fabric containing silver (and sometimes copper) can therefore be used to line curtains, anti-radiation paint can be applied to walls and there's even a form of metallic mesh that can be laid underneath carpeting to effectively create your very own EMR-busting habitable Faraday cage!

CLEANSE: WHAT TO CLEAN UP

When you start to look around your home with this chapter in mind, you might begin to feel a little paranoid! But rest assured, every micro-step you take to purge your home, and especially the kitchen, of any inadvertent energy sappers, is a move towards a healthier you. Bear in mind, too, that it's more useful and motivating to effect one small change that endures for the long term than make a big shift that lasts only a month. To ensure you keep up the good work, let's look at some new habits to introduce.

CLEAN COOKING

The more you can steam your food (from veg to fish), the better in terms of locking in nutrients and safeguarding your pans. And steaming need not involve any fancy pots: instead purchase a collapsible stainless steel steamer basket, which is designed to be dropped into any existing saucepan, expanding to fit and instantly converting it into an inexpensive steamer. But if the lure of a good roast is just too much to forgo, then in order to keep your oven as pristine (i.e. toxin-free) as is realistically possible, always grill or roast on the bottom shelf to minimise any spitting fat catching the exposed heating elements. A chicken can easily be cooked in a roasting bag (simply split the bag open for the last 20 minutes to crisp up the skin if so desired).

CLEAN WATER

Sadly a lot of the water supplied to our homes is not as clean as we'd like it to be. Chemicals are added to kill bacteria, old pipes may throw in delights of their own, not to forget the presence of hormones, nitrates and pesticides, all of which render a filter essential for your drinking water. You can test your water yourself with an easily available TDS (total dissolved solids) meter, which gives a reading in parts per million (ppm). Generally, water with a reading of greater than 500 ppm would be considered undrinkable. I use a ZeroWater filter jug at home, a system that guarantees to remove 99 per cent of all TDS and routinely gets my water down to a reading of 0 ppm. What's slightly scary is how different it tastes once freshly filtered.

CLEAN PRODUCTS

What you put on to your body also goes into your body, because anything applied to your skin is rapidly absorbed by it and therefore becomes a factor in your health and wellbeing. So it's not just about being careful about what you eat, drink or use to cook with, but also any lotions and potions that you use, from make-up to hand wash. Check the labels of these too, or search out certified organic brands. Two key baddies to watch out for include sodium laurel sulfate (which can unnecessarily strip the skin of its natural barrier oils and render it more susceptible to eczema) and the group of antibacterial preservatives known as parabens (some of which have already been banned in Europe due to a potential link to cancer, though they are still used in the US).

CLEAN MATERIALS

The desire to reuse and recycle is laudable and pre-loved items can be an inexpensive way to add unique charm to a home. However, be mindful of the content of any varnishes or sealants that may have been employed, especially on thrift or vintage furniture and other salvage or garage-sale items whose provenance cannot be accurately tracked. While anything gaseous and noxious in coatings will probably have completely evaporated, older glue formulations and other materials may not be as wholesome as you think: consider the widespread use of asbestos for insulation before its dust was discovered to be dangerous, or the common use of high levels of lead in metallic objects and paint. Be particularly careful with stripping or sanding old paintwork for this reason, and think twice about antique crystal decanters, vintage plates and bowls for active use as they are all likely to have been crafted with much higher levels of lead than would currently be permitted (DIY hand-held lead-testing kits can be used to quickly ascertain levels in anything currently owned). Old cutlery, too, may cause unsavoury chemicals to leach into your food, the only exceptions being solid sterling silver or stainless steel, both of which are safe to buy old or new. Also, vintage upholstery may contain outdated and thus harmful fire retardants, along with mould and other nasties; likewise never use antique furniture (especially not a crib) in a nursery. •

COMBAT: WHAT TO INTRODUCE

In Chapter 2, on defining your palette, I stated that synthetics are banned and elemental materials are to be embraced in pursuit of a healthy home. Related to this is biophilic design, an approach that puts increasing our contact with nature at the top of its agenda. And with more and more people now living and working in completely urbanised surroundings – it's even estimated that, by 2050, two-thirds of the world's population will be living in cities – a tangible sense of the natural world nearby is being lost, with a highly negative impact on mood, behaviour and emotions. Luckily, biophilia (meaning 'love of nature') can be brought into any environment by mimicking the natural world in three main ways: experientially through the very architecture of the space around us (curves, natural materials and the use of wood in particular); indirectly through the use of colours, patterns and textures that evoke nature (from leafy prints on fabric or wallpaper to textured flooring that looks like moss); and lastly through a direct connection to nature via natural light, plants and water features. In hospitals such an approach has been proven to help patients recover more quickly; in schools children learn faster; and in the home it contributes to making our surroundings more restorative, energising and relaxing, which is exactly what we need. In this section we'll look at various natural ways to increase the positivity of our places (and ourselves) and other more high-tech solutions that might help as well.

HOUSE PLANTS

There was a time when house plants were considered deeply uncool, something only for the mad lady of yore and her cats. Today, much as our parks are considered the lungs of our cities, so house plants are now seen as veritable indoor air-cleaning Ninjas. Research by none other than NASA has revealed that they can remove up to 87 per cent of air toxins within 24 hours, as well as turning carbon dioxide into clean, pure oxygen. While these studies were originally undertaken to investigate the sort of support that might prove helpful in designing sustainable living environments in space, many of the findings can clearly be applied right here on Earth too. Some commonly available (and beautiful) plants to get you started are listed opposite. And please note the complete exclusion of cacti. Despite the rapid rise of these prickly plants to the top of the pot-plant charts, their very spikiness runs completely counter to the creation of a relaxing environment. Sadly, I feel their popularity in our increasingly fraught, time-poor era has more to do with their resistance to neglect than a true appreciation of their form.

ALOE VERA
(Aloe barbadensis)
A nocturnal oxygenator, so a good one for the bedroom. An evergreen succulent, it requires more light than the snake plant below, though, preferring full sun to semi-sun.

ARECA PALM
(Chrysalidocarpus lutescens)
Also known as the yellow palm or butterfly palm. With its feathery fern-like leaves, this is consistently rated as among the best house plants for removing many indoor airborne toxins.

BAMBOO PALM
(Chamaedorea seifrizii)
A cross between the areca and lady palm, with its slender canes and delicate fans of leaves. Great at pumping moisture back into the air.

BOSTON FERN
(Nephrolepis exaltata 'Bostoniensis')
A beautifully soft, feathery fern that has been popular since the Victorian era. Requires more regular care and maintenance than other plants.

ENGLISH IVY
(Hedera helix)
Particularly effective at removing airborne formaldehyde, ivy is quick growing and great for hanging baskets.

DRACAENA 'JANET CRAIG'
(Dracaena deremensis) 'Janet Craig'
A member of the agave family, with long tapered leaves, it's good for shady sites and is easy to look after.

LADY PALM
(Rhapis excelsa)
With thick brown stems and broad fans of leaves, this looks like a typical palm. Slow-growing and easy to maintain. Best in semi-sun.

PEACE LILY
(Spathiphyllum sp.)
Practically indestructible, this is a great starter plant. Tolerant of even complete shade, it will obligingly droop when it needs watering, and reward you with elegant white flowers.

RUBBER PLANT
(Ficus elastica)
One of the best plants for removal of chemical toxins in the air.

SNAKE PLANT
(Sansevieria trifasciata)
Also known as mother-in-law's tongue. Tall and spiky, or elegant and proud, depending on your point of view, it's good for mixing with other varieties. As it releases oxygen and absorbs carbon dioxide at night, it's ideal for a bedroom.Can tolerant complete shade.

*'I am a firm believer in the maxim that where the
mind goes, the body follows. After all, if you watch something sad,
this provokes a physical response – tears.'*

HERBS

As well as house plants, potted herbs can make a wonderful addition to the home, especially on a table top as a fragrant (and edible) centrepiece. Rosemary is naturally invigorating; mint leaves can be plucked and dropped straight into hot water for a refreshing tisane; and parsley can be added directly to food, as can basil and sage. They each have their own distinctive look and smell and it's a shame to relegate them only to the kitchen.

HIMALAYAN SALT LAMPS

On an empirical scientific level there is little to support the claims that salt lamps purge the air of toxins by attracting impurities and neutralising them, but they are relatively in-expensive and beautiful to look at as they emit a wonderfully soothing pale pink light. For sure there is as much literature passionately vouching for their efficacy as there is declaring it to be utter bunkum, so it may well be a placebo effect (and I'd pop crystals and homeopathy into this category too). But then, defined as something entire-ly inert in the guise of a healing medicine, a placebo can be therapeutic in the way

it connects mind and body. And I am a firm believer in the maxim that where the mind goes, the body follows. After all, if you watch something sad, this provokes a physical response – tears; likewise laughter occurs at the stimulus of seeing or hearing something perceived by the brain as funny. Both are perfect examples of mind–body connections. And the placebo effect has been proven time and time again through rigorous scientific investigation. So if you like the look of the lamps, why not add one to your indoor air-cleaning repertoire? It certainly can't hurt.

BEESWAX CANDLES

As they are made from 100 per cent natural beeswax, burning these candles is reputed to release negatively charged ions into the air (remember them from our metaphorical seafront walk?), which may keep common allergens such as dust and dander at bay. They smell delicious and are completely toxin-free, so again, why not give them a go?

SAGE SMUDGING

Much like Himalayan salt lamps, who knows if this actually works – its origins lie with the Native Americans, who used it to clear bad feelings or negative spirits from their homes – but if just to infuse your home with the sweet, cleansing scent of sage, smudging can be a powerful exercise. And if your home is within a converted building, such as a former hospital or deconsecrated church, as has become increasingly popular, then it could be a good way to help you claim the space as that of a proper home. But treat this ancient ritual with the respect it deserves, or don't try it at all. Instructions follow on how to go about it.

• **Step 1.** Buy a certified organic smudging bundle of white sage from somewhere reputable. If you find a good supplier and it offers an online service, then that's worth bearing in mind for the future, but in the first instance it's better to buy from an actual shop, where you can physically see, and smell, what you're getting, and can check that it was harvested in a manner that respects the traditions. Although white sage is the most commonly used herb for domestic smudging, cedar or even lavender can also be used.

• **Step 2.** Concentrate on your intention to purify your home, then set light to one end of your bundle and allow the leaves to glow hot until they start producing smoke. Next gently stub out any flames in a small bowl – the idea is for the leaves to smoulder, not be on fire. Some people like to use an abalone shell as their 'bowl', but any small natural clay or stone vessel specially designated for the purpose will do.

• **Step 3.** Different traditions have differing and very precise protocols about where to start and the direction to follow, but the basic idea is to walk slowly around the perimeter of your home, wafting the smoke into corners and from top to bottom, moving from room to room in a clockwise direction. Your front entrance is a good place to start, and as you pass other doors or windows, gently push the smoke through and outwards so that it 'carries' any negativity with it. Take your bowl with you to collect any ash, and when you have finished, extinguish the smoking bundle by stubbing it out in the bowl. Return any ash or broken fragments to the earth, and store the remainder of your sage somewhere special.

Used for millennia to purify and heal, some oils are also believed to neutralise airborne bacteria. Eucalyptus and tea tree oil are probably familiar in this respect as cold remedies. But did you know that, due to their allegedly potent antioxidant and anti-inflammatory properties, oregano and frankincense oils have also been touted as alternative cancer 'cures'? While I very much doubt this can be proven, aromatherapy – using an essential-oil burner – is the best way to experience the positive effects of any such oils in the home, as our noses are replete with highly sensitive nerve endings all primed to pick up the positive olfactory messages and send calming thoughts direct to the brain. I've listed opposite some of my favourite oils and their individual qualities. They can be happily combined to enhance their effects, and together they make a great scent starter kit. There are also many ready-made bath oils and beauty products incorporating essential oils, offering another wonderful way to absorb their benefits. However, be sure to stick to reputable, organic brands.

BALANCING OILS

BERGAMOT
Uplifting yet cool and familiar
from Earl Grey tea.

GERANIUM
Sweetly scented and obviously
floral; mixes well with rose.

ROSE
Inherently calming and soothing to
the soul; a good base for other oils.

RELAXING OILS

LAVENDER
Popular, soothing and effective.

CLARY SAGE
Blends beautifully with lavender,
with a slightly richer, almost spicy
fragrance.

CAMOMILE
No doubt familiar from the tea,
but mellow and soothing as a
scent too.

ENERGISING OILS

ROSEMARY
Strongly scented yet renowned for
its ability to aid concentration.

BLACK PEPPER
Warming and spicy, it blends well
with lavender or rose for a more
balancing effect.

ORANGE
Uplifting and sweet, revitalising
and gently detoxifying.

FRANKINCENSE
Heady yet fresh-smelling,
like a lighter version of patchouli.

CLEANSING OILS

TEA TREE
Quite medicinal-smelling,
so you'll either love or loathe it.

EUCALYPTUS
A gentler version of the above.

LEMONGRASS
Energising and zesty; plus whole
sticks steeped in hot water make
a tisane that's fantastically good
for the digestion.

MYRRH
Earthy-smelling and vibrant;
alleged to be a potent hormone
balancer and liver cleanser.

Translated literally as 'taking in the forest atmosphere', this concept was developed in Japan in the 1980s and has become a cornerstone of preventative health care and healing in Japanese medicine. It feels relevant to mention it in this chapter on energy because you are yourself a vital component in the energy metric of your home, and well-being is nothing if not a 360-degree pursuit. Shinrin-yoku, then, is the act of taking a leisurely walk in the countryside, preferably in a wild and natural area of woodland with a canopy of branches overhead, to benefit from airborne organic compounds known as phytoncides. Emitted by trees and other plants, these have been demonstrated to have a whole range of therapeutic effects, from reducing blood pressure and stress, improving mood and increasing focus to accelerating recovery from illness and supporting immune function and thus boosting energy levels. Shinrin-yoku may thus be regarded as a botanically-based form of walking self-medication.

Spending time in nature is also thought to be beneficial because, in a world of relentless demands on our attention, it exerts a 'soft fascination', a term coined in the 1970s by US academics Rachel and Stephen Kaplan, professors of psychology at the University of Michigan who studied the effect of nature on people's health and relationships. What they meant by this was nature's ability to generate 'cognitive quiet', in which your mind is effortlessly occupied in a way that fosters recuperation. Thus, as much as we can bring plants into our homes to combat toxicity, shinrin-yoku could be thought of as a means of taking ourselves to the very source of nature, to bathe in all its multi-sensory benevolence – the sounds of bark crunching underfoot, the smell of the earth, the quality of light filtering through the leaves, the reassuring solidity of tree trunks and the taste of fresh, clean air – the very purest version of biophilic design, in fact.

HIGHER-TECH SOLUTIONS

Shifting to the opposite end of the scale, and back inside our homes, you could introduce a technological approach to air clearing with one of four types of domestic air purifiers: mechanical filters, electrostatic precipitators, negative-ion generators and the less common UV filters. However, any filtration system is rarely able to remove gaseous irritants such as VOCs or radon. For this you'd require the addition of an adsorbent, such as activated charcoal. The extremely porous nature of the charcoal is capable of trapping such molecules, hence it's available as an optional ingredient in some purifiers. If you decide to invest in such a system, or a dehumidifier, it's essential to regularly check the filters and keep all components clean, as standing water and high humidity quickly attract mould and mildew and, before you know it, you'll be back where you started. Opposite is a quick guide to what's what.

MECHANICAL FILTERS

These have a 'dirt'-collection bag or paper filter through which internal fans pull the air in order to clean it, before circulating it back into the room. These are best for low-dust environments as the filters must be regularly replaced to ensure efficacy. To note, some purifiers may be termed HEPA (high-efficiency particulate air) filters. Airtight and designed to capture the very smallest particles, such filters can be beneficial for severe allergy or asthma sufferers. Be wary of anything described as a HEPA-like or HEPA-type filter, though, as it will not be industry certified.

ELECTROSTATIC FILTERS

This type of filter electrically charges air molecules as they are pulled through the unit, converting what are generally neutral airborne irritants to either positive or negative. Metal plates inside the unit then serve to attract and capture them. As long as both the collection cell and charging ioniser are kept clean, these can be very effective in removing particles such as smoke, pollen, bacteria and other contaminants.

NEGATIVE-ION GENERATORS

These feature an ioniser (pumping out those beneficial negative ions) and use an electrical charge in a similar fashion to the electrostatic cleaners, but they do not have a collection capability. Instead the newly charged particles are believed to gradually clump together and become heavier, which causes them to drop to the ground (where they can be vacuumed away), rather than floating freely in the air for you to breathe in.

ULTRA-VIOLET FILTERS

These incorporate a UV light that bathes the air as it passes through, thereby rendering certain airborne micro-organisms and viruses harmless.

BUT GIVE ANY AIR PURIFIER LABELLED AS AN OZONE GENERATOR A MISS

Manufacturers claim that ozone can deodorise and disinfect the air, and while this may be true, ozone molecules are also highly unstable and could readily combine with other airborne chemicals to form new compounds that might be more dangerous than what you are trying to remove in the first place. Ozone also oxidises metals and causes corrosion!

While there's no doubt that air purifiers work, a more direct approach would simply be to eliminate as many sources of airborne toxicity as you can to begin with (as previously detailed), and then carefully monitor the quality of your air afterwards to check how well you're doing. Here are a few last thoughts to help with that:

INVEST IN AN INDOOR AIR-QUALITY MONITOR

If you live near a busy road or have any other reason to be concerned, this can tell you exactly what's going on in the air around you. In some areas, a radon monitor might also be advised as, after smoking, this odourless, invisible gas that comes up from the ground (a result of the radioactive decay of the small amounts of uranium that occur naturally in all rocks and soils) is thought to be one of the leading causes of lung cancer; nevertheless, if found, your house can be effectively proofed against it.

TAKE THE SMOKING OUTSIDE

If anyone in your household is still smoking, then at the very least do it outdoors, and that goes for vaping as well. It might not be as harmful as cigarettes but e-cigarettes still contain toxic chemicals and you don't want those inside.

A CARBON MONOXIDE DETECTOR

Fix this near any fuel-burning device (your boiler, gas oven, certain heaters) as old or faulty appliances can be lethal if this odourless gas leaks out.

SWITCH OFF CAR ENGINES

Never leave your car, or any other fuel-burning vehicle, idling with the ignition on in an enclosed space like a garage.

NEVER USE A CHARCOAL GRILL INDOORS

And when setting them up outside, position them so that any breeze blows fumes away from your house.

KEEP CHIMNEYS SWEPT AND CLEAR OF OBSTRUCTIONS

If you have an open fireplace or wood-burning stove, make certain it is safely vented to the outside, chimneys are regularly swept and the stove is kept in good condition with no leaks from the flue.

ALWAYS INSTALL AND USE AN EXTRACTOR FAN IN THE KITCHEN

One that is externally vented would be ideal, but if that's not practical, models that suck air through a filter can be very effective. Be sure to regularly clean, or replace, the filter pads, though, as they can't work if they are coated in grease.

CONTINUE:
HOW TO KEEP
THINGS MOVING

You are probably familiar with the notion of engendering flow in your work, a state of being in which you are so fully absorbed in the task at hand that time flies. In the home, flow can be regarded as a visual and physical property. One that, as you look around a room, ensures not only a seamless decorative flow, with nothing to jar or distract, but also, as you move from room to room, enables the free flow of air, as well as your unimpeded passage; no catching your jumper on a door handle, your hip on a table corner or your shin on the edge of a bed. It may seem self-evident, but it's remarkable how many people arrange their furniture so that getting in or out of a room involves an elaborate jiggle, squash or squeeze. Sometimes this is because the offending piece is simply too large for the room in question, but often it's because it's in the wrong place.

So in this last section we'll look at ways to keep the energy moving, starting with efficient space planning.

This is a completely pragmatic approach to good energy circulation: making the most effective use of space by ensuring that all items of furniture are carefully positioned so as not to unwittingly limit, block or trap energy. Think of it as constructing a heat map of your home in which the goal is an even spread of energy, avoiding any unduly hot or cold spots.

But it's also about an honest appraisal of how you really use your home, rather than how you think you might, or ought to, use it. A good illustration of this is that despite the trend for kitchen-diners, I prefer to place my dining table away from the kitchen, at the opposite end of an open-plan living area. For my family the table is the focus of much activity, from eating and work to creative play, and I didn't want all of this energy bottle-necked at one end, leaving a big chunk of the ground floor potentially underused (quite apart from it being important to separate food prep from food consumption – but more about that in Chapter 7). Following are some further suggestions to help you create an energetically balanced home:

• **Take that initial whiting-out instruction seriously.** In Chapter 2, I advised painting any space completely in white before you begin, so that you can see the natural areas of dark and light, and how they change throughout the day. Consistently sunny or well-lit spots will intuitively draw us to them, making them perfect for placing tables around which to gather. Shadier corners can have their own seductive qualities and be wonderful for quieter reading nooks or for a dedicated display of personal treasures lit by a lovely lamp. Follow the light and let it dictate where you sit and eat, rather than convention. For example, because I need help to wake early and my idea of luxury is to take a bath at sunset, for me an east-facing bedroom (to catch the first rays of light) and a west-facing bathroom are a must, even if another bedroom might have been larger.

• **Small square tables are banned.** Why? Because they are a nightmare for your shins and small children, and their very angularity cuts off space rather than encouraging flow. Wherever possible, buy circular coffee tables and round or oval side tables; I love a round dining table too as it invites equality, and regard Eero Saarinen's 1950s Tulip table, with its single swooping central pedestal leg, as one of the most iconic designs of all time – it also eliminates the visual clutter of a standard four-legged table surrounded by several chairs; something Saarinen referred to as 'the slum of legs'!

• **Armchairs invite solitary sitting; choose small sofas instead.** Better still, opt for a corner sofa arrangement or a three-seater at least, with a large pouffe or footstool in front of it. The aim is to construct cosy corners in which to snuggle up, not have everyone sitting separately or poker straight (more in Chapter 6 on this). Any lounge chair needs to have one main purpose in mind – supreme comfort – and it should therefore be big and deep enough that you can curl up in it, otherwise it's basically a dining chair.

• **Never place any form of seating with its back to a door.** The primitive part of our brains, the amygdala, conditions us to be alert when we cannot see behind us, meaning that subconsciously you will not be able to relax. It's also why properly old-school restaurants often have eye-level mirrors at seat height around the periphery of a room for the benefit of those diners who will inevitably be seated facing backwards. A small touch that ensures everyone feels comfortable. To add: chair placement is particularly pertinent in home offices and studies, where the need to concentrate is paramount – impossible if subliminally your brain believes you're in danger!

• **Do not store things underneath furniture.** Things stuffed under sofas, those drawers that slide beneath a bed: ideally no and never. Using these spaces to store rarely touched items is to introduce stagnancy right below where you sit or sleep. Keep them clear and let air flow freely underneath them. However, beds that lift up with storage concealed under the mattress are permissible as long as there is a degree of clear space between base and floor, but they are only to be used to store clean, neatly folded, spare bedlinen.

• **Clear rubbish or clutter from around your front door.** We'll look in detail at hallways and the pathway to your front door in Chapter 5, but here I'm referring to the position of an outside wheelie bin, or any tendency to leave 'stuff for later' outside the front door. This is to invite a sluggishness right on the threshold of your home. Things to be recycled, projects to finish, bikes that don't have a proper shelter, scooters, buggies, etc. – try to keep the direct line from the street to your front door completely clear so that, whether walking in or out, you can do so without having to navigate a mountain of obstacles, garbage or unnecessary clutter.

• **Use ceiling pendants to emulate daylight.** By this I mean hanging a pendant directly in front of a window. As night falls, switching on this overhead light will produce illumination from the same direction, if not angle, as the natural light admitted through the window during the day. This creates a consistency that is calming for the brain. Table, floor or task lamps can be used to light specific corners, and spots are useful in certain locations, such as around a bathroom cabinet or over a kitchen worktop. But never use them for overhead lighting; such a blanket of light is supremely unnatural, not to mention deeply unflattering. Lighting should be layered, with most of it set at the level at which the room is occupied, in other words seating height around tables, lower near sofas, and higher in kitchens where you'll most often be standing.

• **Clean your windows!** Easy to overlook this simplest of ways of admitting more daylight, and thus living energy, into our homes. And yet quite often our windows can be coated, inside and out, with a thin film of grime that acts like a fine-mesh screen, blocking natural light. To be able to see the dawning and passing of each day is to sync our natural biorhythms with the world at large. We can't do this if we're effectively shrouded in gloom.

• **Avoid basements if at all possible.** If there are other options, never rent a basement flat, anywhere, for any reason. It is deflating to your very soul to walk *down* to your front door. The only upside might be if it means you get a decent amount of garden space to yourself at the rear of the property. Otherwise, steer clear.

• **But I live in a city-centre bedsit with little natural light and certainly no green views.** Then you must fake it till you make it out of there! Cover a wall with a foliage-heavy wallpaper. Paint everything else white. Strategically place a mirror to reflect every possible bit of light into your space. Buy

'A house is never empty with a pet in situ, nor is an owner alone –
a pet provides security, companionship and affection too.'

a couple of peace lilies (which can survive almost any internal environment) and a foldaway table. Keep everything else super-simple to engender a feeling of expansiveness. But, most importantly, make that mood board, define your palette, allow yourself to picture yourself somewhere better, and continue to dream.

• If you're building new. One of the primary advantages is the chance to plan the size and location of every room, and to determine the position of everything inside it, from light switches to sockets, based on a precise understanding of how you intend to use your space. So if this opportunity exists, be wary of falling into the trap of convention. One of the best homes I've ever visited was one that turned tradition on its head by putting an open-plan lounge/kitchen on the top floor to take advantage of the light and views, while bedrooms were kept on the lower and basement floors. It was incredibly effective for these home owners as they loved to entertain, so for them it was obvious to keep the best spot in their home for where they'd spend most of their time, with their eyes open rather than fast asleep!

THE SUPERPOWER OF PETS

Dander aside, pets are good energy. A pet that is well looked after and loved, whether a goldfish, hamster, cat or dog, brings good vibes into the home in a multitude of ways. From a psychological point of view, a house is never empty with a pet in situ, nor is an owner alone – a pet provides security, companionship and, in the case of dogs and cats, affection too. Stroking a pet lowers blood pressure and naturally increases the release of oxytocin, that love hormone again, which has an overall soothing effect on the nervous system. Having a dog is also proven to increase longevity, no doubt because you have to get outside and walk it, providing exercise for yourself too and the social element of community interaction. And if somewhat less appealing, but equally important, the divergent bacteria of our pets is thought to add to our own, strengthening our immune systems.

Animals also have an uncanny ability to seek out the best spot in the house; probably because they respond to space on a purely instinctual level, so it's interesting to see where they like to curl up to snooze and, equally, if there are any places that they studiously avoid. These could be sites of dampness or particularly stagnant or even negative energy – it's said that cats particularly are drawn to areas that resonate with especially strong bad vibrations, which makes you wonder if this is why they purr so loudly in some spots and not others. Bad-vibe-cancelling cats, anyone?! Here are a few further guidelines on healthy ways to share your space with pets.

'You are a person with a pet, not a pet's person. And you certainly don't want to end up being a person with a pet's diseases.'

• **Establish from the beginning where pets can sit and sleep.** Hierarchy and boundaries are important for instilling good behavioural traits, so be consistent, and ideally keep dogs off your human seats and sofas.

• **Never allow a dog or cat in your bed.** You are a person with a pet, not a pet's person. And you certainly don't want to end up being a person with a pet's diseases.

• **Keep animal beds and eating bowls as clean as you would your own things.** Use a different scrubbing brush, though, and invest in decent grooming tools, and a lint brush so that you and your home are not perpetually covered in shedded fur.

• **Don't underestimate fish.** According to feng shui, fish represent success and wealth, and thus an aquarium has powerful symbolism; however, if the tank water is allowed to get dirty, then both attributes may elude you. And never keep a fish in either the bedroom (the constant motion will affect your sleep) or the kitchen (wrong sort of energy, apparently).

• **Remember the adage: there's no such thing as bad pets, only bad owners.** Overall, pets are part of your family. As such they are representative of your family values. So if people find your dog threatening, or your cat unduly vicious, what does this do? It inspires fear, and even if only at a very low level, there's no place for that in the *happy inside* home. If you want to share your life with an animal, you need to put in the time to train, groom and look after it; after all, it can't learn to do this all by itself.

WHY EXERCISE COUNTS
IN THE ENERGY EQUATION

A chapter about energy cannot be concluded without a word on exercise. Its many fundamental benefits are well known: positive impact on memory, mood and concentration; greater resilience and better metabolic, mental and physical health. Suffice to say, our exquisitely engineered bodies are designed to move, not slouch around all day. In fact, studies have indicated that inactivity kills more people than smoking! So we all need to introduce more movement into our schedules. The tricky bit is working out what you're prepared to do and when and where to do it. Interestingly, though, according to psychologist Ellen Langer in her book *Counterclockwise*, the positive effects of exercise may be as much to do with priming the brain with the belief that it will do you good, as actually doing it. In an experiment she conducted with hotel chamber maids, half the group were informed that their daily cleaning activities satisfied the recommended levels for an active lifestyle, and they were given information about the links between health and happiness. A control group was given the same information but without being told that their current levels of activity already constituted an exercise regime. The results were startling. Four weeks later, with no additional external exercise, changes in diet or hours, the first group not only lost weight, but also gained muscle mass and lowered their blood pressure. As Langer wrote, 'It seems that health follows a change in mindset just as is the case with placebos.' Here, then, are my top exercise hacks so your mind can get your body to follow:

• **No gyms required.** If you have a TV and a DVD player, or a smartphone, then you have a personal trainer at your command with no pricey gym memberships required, only the motivation to switch it on and do it. From yoga and pilates to HIT (high-intensity training) or boxercise, there will be an exercise class to download or buy that you can follow and make into your own programme. For most you'll need only a space the size of a yoga mat, 61cm by 173cm (about 24 inches by 68 inches), and enough ceiling height to be able to stretch up with arms extended – so standing in front of your sofa is probably your best bet, or alongside your bed, if space permits and you're using your phone for guidance.

• **Nor fancy kit.** A folded bath towel could replace the yoga mat, and a kids' beachball (the sort you find at discount toyshops) can be your exercise ball. A pair of large tin cans make great starter weights and if you're doing this at home, you can work out in your pyjamas. Although I strongly recommend a good sports bra for women.

• **Know when to turn to the experts.** However, for both yoga and pilates it's a good idea to attend a few classes first because posture is everything and you learn a lot by having a qualified instructor to correct your positioning. You don't want to teach your body bad habits. So start with a class but keep it up at home.

• **Work up slowly.** For home exercise, routines that come in blocks of ten minutes are long enough to do you good and great for starting out so that you don't get bored or lose heart too quickly. Work up slowly to 30 minutes a session of any moderate exercise (equivalent to brisk walking – 10,000 steps a day is the golden number – or a workout to music) and the medically recommended adult goal of five sessions a week (150 minutes).

● **Get into strength training.** Don't conjure up images of steroid-pumped he-men or hyper-sculpted models, but rather a pair of 3–5 kilo (7–11lb) hand weights and a gentle routine of squats, sit-ups, arm bends, or push-ups against the kitchen counter, at least twice a week. Physically inactive adults can lose 3–5 per cent of their muscle mass every decade after the age of 30, and if that wasn't motivation enough, a 2018 study from the University of Sydney has shown that regular strength training can reduce the risk of dying from cancer by up to 31 per cent! As they say, use it or lose it.

● **Make it fun.** At the time of writing, my current favourite indoor activity is rebounding: a workout on a small trampoline that not only boosts circulation but also jump-starts the lymphatic system because the bouncing action actively pushes lymph around your body. One 30-minute session feels like the equivalent of a deep-cleansing lymphatic massage!

● **Make it easy.** I also love English TV presenter Davina McCall's *Toned in Ten* DVD (released in December 2017), a series of exercises devised by trainer Sarah Gorman that blends barre, boxercise, HIT (high intensity training) and more in very digestible ten-minute segments that you can mix and match to keep it interesting. I sometimes only do the ten-minute warm-up, which is a workout in itself, on the basis that doing something is better than nothing!

● **Do the minimum.** As above, even ten minutes of vigorous aerobic activity a day (that which significantly increases your heart rate) is enough for you to notice, and feel, a difference. Think of it as exercise snacking: ten minutes of stretching here, ten minutes of strength training there, and seize every opportunity to walk – up stairs and escalators – and you'll be hitting those daily recommendations without even noticing. Ultimately it's a matter of discipline. Whatever your age and usual level of activity, but especially if you lead a more sedentary life, the benefits are so widespread you simply cannot afford not to do this. ●

SUMMARY

Energy is such a mutable entity – unseen yet profoundly felt. In our bodies, when we lack it, everything becomes arduous and overly complex; when we feel it in abundance, life itself becomes lighter and we are more able to shake off incumbent pressures. In our homes it can become stuck too, making everything we do there harder and more likely to be fraught. It's also contagious: whether good or bad, personal or environmental, we pass it on.

In many ways, the traditional spring clean was a way of initiating a fresh energetic start in a home. New-season air was encouraged to blow away the accumulated dirt and dust of winter. Furniture would be taken outdoors to be thoroughly refreshed and every inch of a home would be revitalised and readied for the coming months. But as a tradition to maintain, it presents more than just an opportunity to clean. It's also a chance to rearrange every component of your home. Too often furniture is placed in a room according to one need and then never touched again for years to come, even as our familial requirements change, so much

so that we forget we are in fact permitted to shift layouts around any time we like!

So, ask yourself what might happen if you swapped bedrooms? Or if the sofa was moved to face a window in summertime or a fireplace (if you have one) as autumn draws in? And is the dining table really in the best spot?

We must also avoid having rooms that are seldom used and ensure there are no forgotten corners in which the air is allowed to become stale or dust to collect. What might they become instead? And to be clear, energetically evaluating your home is different from looking at individual pieces and deciding whether you still like them or not (besides, following Chapter 1, all your possessions should now be carefully edited and cherished). The goal is the enthusiastic questioning of how to improve the energetic *soul* of your home.

To recall the opening paragraph of this chapter, our homes are holistic entities, so if one room pulls you down, the whole will be pulled down, and you with it. Lift the whole and you will surely rise up too. •

4

ACTION

'WHEN IT IS OBVIOUS THAT THE
GOALS CANNOT BE REACHED, DON'T
ADJUST THE GOALS, ADJUST THE
ACTION STEPS.'

CONFUCIUS
CHINESE PHILOSOPHER AND POLITICIAN
(551 BC-479 BC)

Ultimately, all of the clutter-clearing, palette-composing and thinking about energy and flow is about getting yourself organised to really enjoy your home, and to decorate and furnish it in a way that promotes happiness. But before we can get into the exciting specifics of individual home zones, in this, the final module of your foundation course, a word or two on home maintenance and management, plus getting to grips with cleaning.

GETTING
ORGANISED

Of course, in past times it would have been common practice for even a relatively modest household to employ a housekeeper to clean and manage a house. Today we are statistically more likely to be a single parent/person outfit, or, if a two-adult household, then both people will probably be working, and even if one person stays at home, they will still be working, whether professionally or as a full-time parent. Therefore, to run a home in the twenty-first century you need to get on the efficiency fast-track quite simply because *a well-organised home allows you to spend more time doing the things that charge your soul, and less on things that do not matter.*

And yet we expect so much of our homes: to keep us warm and dry, to battle all of the elements on our behalf, and to stay free of leaks and draughts. But do we regularly put in the time to check them over, as we're legally obliged to do for our cars every year if we want to keep them safely on the road? Do we regularly clean out gutters, oil wooden floors, check for broken sealants or book a boiler service? And then we're surprised when something bursts, breaks or packs up. Household maintenance needs to be a case of little and often, not wait and see with fingers crossed that disaster will not strike. And it's the same with cleaning. If you can afford a cleaner, then marvellous, book them weekly for the basic stuff and that's a load off your plate. However, I prefer to do the cleaning myself for several reasons. One, my home is not so large, so it can be done relatively quickly (as long as I stick to the 'little and often' and 'do it now' mantras – see following). But most importantly, this is how I keep on top of maintenance: by regularly inspecting the whole house from top to bottom, I'll spot signs of anything going wrong before it becomes something that requires a more intrusive investigation.

It is the same with our personal health. If we consciously ignore the nagging pain, that oddly pigmented mole, the recurrent headache or simply being tired, and push through regardless, under the surface, our bodies hold on to our emotions. A state of latent anxiety and stress will inevitably agitate what is being repressed, and at some point your body will indicate that enough is enough and you'll find yourself laid low, ill in bed or, worse, in hospital. Our bodies are not infallible. We need to maintain awareness of their variability. After all, it

is a rare individual who has perfect health and optimum vigour every single day, but if we can notice that we feel more off than usual – that we have varied significantly from whatever is normal for us – we have more chance of a speedy recovery. What we need to ensure is that we have enough space in our heads and schedules to check in with ourselves. Am I overdoing it a little? Did I skip breakfast too often this week? How much sleep have I had? Could I have picked up that virus that's going around, or is it more than that? In this respect, our doctors and health-care practitioners should be seen as our health *partners* in the quest for a healthy life, rather than people we rely on to patch us up, or even all-knowing medical sages trained to guesstimate what's wrong with us in the first place. Medicine is an inexact science. It's obviously based on extensive study and experience, but this doesn't extend to absolute factual knowledge of *your* unique body. Your body is amazing at adjusting and adapting, but keep pushing the wrong buttons or not oiling those cogs, and something will eventually give. If you're in this for the long game, you ignore what your body tries to tell you at your peril. •

MAINTENANCE AND
MANAGEMENT

As it is with your body, so it is at home: know it, look after it, and it will best be able to look after you – prevention really is better than cure. For while you can't feel the aches and pains of your environment, you can see cracks, damp and flaking paint, all of which signal that something is a little amiss. And even if you choose to delegate some aspects of the cleaning, be aware that tidying is a discipline that benefits from practice, and vigilance is everything when it comes to home maintenance. The following are my top tips for time-efficient home care.

SIGN UP FOR
HOME DELIVERY SERVICES

Frankly, in my household were it not for a combination of Amazon Prime and various food-delivery services, we'd be permanently starving and living in the dark. And if you feel queasy at the idea of capitulating to mammoth conglomerates for your shopping, appease any guilt by logging in through AmazonSmile: it's exactly the same as the regular portal, with the same prod-

ucts, prices and shopping features as the main site, and you can transfer all your account details instantly, but the difference is the AmazonSmile Foundation will donate 0.5 per cent of the purchase price of eligible products to the charitable organisation of your choice, for free! Nominate something meaningful to you and your quest for efficiency will give back in more ways than one.

ANYTHING THAT CAN BE
DONE IMMEDIATELY, MUST BE
DONE IMMEDIATELY

An ornament breaks, whip out that tube of Super Glue. A bulb or battery fails, replace and reorder right away, so you're never left short. And right away means flipping open your laptop, or swiping that app, the very second you've recycled the old carton. Often these things take less than a minute, especially if you've ordered them before, but they're also the things that we think, 'Oh, how annoying,' then keeping on walking out the door. When you return, tired and ready for dinner, what happens? There it is, still, the non-working light or the ornament in pieces – and your mood? Grumps, the sequel. Why go through this? Just fix it right away and give yourself a pat on the back. You'll be boosted by your efficiency and when you come home, you'll be reminded of how smart you've been, and you'll smile.

MAKE A HABIT OF INSPECTION

It's easy to make assumptions about your home. The windows were painted last spring and the boiler is practically brand new, so everything must still be tickety-boo. Sadly, this is seldom the case. Depending on its age and type, your home will be exposed to the elements to some extent, and while the basic objective of roofs, floors and walls is to keep out wind and rain, both can be tenacious predators, worming their way in wherever they can. And you will always find something, inside or out, that needs your attention, because wind blows things over, drains get blocked and wood warps. So, whether the persistent drip of a tap or a growing patch of damp, the sooner you spot it the quicker you can sort it. Even if you rent, better to promptly point out such problems to your landlord while making the same point: would they rather do a small efficient repair right now with you in situ, or have the flat unoccupied (and unprofitable) for some time in the future because major renovations have become necessary? And if a landlord will not take you seriously, for the benefit of your long-term wellbeing you need to plan to move.

GET INTO CLIPBOARD ORGANISATION

Kitchen worktops magnetically attract anything that doesn't quite fall into the can-it-be-done-immediately category: bills to pay, leaflets to read, classes to book for your children, and so on. And if you work freelance, then add to that receipts, job briefs, tear sheets and all those other random bits of paper that seem to multiply prodigiously of their own accord. Well, no longer, because you're going to buy yourself two A4-sized clipboards. Nice simple ones, nothing fancy. Mine are in stiff brown cardboard with silver clips. Designate one for work and one for home, and from now on all those miscellaneous 'bits' get clipped on to the relevant board in order of

'It's easy to make assumptions about your home. The windows were painted last spring and the boiler is practically brand new, so everything must still be tickety-boo. Sadly, this is seldom the case.'

importance. So an interesting article that you've ripped out of a magazine but haven't got round to reading yet? This could probably go at the back. Whereas receipts to file for your VAT are probably best further towards the front. And keep like with like too: if you find another receipt, for instance, clip it with the first ones. If you want to, you could hang your clipboards on the kitchen wall so they are off the work surface. But it doesn't really matter where you keep them (as long as it is a permanently designated spot – see 'A place for everything' overleaf) because the point is that all this 'stuff' is now securely contained, so when you take a moment to tackle household admin, or the water supplier calls because you appear to have forgotten to pay your bill, you know exactly where to find what you need.

UNDERSTAND THE FUNDAMENTALS OF FILING

This follows on immediately from the above. Where do all those important bits of paper go *after* you've eventually dealt with them? Here you need a set of standard box files, the narrow vertical sort with a lid that opens like a door. Designate one for each

'Instil from the start that the magic laundry fairy does not in fact exist, and neither is toothpaste available in never-ending tubes.'

main area of your life: for example, household, car, pets, health and one for each of your children, if you have any. I also have one marked 'documents' for certificates and legalese that don't quite seem to fall into other categories, and one labelled 'manuals' for all the booklets that come with electronic equipment. I also have a set that relates to work, finances and insurance. I have colour-coded mine too: for example, all financial stuff is red (I should perhaps have filed these in black boxes!), anything related to the house is yellow, family stuff is blue and everything else black. This is to easily group them. Then, once a year, go through each box and throw out anything that's become outdated. I always do this in the gap after Christmas, so I'm all sorted before the New Year. Keep about seven-years' worth of records for things such as your mortgage, bank statements and such like, but in excess of that, bin. Caveat: if you ever close a bank or credit card account, be sure to keep one sheet that shows the account number and final balance and confirms the date of closure, in case you need these details at a later date.

LITTLE AND OFTEN IS THE WAY
This applies to so much. Exercise. Walking. Treats. Admin and filing. And it also follows on from the can-it-be-done-immediately mantra. Dust gathered on a lampshade? Quick spritz and dust begone. Doing such things little and often means you keep on top of everything, which is a much nicer place to be than overwhelmed because it's all mounted up. Crucially, if you do not live alone, get the whole of your household on board with this – see yourself as a team and thus it's everyone's responsibility to keep the home shipshape day to day. Instil from the start that the magic laundry fairy does not in fact exist, and neither is toothpaste available in never-ending tubes. And, besides, kids (and sometimes grown-ups) need to understand that things left on the floor might get lost or broken, so they should pick them up at the end of the day.

INVEST IN A QUALITY CORDLESS, HAND-HELD VACUUM CLEANER
This will be a life-changer. Mine is a Dyson Animal Cordless vacuum cleaner. I'll admit, it's expensive in comparison to

other brands on the market, but its efficacy makes it absolutely one of the most revered items in my home (alongside my Vax steam mop!). It's tucked into a corner of the kitchen, permanently on charge on a wall-mounted bracket, so it's easy to grab and dust-bust without a second thought. And this is what you need to be able to do too. Don't overcomplicate the issue with a surfeit of suction and brush-head attachment options, although they seem to come as standard these days; work out which ones are best for your particular flooring, and get shot of the rest – a small stiff brush head is ideal for carpets, a nozzle to do corners, and a soft rotating sponged head to collect dust or dog hair from any hard floors downstairs.

A PLACE FOR EVERYTHING AND EVERYTHING IN ITS PLACE

For example, all spare batteries should be stored together in one box, in one place, so that everyone knows where it is. Likewise everything from spare toilet tissue and kitchen towel to extra sponges, tea cloths or matches. However, when it comes to your cleaning solutions, keep these near to where they will be used. In other words, bathroom cleaners need to be in the bathroom, washing tabs near the washing machine and so on. It may seem obvious, but so often people have only one of each cleaner type, and they are all stored together, often in the kitchen. Give yourself a break. This is the one item you are allowed to purchase multiples of! After all, you won't want to give your bathroom mirror a quick polish after you've brushed your teeth if you first have to troop downstairs to retrieve the correct solution. Finally, invest in nice cloths and sparkly scrubbers so they look pretty too. Sounds silly? It's not. Every time you open a drawer or cupboard, no matter what you're looking for, it'll boost your mood to see things that you consider attractive, and that applies to your cleaning equipment too.

HAVE TRUSTED (AND TESTED) TRADESPEOPLE ON SPEED DIAL

Ask for recommendations from friends by all means, but the best suggestions often come from hardware-store owners. If you have a local electrical store, then they are the people to ask about electricians, and so on, simply because they would be unwilling to stake their professional reputation on anyone they didn't trust. In addition, said person will probably be able to access any spare parts quickly and easily because they already have a connection to your local supplier. This aside, for bigger jobs always interview a minimum of three people, and ultimately choose by trusting your gut on who you feel the most comfortable giving your house keys to. You are letting this person loose on your most valuable asset (after your body), so you must feel not only that they can do the job in hand, but also that you are 100 per cent confident about leaving them to their own devices should you have to pop out for any reason. There are many plumbers, electricians, chippies et al. out there; keep interviewing until you find the one for you. And then never lose their number! Likewise for any other tradespeople you may need to use regularly: window cleaners, chimney sweeps or gardeners. And pay them what they quote. Trust is worth every penny, and it's unlikely that someone that you feel you can trust will rip you off. Plus, if you interviewed three people and one person's price is way out of line, whether under or over, you know to ask them why. However, make sure everything you need doing is included, and in writing. Always negotiate a price per completed job, as opposed to a day rate, as then the onus is on them to get it done promptly, and *never* pay anything up front (or before you've properly inspected finished work). Instead, if necessary, agree a system of part payments per satisfactorily completed task before you start – reputable tradesmen should always have enough of a float to start work, and

they should also be open to handing over receipts to prove the costs of anything substantial they purchase on your behalf. However, if something unexpected crops up as work progresses, then be fair on what additional supplement you may need to pay. The challenge of houses is that we do not have X-ray vision, and sometimes horrors really do lurk within, although less likely if you 'Make a habit of inspection' (see previously)!

TIDY BEFORE YOU GO TO BED

Every evening, wash any dirty dishes or load the dishwasher and set it running. Clear and clean table tops ready for breakfast. Deadhead any flowers. Tidy away any magazines or newspapers or stash them straight into your recycling bin. Close all your curtains, switch off the lights, power down your Wi-Fi router and ready yourself for sleep (more on this in Chapter 8). Thus, on waking, your home is refreshed and ready to greet you for a new day, not still covered in the detritus of yesterday. After all, would you go to bed without washing your face or cleaning your teeth? And if you did, how would you feel in the morning – grubby, and on the back foot. While we might not wake and be natural morning beauties, we are at least clean and ready to face the day. And so it should be with our homes. •

CLEANING AS
A RITUAL

One of the best ways to appreciate your home is to literally touch it. Through the gleam of freshly polished wood to the sparkle of a clear window you can begin the all-important journey of emotionally engaging with your home. And we could do worse than take inspiration from Buddhist monks, for whom the act of cleaning is much more than the removal of daily dirt. As Shoukei Matsumoto, a monk in the Zen Buddhist tradition, explains in the introduction to his book *A Monk's Guide to a Clean House and Mind,* a monk's day begins with the cleaning, sweeping and polishing of their temple and its grounds. However, as he writes 'We don't do this because it's dirty or messy. We do it to eliminate the gloom in our hearts. We sweep dust to remove our worldly desires. We scrub dirt to free ourselves of attachments.' The belief is that by living simply and mindfully (as touched upon in Chapter 2) the monks create space to 'contemplate the self'. Something he believes everyone in today's busy world needs to do. As he puts it, 'Life is a daily

'One of the best ways to appreciate your home is to literally touch it. Through the gleam of freshly polished wood to the sparkle of a clear window you can begin the all-important journey of emotionally engaging with your home.'

training ground, and we are each composed of the very actions we take in life. If you live carelessly, your mind will be soiled, but if you try to live conscientiously, it will slowly become pure again. If your heart is pure, the world looks brighter. If your world is bright, you can be kinder to others.'

And this is a wonderful concept – cleaning as a pathway to a heightened state of mindful contentment. Albeit one we can take a little more lightly at home where mindfulness can be understood as the art of giving yourself fully to the present moment in order to catch up with how you are feeling. After all, what is gardening but tidying and maintaining an outside space? And yet we don't tend to think of gardening as a chore; we see it as a pleasure and something that relaxes us. Crucially, it is something that often fully absorbs us while we do it. This is the very definition of a mindful activity. So, if we take this inside, why did cleaning, basically the act of tending to the indoors, end up with such negative connotations, commonly described in terms of house*work*, drudgery or duties? It doesn't have to be this way. What would

happen if we started to think of cleaning as the act of tending to ourselves through the medium of our possessions, and what we are nurturing in the process is our sense of wellbeing. Consider too the difference between referring to something as a ritual rather than a routine. The latter can sound onerous, something that *has* to be completed. Whereas the former can have a lightness to it that feels imbued with pleasure. To light a candle on settling down for the evening is a ritual that evokes the spirit of relaxation. Could you reconsider elements of cleaning as such a ritual too?

By way of example, I sweep my entire downstairs floor every morning. It was a great moment for me to have finally had installed the hand-laid wooden parquet flooring of my dreams, and it continues to give me great pleasure every single day. But I also have two dogs who sleep in the kitchen at night. So each morning, I am greeted by a fine layer of dog grime and shed hair covering my beautiful floor. Nevertheless, making into a ritual the necessity of regularly vacuuming, mopping and waxing the floor, to restore it to its former glory, elevates the

'What is gardening but tidying and maintaining an outside space? And yet we don't think of it as a chore; we see it as something that relaxes us.'

task from a need to a desire. It is entrenched in the way I start my day, making me feel organised and on top of things. And because my home is uncluttered and nothing has been left on the floor from the night before, it takes no more than five to ten minutes, with the result that my house is returned to a state of cleanliness that relaxes and thus readies me for the day. But I have made it easy for myself. After reading Shoukei Matsumoto's book, I confess to buying a lovely long-handled soft-bristle broom and a shiny new dustpan, and I set about cleaning and sweeping with much vigour and determination. While it was great as an early-morning workout, it was quite frankly an enormous faff, which quickly became extremely unfun. It took about a week before it occurred to me that just because monks use brushes and feather dusters, it didn't mean I had to. It prompted the installation of the wall bracket for the cordless vacuum cleaner in the kitchen, and hey presto, 'sweeping' was now doable in five minutes flat. And the wash and waxing? It's an all-in-one product that cleans and protects at the same time.

But more than the act of returning my floor, if not home, to order, this is a moment for me to plan the day ahead. As I marvel at the disappearance of the dust and dander, my head too becomes clear, allowing me to contemplate what I must get done that day. It is a little breathing space for my mind – a walking 'n' cleaning meditation, if you will. And before you spit out your coffee in exasperation, fuming that you barely have time to get dressed in the morning let alone take a quick jaunt plus J-cloth around the house before heading off to work, I hear you. I was once in that place too. •

BEGIN AT THE
BEGINNING: MY STORY

In my last few years as editor-in-chief of *ELLE Decoration*, as a single parent to a young child, I'd often get up having had a rotten night's sleep, get dressed, get my toddler son dressed and deal with the dogs (i.e. usher them into the front garden to wee while I sorted fresh water and food bowls), all the while feeling barely conscious. I'd sort what I needed for work and have to be straight out the door at silly o'clock to drop my son at his nursery breakfast club so I could run to catch the early train to London. Certainly no time for breakfast, and definitely no pause for mindful contemplation! However, I viewed pushing the buggy up the hill to the nursery as my exercise routine, clocked my steps and tried to listen to a guided meditation on the train before ploughing into emails. When I reached the office, my working days were full on but focused, so I could leave in time to be able to put my son to bed, after my childminder had brought him home. I loved my job but a sense of encroaching unease that I was busting a gut to pay other people to enjoy the things that meant the

most to me – caring for my son, walking my dogs – was building in intensity.

Against this backdrop, my home was my refuge. And yet come Sunday, while my son napped, I would begin to vacuum and clean it somewhat resentfully. I'd internally berate myself, questioning why I was wasting part of a precious non-work day doing this, missing out on the chance to just sit and read the papers, or – depending on how stressed I felt – why, for goodness sake, had I not yet outsourced this! But I persisted because, in truth, putting my home in order felt like putting myself in order. It was like pushing through some sort of invisible pain barrier to get to the other side – uncomfortable, but it worked. Ultimately the gratification that I felt on seeing everything looking clean and ordered translated into a feeling of calm, which in turn benefited everyone around me, so I knew it was essential to my wellbeing (a bit like exercise). Basically, it was keeping me sane!

Nevertheless, when you are in the flow of an authentic life, what I call choice points appear – profound moments when you are offered the opportunity to consciously change your trajectory. It could be hearing about a new job that makes you evaluate your current position, or something as extreme as discovering that your partner has been cheating on you. One seems positive, the other profoundly negative, but both are in fact tremendous chances to evolve, a time to decide which fork in the road you will take – to move on, to forgive, or be wounded. Of course, we could all make life-changing choices at any time, but often it is only when faced with a serious challenge to our status quo that we do.

And so it happened to me. As I juggled my professional and parental responsibilities, my self-care was beginning to fall by the wayside. My home was perpetually in the middle of minor renovations as anything that took longer than a few days felt like an unbearable infringement of my privacy. Increasingly over-stretched, I'd compiled a revised work plan proposing an

additional day working without distraction from home, but before I had a chance to submit it, my publishing house decided to completely restructure the way it produced magazines. I disagreed with the proposal from the very core of my being, and knew then that I needed to leave, rather than just tweak my commute. And such is the way of life, in the very same time frame my father was unexpectedly diagnosed with advanced prostate cancer. As a family we didn't really know what this meant, having never been previously touched by this insidious disease. He died under a year later, just before Christmas and one week after my employment contract officially ended. Thus, instead of being stuck inside the office navigating one of the biggest forthcoming issues of the year, I was at his bedside, holding his hand, as the last breath left his body. A privilege that knows no bounds. And there has never been a single second that I doubted I made the right decision. •

NOW BACK TO CLEANING!

And the moral of this tale? There is no one-hit wonder solution to the always-on nature of contemporary life, apart from the decision to change the degree to which you wish to interact with it. We always have more choice than we imagine. It's just that often we become so caught up with maintaining our status quo that we lose perspective; we become unable to assess our true priorities, usually until life intervenes and forces us to stop and take stock. As Bryan Dyson, former president and CEO of Coca-Cola Enterprises, memorably said in a commencement address he delivered at Georgia Tech in 1991: 'Imagine life as a game in which you are juggling some five balls in the air. You name them – work, family, health, friends and spirit – and you're keeping all of them in motion. You will soon understand that work is a rubber ball. If you drop it, it will bounce back. But the other four balls – family, health, friends and spirit – are made of glass. If you drop one of these,

they will be irrevocably scuffed, marked, nicked, damaged or even shattered. They will never be the same. You must understand that and strive for balance in your life.'

And only when we are able to do this, without worrying about the *how* of doing it, will we achieve it. To put it another way, once you recognise your purpose, as suggested right back in Chapter 1, you have the ability to clarify your intentions and the way will duly present itself. It is, as Shoukei Matsumoto, our cleaning monk, says, a case of 'Once you learn to see how your inner turmoil manifests itself through your surroundings, you can reverse engineer this, mastering yourself by mastering the space in which you live.' As such, from the perspective of this chapter, I'm not advocating obsessional organisation nor a full-on daily cleaning blitz, merely extolling the virtues of incorporating an element of each in your life as a daily ritual to acknowledge the importance of your home as your sanctuary. •

SUMMARY

You might well have read this far and still conclude that you simply do not have time to tidy in the evenings or to clean in the mornings; or that you have employed a cleaner, so that's that. But could you be open enough to entertain the idea that this *might* be a rewarding exercise? That great joy *could* be gained from taking the time to tend to what you have now carefully chosen to surround yourself with? It's certainly not about becoming a rubber-gloved martyr cleaning away while everyone else has breakfast and wonders what on earth's wrong with you! Rather it's about taking a brief pause to enjoy your things, carefully maintaining them to express gratitude for their secret stories and the protective force-field of strength that they can now provide for you. After all, what was the point of acquiring them if you don't take a little time

'At the end of each of the following four chapters I will suggest a ritual that I invite you to make your own with the intention of helping you to more wholeheartedly align yourself with your home.'

out to appreciate them? Perhaps it's something that could be done while waiting for the kettle to boil rather than idly standing by, perhaps lost in a whirl of thoughts or fuming with impatience that it takes so long to heat. Instead, could you take a moment to reminisce on a thoughtful gift as you polish its surface, or recall where a photograph was taken as you carefully wipe its frame? Or more pragmatically, could you empty the bin and quickly spritz the inside with a fragrant spray so that this is the aroma that greets you, or the next person to use it, not the stink of yesterday's trash?

Admittedly, the busier we are, the harder it can feel to deliberately make time to slow down, but it is usually the busy who are the most in need of such self-nurturing, and for them rituals can be the quickest route to a soothed mind and boosted happiness. Whether it's weekly watering of your plants to everyone bundling up on the sofa to watch a special programme together, rituals are important. They ground us, and can become comforting frameworks for our lives. Besides, human beings thrive on routine, from sleep to exercise; so develop good habits, then elevate them to rituals. And as we now move forward to look at individual home zones in greater detail, at the end of each of the following four chapters I will suggest a ritual that I invite you to make your own with the intention of helping you to more wholeheartedly align yourself with your home. You will obtain the maximum benefit if you can find a way to do them regularly, but even if you can only make time at the weekend, I believe that they will reap lifelong rewards for both you and your home and all who visit it. •

5

WELCOME

'WELCOME OUT OF THE CAVE, MY
FRIEND. IT'S A BIT COLDER OUT HERE,
BUT THE STARS ARE JUST BEAUTIFUL.'

PLATO
CLASSICAL ATHENIAN PHILOSOPHER
(428 BC-347 BC)

Mood breaker or mood maker, the entrance to your
home is a space of great subliminal power. Why?
Because the creation of a truly supportive environment
involves harnessing every possible opportunity to give
yourself an energy boost. And this begins the minute
you cross your threshold. It is therefore the first home
zone that we shall consider in detail. As the saying goes,
'Home is not a place, it is a feeling', so how do you want
to feel when you first come home?

FIRST
IMPRESSIONS
COUNT

In many Japanese or Buddhist homes, you will often find something called a *butsuma* near the entrance. This is a sort of indoor altar that honours the Buddha and the memory of deceased family members in the form of a small shrine set upon a dedicated cabinet that's regularly adorned with flowers, candles or incense burners. It's considered a sacred space that must be kept spotlessly clean. Important family documents may be stored inside the cabinet, but nothing else is allowed to loiter here – no piles of abandoned newspapers or any sort of clutter. It's a wonderful set piece dedicated to faith and family that's usually easily visible on arrival home. And this notion of something so symbolically powerful placed at a key axis point is one of the underlying principles of this chapter.

So, what do *you* see when you walk through your front door? A tangle of shoes and a pile of post? In so many Western homes, hallways are Cinderella spaces, forgotten and overlooked in favour of larger rooms, even though it is actually here that the story of your home starts. Your hallway can be thought of as a kind of stage set, one that should put you at ease as soon as you get home, as well as providing a thoughtful tableau for anyone else who comes to the front door. It is both the fulcrum around which a home revolves, as well as its physical spine. How important, then, to make it a strong and cherished zone in its own right, rather than somewhere to pass through as quickly as possible.

Equally vital is the need to imbue a hallway with a sense of openness and expansion, rather than enclosure and constriction. In other words, carefully considering your palette choices so that the decoration encourages you to literally exhale, to feel lightened and able to catch your breath; permitting yourself a moment to give thanks for being safely home.

However, this might seem like an impossible proposition to some. Indeed, I've rented many a property in the past where

'In so many homes, hallways are Cinderella spaces, forgotten and overlooked in favour of larger rooms, even though it is actually here that the story of your home starts.'

the front door opened on to a 'hallway' no bigger than the door swing, or one so narrow that two people would be unable to pass each other in it. And they were always utterly blank, often beige and with closed doors all around. Thankfully, there are ways to make even the most diminutive or unprepossessing of passages into a space that lifts rather than dampens the spirit as soon as you get home.

First, in most homes today there's no reason to close everyone in. Even in shared accommodation, while bedroom doors may be shut to safeguard privacy, the door to a communal living room may be unnecessary (fire regulations notwithstanding). Historically, doors were installed to retain heat and minimise draughts. Today, with central heating, or better yet, underfloor heating, this is no longer such a concern. The removal of even one door can lend that feeling of openness that we're after here, with no need to knock down walls or go fully open plan, so it's worth taking a lateral look at your layout to see if this easy tweak might be possible. Besides, as already covered in Chapter 3, encouraging a free flow of air throughout your home is a lot healthier than trapping it inside separate rooms.

In fact, one of the most soul-rousingly perfect entrances I've ever seen on all my home-shoot travels had a standard front door that opened on to a very unexpected three-storey light well, encircled by a stunning pale oak staircase. Opposite the door was a long table that led your eye to an enormous double-height window that framed an ancient oak tree outside. The effect was almost spiritual in its majesty. And instantly soothing.

But even if your hallway stops a touch short of this heavenly idyll – certainly mine does – it shows what's possible. The point is that when we truly understand our homes as a series of interconnected energetic zones, with each room and every item contributing to the feel of the whole, why then have a hallway that's effectively a cold hard spike thrust through its very heart?! Your hallway has the power to set the tone of your entire home, so this urgently needs to be turned on its head in favour of the deliberate engendering of a sense of warmth, lightness and calm right from the off. I have therefore spent many an hour picturing the ideal entrance and the four key takeaways are as follows:

1. THE IMPORTANCE OF THE FLOORING

2. BEING GREETED BY SOMETHING INSPIRATIONAL (MY VERSION OF THE *BUTSUMA*)

3. CONSIDERATION OF YOUR ENTIRE ARRIVAL SEQUENCE

4. THE IDEA OF A HALLWAY AS A PAUSE POINT FOR CONTEMPLATION

'When we truly understand our homes as a series of interconnected energetic zones, why have a hallway that's a cold hard spike through its very heart?!'

THE
IMPORTANCE
OF THE
FLOORING

Your hall floor is crucial. It will see a lot of wear and it is your first chance to make a statement of intent about your home, but bear in mind your overall palette and spend as much as you can afford here to get exactly what you want. Remember, though, from Chapter 2, that in a flat or smaller home, using the same flooring throughout all public areas will make them feel larger. What's fundamental is that, whether clickety-clack, easy-clean tiles or reclaimed wooden parquet, it's laid so that it's perfectly centred to the front door behind and flows straight through into other rooms. This contributes to the impression of a seamless transition from outside to in. But if your hallway is very generously proportioned, and your home large, then by all means distinguish it in its own right with the flooring.

And if you're a renter with a grotty carpet in situ, consider buying a simple runner to cover it up, something natural like sisal or rattan, as this can easily be taken up and reused elsewhere. Or, as we've discussed before, look out for a brightly coloured offcut from a local carpet retailer, which you can repurpose as a 'rug' to add something cheering underfoot. To be able to walk happily barefoot in all areas of your home is to be able to ground yourself from the feet up. Do not underestimate the significance of this: the soles of our feet are the foundations of our bodies; keep them happy and you're one step closer to keeping yourself happy (this is also why underfloor heating can be so soothing). And regardless of covering, the floor of your hallway must always be kept scrupulously clean. Wax the wood, mop tiles, vacuum carpet, and do it daily. Dirt may not be allowed to settle here. This is the main artery of your home – it cannot become clogged! •

BE GREETED BY SOMETHING INSPIRATIONAL

In a dream hallway, there would be a centrally placed circular table – remember, no sharp edges to catch an unsuspecting hip or impede the visual flow – and on that table fresh flowers and greenery would be displayed, being both beautiful and useful (a fragrant, natural air purifier). Beyond this centrepiece would be a wall on which an inspirational artwork might be hung, or else we would see straight through to a view of a garden beyond, because what greets you at the end of your entry vista has great impact.

But what if there's no room for a table, or you lack a view of any sort? The simplest solution for small hallways – paint whatever lies directly ahead (whether a wall or a door) in an uplifting colour, and hang a picture here instead. Alternatively, could this be the perfect spot for that fabulous wallpaper you've selected as one of your statement finishes? Or could you create your own version of a *butsuma*, in

a nod to the idea of the welcoming altar, to endow your hall with a spiritual focus? In my home, directly opposite the front door, at the end of the hall, I have combined all of the above. There are a set of four simple wall-hung cupboard units, topped with marble tiles and joined together to make a floating sideboard. I use it to display flowers and a few treasured ceramics. Above it, hung on the wall (textured and painted deep fir green), are an assortment of favourite framed artworks. This careful arrangement immediately brings a smile to my face the minute I get home. It could have been a single shelf, but making it into storage created additional space to keep vases, candles, tea towels, kitchen roll, cleaning utensils and serveware – all items devoted to display or cleaning, reflecting the Japanese convention to not store clutter in this area. •

THE ARRIVAL SEQUENCE

Because you can positively affect all of your senses as soon as you come through your gate or cross the line that marks the boundary of your home, let's now step outside and look at the path that leads to your front door, however long or short that may be. Even if only a few steps, such a path and its surroundings are as important as what takes place once over your threshold. Spend some time thinking about what could be done to heighten this arrival sequence. Is there room for something simple such as hanging baskets? A pair of low-maintenance geraniums in pretty pots? Perhaps hyacinths in the springtime, so that their magical scent can greet you as you unlock your door? And if natural light is an issue for living plants, then why not take advantage of the wealth of increasingly realistic faux flowers now on the market. Basically, you have no excuses! It's also good practice to keep your front door in a state of sound repair – no peeling paint, wonky handles or rusty locks. This is about claiming ownership of your space from its very periphery and making a pos-itive impact, even if it's just you and your postman who will appreciate your efforts. Think of it as a deliberate act of kindness to yourself, which may trigger a random trickle effect of joy for others.

If you have the opportunity to do more extensive remodelling, then a generously proportioned door, one that's wide enough to carry furniture through, about 85cm (33 inches) minimum, is essential for obvious reasons. Even if it's only slightly oversized, it will add to a first impression of spaciousness. However, as well as being practical, it must also be pretty, so stained-glass panels on either side – visually widening it still further, as well as admitting extra light – and a simple pitched-roof porch overhead, to keep you dry while you hunt for your keys when it's raining, would be the height of sophistication. Built-in seating niches to left and right (useful for depositing bags as well as bottoms), with cupboards underneath for the postman to safely leave parcels, would be the cherry on top.

Once inside, what happens along the route of your hallway? It's habitual in many homes to hang coats and leave shoes here, to avoid bringing external dirt further inside. Obviously, if there's been bad weather you want to remove outerwear as quickly as possible, but that doesn't mean it has to live here permanently and be the first thing that you see. Is there room to create a skinny wall-hung closet to conceal them inside instead (be sure to set it an inch above any skirting to protect the integrity of the floor)? Could you build a cupboard under the stairs into which coats could go? If not, ask yourself whether all these coats are in active use, or is the hall simply being used as a convenient dumping ground. Which ones could be put away (especially important when the seasons change), or possibly even given away? The same with shoes: do all those pairs of trainers really need to live here? At the very least, tuck them out of sight, even if just inside an adjacent room. Your mantra should be 'minimise and contain', because if your hallway is narrow, to be greeted by

such clutter will immediately contribute to a feeling of distraction, overcrowding and physical constriction.

However, this isn't about trying to obliterate all vestiges of the inevitable chaos of family life; keeping the hallway clear simply prioritises an ambience of calm and order for that crucial first moment of arrival home. Because of this, in terms of decoration, light 'n' bright colours are *always* preferable, despite the enduring trend to add 'drama' by finishing hallways in dark hues. I'm totally against this. I think the effect it creates on entry is to dampen or deflate, with any sense of uplift delayed until you've passed through. Even if the intention is to emphasise a sense of light beyond, the subliminal mood will be one of heaviness. Two exceptions would be if your overall home vibe is deliberately dark, such that a moody entryway would be an authentic opener rather than something driven by fashion, or if the dark colour is restricted to a single wall and intended as a contrasting backdrop to a *butsuma* or displayed artwork.●

FINISHING TOUCHES

If your hallway is wide enough, then a nice touch is to add something to sit on when removing shoes. A narrow bench or long wooden seat such as a reclaimed church pew would suit, but beware of this being gradually co-opted as a convenient place to drop bags, parcels and other such items. Likewise, if you have radiators, a beautiful cover can come into its own in a hallway by doubling as a handy shelf. Again, though, while a strategically placed tray for relieving yourself (neatly) of all your daily bits and bobs is to be applauded, nothing else should be left here. And don't use it for propping pictures or post on, either. Pictures must always be properly hung on the wall, and post should be dealt with immediately (remember the golden rules for getting things done in Chapter 4!). I have a simple but beautiful hook, tucked just to one side of my hall, on which I hang my keys and handbag as soon as I come home. I bought it for about £3 in a French hardware store – veritable treasure troves for such things – and it's probably one of the most useful

things in the entire house. Alternatively, the slimmest of wall-hung shelves can happily accommodate keys and wallet and you'll never waste another second hunting for either of them again.

On the dilemma of how to make a narrow space feel wider, mirrors can be brilliant. However, it doesn't work to simply hang one on a side wall. As you look down your hallway, the lean of the mirror *away* from the wall, however subtle, will interrupt the vista, and its light-reflecting ability will be negligible anyway. The only effective solution in a situation like this is to have mirrored glass professionally set, top to bottom, directly onto a side wall so that it sits absolutely flat against the wall and within the depth of existing skirtings, not in front of them. It will then reflect the entire wall opposite and visually double the width of the hallway in the manner of an optical illusion.

However, don't be tempted to place a large mirror opposite the front door, even if it's glazed and you're trying to bounce more light around. I did this in iteration 1.4 of my hallway planning and was routinely thrown by seeing my reflection through the door as I unlocked it. 'Who's that in my house?! Oh, it's me,' sort of thing. You don't need this kind of confusion in your life. Painting your ceilings in gloss will produce a better effect and be a more subtle, yet unexpected, touch that really helps to bounce all available light around. And if you're lucky enough to have a window at the end of the hall, then apply the same sense of attention to both how you screen it and how you draw attention to what lies beyond. Does the window have a sill big enough on which to display fragrant herbs or other house plants? If not, could it be widened to make it more useful? Maybe a narrow glass shelf, installed *across* the window itself, could be used to display coloured bottles so that they catch the light like an improvised stained-glass window. Could you put a seat here, covered in gorgeous cushions? How about a window box on the outside? Or plant something externally so

that it's directly in view as you look out of the window, like the aforementioned ancient oak tree? Even a blank wall beyond could be painted Schiaparelli pink or Yves Klein blue! Consider this view carefully, give it a deliberate focus and think laterally if required. Remember, this is a view you will see over and over again, so make it catch the eye, and make it special.

Finally, remember to turn around and check the view the other way too, by which I mean, what do you see when you stand at the end of your hallway looking *back* at the front door? After all, this is a view you'll see as much as the other way around. And if you have a glazed front door, what might it feel like at night? I installed a full-drop, fleece-lined velvet curtain that pulls across the entire width of my entryway in the evening. It has a dual function. It makes the view back down the hallway equally restful, and it's a great draught excluder/ privacy provider at night. Without such a screen to cover it, my semi-glazed door could leave me feeling rather exposed.•

WHERE TO START

How to apply this to a whole wall depends entirely on the thickness of the mirror, the flatness of existing wall finishes and the depth of skirtings. The aim is for a seamless finish whereby the wall appears to be covered in a mirrored surface that sits neatly on top of any skirtings without protruding. This will give the most transformative effect. If you have nice deep skirtings, then one of the simplest options is to fix a J-shaped bracket above the skirtings into which large mirrored panes can be slotted, fixed at the top of the wall with clips to hold everything tightly in place and with glue applied to the back of each pane for added security.

WHAT IF MY SKIRTINGS ARE SKIMPY?

You really do not want the mirror to overhang your skirtings, so if they're not deep enough, depending on your wall finish, you could contemplate carving out part of the wall itself to give you the additional depth required (a bit messy, however, and not ideal), or what most builders would probably prefer, remove all existing skirtings and surface finishes in order to overlay a new and perfectly flat infrastructure. Basically, the bigger the tile, the flatter your walls will need to be beforehand. Good prep is therefore essential.

NEAT EDGINGS ARE ESSENTIAL

If you end up removing skirtings, you may wish to dispense with them altogether and have a neat shadow-gap detail (see Chapter 2 – 'The seven principles of *happy inside* decorating') as a bottom finish. However, my preference would always be to have the tiles sitting neatly on top of a standard trim, so be sure to choose new skirtings in advance if the old cannot be reused, so you know exactly how much space to leave.

A CHEAPER DIY ALTERNATIVE

If you have lovely flat walls, you could use thin mirror tiles – again, only if they sit within the depth of any existing skirtings or cornices – then frame the whole thing, top, bottom and sides, with lengths of a skinny wooden trim to give the effect of a single massive mirror adhered firmly to the wall. Top tip: paint the trim to match the surrounding walls *before* you attach it! And because most walls aren't strictly orthogonal, the trim has the added advantage of allowing you to sneakily square up the whole and cover any gaps.

SUMMARY

In the musical analogy of Chapter 2, hallways are given great importance as the opening movement of your healthy home, as it's essential to strike the right note from the start rather than neglecting them or leaving their decoration until last. No matter how small they are, there's always something you can do to improve them. So from this moment on, a welcoming hallway must be your number-one priority: purposefully decorated, as open as possible, clean, clear and uplifting – at the very least install a hook for your keys, and never paint the walls beige!

With this in mind, what could you instigate here as your first ritual? For example, I regularly shake out my doormat and sluice down the path from front door to street with a mix of baking soda and hot water. I do this primarily (and practically) to rid the path of any lingering odour of wee (courtesy of my dogs!), but it also serves as a means to prepare myself for the week to come, clearing the way ahead by washing away the past, literally and metaphorically. Perhaps there is some version of this that you could adopt – whether wiping down the front door to ridding a pathway of dirt? And while it might sound a little hocus-pocus to some, the act of physically engaging with an activity also assigned a spiritual connotation can be profound; and such things are tremendously powerful in affirming the link between body and soul, heart and mind – something core to the *happy inside* philosophy. •

6

HARMONY

'NATURE REQUIRES US NOT ONLY TO BE ABLE TO WORK WELL, BUT ALSO TO IDLE WELL.'

ARISTOTLE
CLASSICAL GREEK PHILOSOPHER
(384 BC-322 BC)

In an era when Fear of Missing Out has its own universally understood acronym, recuperative rest and relaxation are not always regarded as the intensely worthwhile pursuits that they are. Instead, we are harassed into believing that we must be constantly available to be of value, that peak productivity and performance are directly related to presenteeism, and that to snooze is to lose. This couldn't be more wrong. Instead, we must recognise that to stop is to succeed; and we must arrange our homes in such a way as to make this easy for us. Therefore the focus of this chapter is on your main lounge spaces, but from the perspective of their private as opposed to public use. After all, it's only when we have our homes to ourselves that we can take maximum advantage of them as an aid to relaxation. And this, more than anything, is the primary purpose of the *happy inside* home, but particularly our living rooms.

MAKING SPACE
TO REJUVENATE

Technology has accelerated the speed of life beyond our capacity to cope, and being constantly on the go, juggling jobs and home life, tying ourselves to our desks and clocking ever more hours in pursuit of 'a good life' is completely counterproductive. Instead of working to support our wellbeing, we're allowing work to take over our lives, dominating our thoughts and percolating as a persistent drip of dissatisfaction into our off-hours.

And yet, as Dr Alex Pang says in his book *Rest: Why You Get More Done When You Work Less*, 'by seeking out rest we get more out of life, are more effective and more creative'. He cites examples of many world-renowned leaders in the fields of research and creativity who have made it a habit to work for no more than four or five hours a day before setting aside their pens or experiments for extended periods of considered musing. Of course, that all sounds wonderfully doable if you don't have small children constantly vying for your attention, or if you work from home so can freely excuse yourself for a walk whenever you please. But what if you don't? Then you need to learn how to deliberately detach yourself from your work, as well as how to actively engage in rest. •

DELIBERATE
DETACHMENT

But before we explore how to achieve such rest, let's clarify that it is not simply the absence of work (however that might be defined, from childcare to being in an office). Nor am I referring to sleep, which we will cover in depth in Chapter 8. Here rest refers to the space *between* work and sleep – how we spend whatever moments of wakeful downtime that we have, if you will. However, such rest does *not* consist of being slumped in front of the TV mindlessly watching daytime soap operas or evening box-set marathons. In fact, it is not a passive pursuit of anything, though it should not be confused with, say, cloud-watching. To be actively engaged in noticing the shifting patterns of light in a room, or outside marvelling at any form of nature, is to be fully present in the moment and using all your senses. Prostrate on the sofa, eyes glazed, watching something forgettable, is to be barely conscious. Better to go to bed. In contrast, curled up on that same sofa with a loved one, adult or child, watching a favourite programme together – this exemplifies considered choice. This applies even if you're on your own. It's mind*ful* versus mind*less*. What Dr Alex Pang calls 'deliberate rest', which is differentiated from mere distraction by virtue of you being completely detached from your 'work' and purposefully engaged in something else, albeit something that still requires a degree of gentle concentration or participation, for example a jigsaw puzzle or a video game. This is not to demonise the TV, merely to highlight that being glued to the box, too tired to do much more than randomly surf from one programme to the next, is a sort of suspended animation. The *happy inside* goal is a more fulfilling, and active, use of our rest time.

And yet, perhaps ironically, it is one of the hardest states of being to achieve. Many of us have become hard-wired to oscillate between being in full-on work mode and exhausted. Hooked on constant motion and the completion of never-ending to-do lists, we grind to a halt rather than feeling buoyed up by the prospect of doing something else. This is no way to go on. Here, then, are seven ways to start afresh. •

SEVEN STEPS
TO GOOD
ACTIVE REST

1. STOPPING IS
THE PATH TO SUCCESS

The classical Greek philosopher Aristotle said: 'Nature requires us not only to be able to work well, but also to idle well.' He understood that we are not machines capable of toiling 24/7 like robots. As we touched upon in Chapter 1, constantly pushing ourselves to achieve against all the odds offers no respite for reflection. We need downtime to allow insight to flower. Otherwise, we can persist in striving for something only to realise too late that we are headed in entirely the wrong direction.

Let's take that great philosophical question: what makes a good life? For decades this has been defined as 'success', where that was understood to be a function of money, fame or power. It's always a revelatory moment when we realise that none of these guarantee any such thing, and in fact the pursuit of them quite often ensures the opposite. As the actor Jim Carrey once quipped: 'I think everyone should get rich and famous and do everything they ever dreamed of so they can see that it's not the answer.'

'You have to seize the moment and consciously decide that you want – and, more importantly, need – to partake in active rest more than you want to do something else.'

2. CHOICE, NOT CHANCE, DETERMINES YOUR DESTINY

This is a line from another quote by Aristotle, the full text of which is: 'Excellence is never an accident. It is always the result of high intention, sincere effort and intelligent execution; it represents the wise choice of many alternatives – choice, not chance, determines your destiny.' I am hopeful that reading this chapter will help you understand that the decision to live 'a good life' replete with wellbeing is, thus, entirely within your own hands.

3. ACTIVE REST TIME NEEDS TO BE SCHEDULED

Following on from the above, here comes the but . . . It won't just happen by itself; you have to seize the moment and consciously decide that you want – and, more importantly, need – to partake in active rest *more than you want to do something else*. Determine a time at which you will stop work, no matter what, so that you can go to that life-drawing class, or for a short walk before picking up the kids, or, better yet, for a walk afterwards *with* the kids. Signing up for courses is an excellent way to ingrain a commitment to do something 'other' – you pick something of interest, find a time slot that fits *into* existing commitments, and you show up. It can be a tremendous first step in prioritising time for yourself, and once you realise that you really can do this, perhaps that sliver of time becomes yours for the long term. By putting yourself first in this way, you become more able to give others what they need. And before disillusionment has a chance to sink in, as you sigh and argue that your current commitments

simply do not permit the opportunity to do this, I say that they do. Find a chink of time, however small, and start to drive a wedge into it to open it up as far as possible. It could start with a five-minute walk around the block after you've eaten your lunch or a longer stroll around an art gallery to an hour reclaimed on a Sunday morning for a relaxed bath plus book because you have purposefully allowed your children to watch cartoons. You don't have to dive right in with salsa classes, just as you don't *have* to sign your kids up to a club first thing on a Sunday morning. It's all a matter of choice. And rest is just as important for them as it is for you.

4. DO THE HARDEST THING FIRST

Whenever you have a lengthy to-do list, at home or at work, it is tempting to knock all the smaller items off first so that you feel you have achieved something. Except it never works because gnawing away at the back of your subconscious is the knowledge that the tricky email, essay, article or thing to be mended, is still sitting there, awaiting your attention. By putting it off, you undermine any ongoing attempts at efficiency, let alone rest, because you know that this is the one thing that really must get done. It's like facing a fear: you give it too much power by not confronting it. And most often, as soon as you do this, you realise that it was not that scary after all – the medical test result is negative or the task was not as hard as you thought. Plus, once you have tackled the hardest thing first, everything else is easier! And even if that test result was positive, now you can seek help to get healed rather than causing yourself more strife by worrying about it, or leaving anything to get worse.

It is not possible to do more than one thing at a time and hope to do any of them well. Whether writing notes during a presentation instead of just listening, to driving while talking on the phone (even hands-free), neuroscience indicates that far from effortlessly orchestrating two tasks at once, the brain rapidly switches focus between one and the other in a stop/start process that is inefficient, mistake-prone and highly energy sapping.

Not convinced? Compare the act of listening to a piece of music with your eyes closed to reading a book with the radio on in the background. While we may not have much time to do the former, half of the latter is completely wasted as what you are reading will not be fully absorbed for every moment that you are actually hearing the radio. It follows, therefore, that if you have a specific task to complete that requires your full concentration, switch your phone to silent and turn off all notifications (especially the ones that 'helpfully' pop up on the corner of your computer screen).

If distracted from flow, according to a study on digital distraction led by Gloria Mark, a professor in the Department of Informatics at the University of California, it takes 23 minutes and 15 seconds precisely (*plus* however long you spent occupied by the distraction) to return to full focus. And that's assuming the distraction didn't entail any emotional component such as someone texting to say, 'We need to talk!' As she wrote in her subsequent report: 'attention distraction can lead to higher stress, bad mood and lower productivity'.

6. PRACTISE 'DEEP PLAY'

This is another term coined by Dr Alex Pang, author of *Rest*. He uses it to describe hobbies that offer some of the same psychological rewards as your job but in a different setting and without the frustrations of work – activities that give your subconscious the chance to take up the problems that your conscious mind has not yet been able to solve. As he explains: 'Deep play is especially important for people who don't have a lot of control over their daily schedules, have to work long hours, or who love their jobs but are prone to overdoing it. For them, deep play is valuable because it provides a more compelling alternative to work than just sitting on the beach.' He offers as examples competitive sports and rock-climbing, as well as activities that combine physical respite with creativity, such as playing chess or a musical instrument or painting. I would add to this list DIY and cleaning, both of which can be intensely fulfilling and transformative! And if we observe young children, it is clear that they intuitively understand that time spent in play is never time wasted. A lesson that seems to get lost the older we become.

It recalls one of George Bernard Shaw's greatest quotes: 'We do not stop playing because we grow old; we grow old because we stop playing.' In fact, properly engaged time with a child can be one of the very best and most restorative opportunities to practise our own form of deep play. To escape with them into a make-believe world of a teddy bears' picnic, hide and seek, or building a new Lego set, is to both successfully lose yourself in the moment, and deepen your bond with your child.

7. IT'S A SPRINT, NOT A MARATHON

When it comes to active rest, short bursts are preferable to extended lounging. *How* you spend your rest time is far more important than how long you do it for, with the key factor being the level of escape and detachment it affords from whatever constitutes your daily toil. Whether exercise or play, ten minutes of intense 'otherness' will do you infinitely more good than an hour of passive phone scrolling. •

'If we observe young children, it is clear that they intuitively understand that time spent in play is never time wasted. A lesson that seems to get lost the older we become.'

BUT WHAT'S THIS GOT TO DO WITH MY LIVING ROOM?

It's got everything to do with your living room because this zone of the home is the number-one site for aimless distraction and mindless multi-tasking rather than deliberate detachment and mindful attention. In every other home zone, we take ourselves there for a reason – to the kitchen to cook, to the bathroom to bathe, to our bedrooms to sleep.

For sure we can be distracted in these rooms too, yet we had a distinct reason for going there in the first place. But our living rooms? As adults, these are the places we generally retire to only when hitting that point of exhaustion mentioned earlier. And even then we persist in checking our emails while paying scant attention to our partners or children or scanning our social media with the TV burbling in the background. We seldom go there deliberately to indulge in active rest, let alone 'deep play'. What, then, can we do to proactively encourage this? •

LET YOUR SOFA GIVE YOU A HUG

It's never a surprise to me that very large homes often boast a den as the homeowners' favourite place of refuge, because it fulfils a primal need for a warm, cosy space in which to retire and feel safe. This is the domestic version of the burrow to which an animal retreats to calm itself when it is no longer in flight or fight mode. And because this state of anxious over-wiredness is also evidenced in humans due to the frenetic pace of modern living, we must try to create a new version of the primal den, but openly, in our main living spaces. And this perfect retreat is already to hand – in the form of your sofa.

This is a piece of furniture that should envelop you in comfort and act as a domestic talisman for a more balanced life. It should have a ridiculous number of cushions and plenty of soft throws, because it is to become your wakeful bed, a place to which you will feel compelled to turn *before* you are exhausted. It will become your

secondary point of gathering after your dining table. And you must learn to sit on it like a child, all snuggly with curled-up legs.

As such, in the *happy inside* home, sofas are not immaculate and shaped for an erect posture. Nor are they showpieces or sculptural artefacts with carefully draped antimacassars and cushions tipped en pointe and punched in the middle like a fortune cookie! The *happy inside* sofa is deep, soft and comfy. And I use this last word very deliberately. Let me share a story to explain. I once witnessed a smartly dressed and confident woman enter a high-end Italian furniture store. The woman explained to the sales assistant who leapt up to greet her that she had selected this particular brand because of its commitment to quality. She wanted a sofa that would last. However, having been unable to narrow down her choices online, she had now come into the store. The assistant eagerly began to show her around, expertly describing the provenance of every model, providing information about the various designers and the particular nuances and details of each style. They walked, she listened and I eavesdropped, keen to discover which one she would choose – perhaps the company bestseller in the newly on-trend leather, an older classic or the hyper-modern latest release? But after some minutes of her tour, the woman was starting to look some-what exasperated until, unable to contain herself any longer, she blurted out, 'But I don't care about any of that – I just want a sofa that's comfy!'

I relate this tale because when I edited *ELLE Decoration* we prided ourselves on the comprehensive nature of our captions, carefully listing all of the information per-taining to provenance, size, designer and materials. But had we ever sat on many of the sofas we featured to determine what is ultimately their most important character-istic – their level of comfort? No. In the store that day, well over a decade ago, it was a light-bulb moment. The stark realisation that, for all that design nous, who really cares where your sofa is from and what it refer-ences if it's not comfortable? What we need to return to is assessing our furniture *only* by how it suits us as individuals. The point being that it is essential to try before you buy. Do not be seduced by the latest 'must-have' lists in magazines. These are printed so that you can see the full range of what's on offer, but as the inimitable Coco Chanel once said, 'Fashion is what's out there, but style is what you choose.' And when it comes to furniture, always choose guided by what's comfy. Herewith are my top tips for choosing a sofa that can give you a hug.

'We must try to create a new version of the primal den, but openly, in our main living spaces. And this perfect retreat is already to hand – in the form of your sofa.'

• **Buy big!** That is to say, as big as can be easily accommodated in the space that you have available; a sofa should always be pulled back slightly from the walls if tucked into a corner, and there must be plenty of room to walk in front of and alongside at least one side of it.

• **Consider corner sofas.** A corner sofa – consisting of a standard three-seater with one end extended to form a daybed, or another fixed permutation of an L-shape – is the epitome of comfort *if* it is long enough for you to stretch out on it solo, deep enough for you to be able to sink right back into it and wide enough for two or more people to sit on it without you all being lined up as if you're at the cinema.

• **Consider modular.** A modular sofa is divided into individual seating units (rather than the fixed options described above), much like kitchen cabinets, except here each unit could be a seat, ottoman or daybed with multiple options for backs and arm-rests. The advantage of such a system is that they can be incredibly flexible and you can build them up over time. So if today you can only afford, or have space for, a two-seater section, when you're more flush or move to a bigger house, you can add to it at will.

And why not have each unit in a different but complementary colour? Forget notions of the three-piece suite: your sofa and chairs do not have to match. In fact, it's more hospitable to have a range of seating types (see below), and the overall effect will be more uplifting than a strictly coordinated look.

• **Steer away from solitary sitting.** If you have room for more than one sofa, then consider oversized armchairs or additional two-seater sofas to accompany them. As mentioned in Chapter 3, never buy the sort of armchair that fits only one occupant with feet firmly planted on the floor. These do not promote relaxation. You can still find support in a more capacious chair.

• **Do not fret unduly over upholstery.** When it comes to sofa upholstery, your choice must be guided entirely by personal preference. Leather is supremely practical in case of any spillages, whereas velvet must be treated with a stain-resistant finish or it will be speckled with dirt within minutes; other fabrics likewise. But whatever you choose, see it only as a basic backdrop, for your sofa will, and must, be lavishly draped with additional quilts and throws, not to mention cushions (see next point), so chances are not much of the original finish will be visible anyway. However, the colour is still important as this should always be strictly within the bounds of your palette.

• **It's all about layering.** Much as you would do with a bed, dress your sofa from the base upwards. Seats can be made extra snuggly with soft linen- or velvet-covered pads laid over existing base cushions. There should be enough throws so that each recruit to the sofa can wrap themselves individually. And as for cushions, how many can you stack! Your sofa is an invitation to bring all of your palette together in one glorious celebration of colour and texture, plains and patterns. Don't miss this opportunity to indulge.

• **Try before you buy.** Reiterating this essential guideline, much could be said about tall backs promoting wrap-around cosiness, or low-slung sofas being more grounding, but in the end it's all a question of what it feels like to you when you actually sit in, or on, it.

• **And if you have a partner.** Always shop for your sofa together. For such a significant piece of furniture, the angle of the back, depth of the seat and height of the armrests are vital to how it's experienced, and very personal. For two people moving in together, the purchase of a new sofa can serve to really cement the relationship. Like your bed, a sofa is made for sharing, so be sure that it comforts you both. Stay open-minded in terms of look and feel, and pay no heed to trends or fashion. There are a huge number of sofas out there; one of them will be perfect for you, and it matters not one jot whether it's the latest design or not. •

AND WHAT
ABOUT THE DECOR?

Just because we have determined that our living rooms be devoted to active rest, it doesn't automatically mean laid-back neutrals or quiet pastels in decorative terms. Rather, the idea is the creation of a space in which you can feel free to express the full gamut of your tastes and predilections. Your living room should be devoted to the celebration and acknowledgement of what makes you (and anyone you live with) unique, which makes them a great spot to showcase individual treasures – pieces that demonstrate the independent interests of each member of the household displayed together as one, rather than being squirrelled away in separate rooms. Think of them as visual reminders or prompts to recall your harmonious unity. Plus, if we're going to spend more time here, it helps to have things on show to capture our gaze. The trick is to learn how to do this coher-

ently, and Chapter 9 will serve as your in-depth guide to that.

Meanwhile, the backdrop to all of this will be your signature finishes – chiming with the theme of fulsome self-expression. You may well favour a contemplative mood in colours and materials if the goal is one of calm, but equally you may prefer something more vibrant if this space is envisioned as more upbeat and interactive. Here are some ideas to get you started.

• **Be confident.** It can be easy to lose your nerve in a living room because you are so aware that it will be seen by others, but the whole point of a *happy inside* home is that it's *your* home, no one else's. This is your opportunity to curate a small piece of this world coloured and cut to fit you precisely, so have the courage of your convictions, and go for it!

• **What's your statement?** It's not just about the sofa. The decor might revolve around a single statement such as an oversize bookcase, because you are passionate bibliophiles, or a collection of paintings hung together on one wall. Do you love photography, horses, plants, the work of a particular potter? It could be anything, but your living room is the place to explore such a theme.

• **Paint one wall in a bold colour.** Remembering the seven principles of decorating from Chapter 2, never forget that the wall itself is as important as the objects on display. For example, perhaps you have decided to dedicate a whole wall to a collage of decorative plates. It must be considered as a composition of layers, in which the plates are simply the top layer. And this holds just as much for large pieces of furniture, such as that oversized bookcase. While the books will provide a huge amount of colour and pattern, do not neglect the surrounding wall or even the infrastructure of the shelves themselves – perhaps introduce a unifying finish, an accent colour or some prettily-patterned wallpaper on the back panels, depending on their construction. This is also a fun way to update shelving in children's rooms.

• **Once again, tactility is everything.** Because these spaces are where the public and private areas meet, and as such they combine both the busy and the restful, this should always be reflected in the overall decor, not just the sofa, with a tactile and sensory mix of both the hard and soft, rough and smooth. •

A QUICK NOTE ON
THE JOY OF THE STAYCATION

Now that we are making our homes into the most perfect retreats, will we ever want to leave them? In truth, I have always been a huge fan of the staycation, the art of holidaying at home. For sure, it's not the same as checking into a plush hotel with an abundance of clean towels and room service a phone call away, but, that aside, it's a lot cheaper and it can be a unique opportunity to immerse ourselves in the pleasures of leisurely days off in a familiar place without jet lag or the inconvenience of having to unpack. But it only works if you take it seriously, regarding each day of your staycation as an exercise in doing everything that you would *not* normally do. For example, it can be a chance to discover new facets of your local neighbourhood. You could indulge in ice cream in the morning and cereal for tea, and abdicate the responsibility of cooking by eating out at every meal and trying a new place each time, because you *are* on holiday. Admittedly, if you work from home this may seem less appealing, and one must be

disciplined to not revert to spring cleaning or getting the laundry done. Equally, if your days are ordinarily spent in an office, the idea of 'getting away from it all' at home might seem equally off-putting. Nonetheless, the very purpose of the creation of your *happy inside* home, particularly the reinvention of your living room, is for it always to be a complete pleasure to return to. What better act of appreciation than to deliberately factor in some time to immerse yourself in it? Most importantly, it can be a period to set in motion some of the earlier lessons of this book – whether learning to begin your days more softly, making time to exercise, or starting a do-a-painting-a-day challenge. Cataloguing all your baby photographs can wait for a rainy weekend. And don't forget to enjoy your staycation *detached from all digital devices*. It is only when we experience the sheer joyous freedom of being temporarily uncontactable that we realise just how much unseen pressure these devices exert upon us. •

SUMMARY

It is clear that work and rest are intimately related; we cannot do one without the other. Work non-stop and you will soon burn out. Take to your sofa all day and that novel will never get written. But combine the two and all things become possible. Nevertheless, although we now know that we must make time for active rest, it is also something that we must learn to do well in order to get the most out of it. Exercise is a unique form of restorative active rest, and we have covered this in Chapter 3. But if you adopt only one new ritual from this entire book, then please make it the addition of something like meditation to your life. It's a game changer.

So much has been written about the benefits of meditation that it would be doing it a great disservice to try to encapsulate it all here. Suffice to say, it is the single most powerful tool against overthinking, and the resultant over-complication of life, that is freely available to you. And yet the meditative quest is not a mind free from all troublesome thoughts, but one that recognises those thoughts as something we manufacture, not the essence of who we are. So much anxiety and worry are generated about what has already happened or what may come to pass, along with our ability to cope with it, and yet both are untouchable in the present moment. If you believe that you have done something wrong, or think you may have caused offence, then take prompt action to remedy it – it could be as simple as sending a text to apologise. But get it out of your head, then let it go. You've done your best. As for the future, it'll get here when it gets here and your best preparation is to be calm right now. And if such worrying disrupts your sleep, then this is a downhill slope (read how to tackle this in Chapter 8). So while meditation may not need any additional justification, the need to take the time to do it, does.

To have the best effect, though, it must become a daily habit – something you do as automatically as you clean your teeth. But you don't need to be at it for hours, staring morosely into a candle or chanting, to reap the benefits! Settle yourself in the middle of your now divinely cushioned sofa den and use an app. I use the Calm app as it offers daily guided meditations in 10-minute chunks. I do it as soon as I wake up, before I have time to consider not doing it, and before the rest of my household wakes. I go downstairs, plug headphones into my phone and just sit and listen with eyes closed. There are meditations specifically for addressing anxiety, low self-esteem and stress, along with sleep stories, a children's section and even masterclasses on mindful eating and creativity, so there's lots to choose from, and all at different lengths. There are many other apps available too (InsightTimer is also highly recommended), so take the time to discover what suits you; I find the tone and timbre of the teacher's voice to be the clincher.

And on those occasions when you feel that you're struggling or overwhelmed, turn to meditation rather than alcohol, cigarettes or TV to diffuse the overthinking. Exercise, meditation and rest: make space for them, and they will happen. Make them a habit, and they will change your life. •

7

GRATITUDE

'ONE CANNOT THINK WELL, LOVE WELL, OR SLEEP WELL, IF ONE HAS NOT DINED WELL.'

VIRGINIA WOOLF
ENGLISH AUTHOR
(1882–1941)

The kitchen is popularly referred to as the heart of the home, which has resulted in an increasingly trend-led drive for ever larger and more ostentatious cooking spaces flowing unbounded into our living areas. The dining room has become all but obsolete and an enormous kitchen island is the status symbol du jour. While it's great that kitchens are receiving as much attention to aesthetic detail as other areas of the home, I challenge its designation as the epicentre and champion instead a return to a more pragmatic focus on function.

CREATING YOUR HEART OF HEALTH

The vision of a family all cosily seated around that must-have kitchen island while a cake bakes in the oven, laughter reigns and home-work gets done is an idyllic one, but it's also a fantasy in most modern households. It's more likely that such an island will prompt short-cuts around eating, encouraging breakfasts taken standing up, lunches served from pan to plate and started before the whole family is seated, and ad hoc buffet-style dinners as everyone comes home at different times. In today's busy world, this is inevitable to some extent, and once in a while it's okay. But if we wish to get any-where near that picture of familial bliss, then the action needs to shift elsewhere and your kitchen returned, in terms of function rather than aesthetics, to a straightforward emphasis on food preparation; at the same time eating should be encouraged to be conscious and slow, not convenient and swift. And so, food prep and food con-sumption must be deliberately separated to enable the appropriate focus on what's important – the food. Not quite a reinstatement of the formal dining room – after all, open-plan living encourages easy communication and active engagement – as a call for the timeless tradition of eating together to be honoured and for the dining table around which the whole family sits to be acknowledged as the most important piece of furniture in your home.

As we have already explored, the true beating heart of your home is your hallway – the link between all zones. This is followed by your living and lounging areas in terms of importance. But the kitchen? Think of it as the engine of the home: finely tuned, fully integrated and supremely functional, but in the background. We don't necessarily want to be shut away while we cook, but neither is it a stage for culinary performance. And while the superior slide and click of a quality drawer mechanism is a thing to behold, as are leather-lined

cutlery drawers, sous-vide ovens and large-scale ranges, none of it is necessary. Unless you are a professional chef who needs space to test recipes, you host your own home-cooking show, or food is an absolute passion, you're betting your happiness on the wrong thing if an aspirational kitchen is the assumed holy grail. Instead, picture a camping scene or impromptu barbecue on the beach: a simple tin-foil grill or open fire; the delicious aroma of something roasting; the company of friends, family or perhaps just the stars; all in a naturally energising environment. These are the only four components worth investing in. Nothing else matters. So let's explore each in turn:

- MODESTY OF ACCOUTREMENTS
- THE BEST INGREDIENTS
- A SENSE OF COMMUNION
- AN ENERGISING ENVIRONMENT

THE
'MODEST'
MODERN HEARTH

Cookbooks ride high in bookseller charts regardless of whether readers concoct anything from their pages, and TV cookery shows are consumed voraciously by rapt viewers as they tuck into microwaved dinners balanced on their laps. Entire magazines are devoted to the pursuit of the perfect designer kitchen and they love to talk latest trends as if readers would redo this whole zone every season. This says to me that there is indeed a huge appetite for the joy of food, but also that it's translating into the purchase of unnecessary gimmicks and gadgetry and the elevation of the kitchen to domestic trophy. And so we find ourselves at a crossroads, for while the facilities may be initially complex to arrange, the purpose of the kitchen itself is, and always has been, really quite simple.

A kitchen needs to be able to house the means to store, prepare and cook food, and clear everything away afterwards. In many homes, it must also accommodate washing machines and dryers, and it is therefore also a hub for housework. Anything beyond this is superfluous and mere whimsy. There was a reason why clutter-clearing was addressed right from the start in Chapter 1: hoarding is a habit that merits being repeatedly challenged, and kitchens are particularly bad when it comes to harbouring both just-in-case and used-only-once items, as well as often being elaborately over-designed for purposes way beyond the remit of the actual users.

Certainly it's important that our kitchens feel fully integrated within our homes as a whole, regardless of whether they're exposed in an open-plan layout or cloistered away in a room of their own. Their design can be a complex balance between the useful and the beautiful, and the best results always lie finely poised between these two demands. But we'll come to this point last.

THE PURPOSE
OF YOUR KITCHEN

In order to properly evaluate what you need, you must start by asking yourself, 'What do I really do in my kitchen?' Or to put it another way: 'How is it used for the way I truthfully live my life?' As you may have found in earlier chapters, when you take an honest look at yourself, you may come up with some surprising answers. Do you regularly make meals from scratch several times a week, order in takeaways or dine out most often? Do you usually work with a vast array of ingredients, or stick to a bit of a fixed repertoire of favourite dishes? Do you love to host dinner parties, or is this just a dream? But if you do, are they formal dinners or impromptu suppers? Do you in fact even like cooking? There is no judgement to be made on any of the above, only the acceptance of reality so that your kitchen can be designed to fit, or scaled back accordingly. After all, if you rarely cook for more than six, do you need a hob with more than four rings? If you are a couple, would a slim dishwasher no more than 45cm (18 inches) wide not suffice, rather than running a standard 60cm (24 inch) unit half empty every night? It's worth reassessing, too, the assumed required sizes of fridges and freezers. How much fresh food do you throw away each week because it's gone off before you got round to eating it? If your fridge is too big, you're probably filling it regardless of need. Likewise the freezer. •

HOW TO WORK OUT
WHAT YOU REALLY NEED

All those gadgets used once, kit for recipes you'll never try again, unthumbed cookbooks – they are tokens of a life that does not belong to you, whether future fantasy or past. And while they may seem harmless enough, keeping such things around 'just in case' drags you away from who you truly are, here in the very real present. Plus, by physically cluttering your kitchen, they prevent by proxy the wholehearted enjoyment of an energetically efficient space in which nothing is in excess and everything is easily to hand. There are few things more frustrating while cooking than going to strain vegetables and struggling to retrieve a sieve that has worked its way right to the back of an overcrowded cupboard. As such, the clutter-busting must extend to the kitchen – no superfluous tools, outdated ingredients or crowded work surfaces here, please. For example, if you have a sharp knife, who needs an egg slicer? As the engine of your home, it should be kept streamlined and in good order, and in return it'll help you to do the same for yourself. And as you will by now have already carefully inventoried all of your possessions, you'll be ready to take it a step further here as a fine-tuning cross-check to ensure that nothing has been missed, and you really are holding on to only that which you truly need.

- **Step 1: Empty your closets.** Take everything apart from crockery and cutlery out of your closets: utensils, pots, pans, oven dishes and anything else used to prepare and cook food, from cupcake trays and serving spoons to egg whisks and blenders. Stack all of it together, ideally not in the immediate vicinity of your kitchen space, but somewhere easily accessible (on the floor is fine), and stack like with like, i.e. all saucepans together, all serveware and so on. You want to make it straightforward for you to find what you need, without having everything too conveniently to hand.

- **Step 2: What do you actually use.** For a full ten days, from the first piece of toast to the last roast lunch, you will select only what you need from this stack and, after use and prompt cleaning (recalling the tips of Chapter 4), replace it, and it alone, into one of your now empty closets (cupboards that you will also have taken the opportunity to give a good deep clean while they are clear). What is of primary importance is that in going to make each subsequent meal you do not revert automatically to the stacked stash of equipment, but straight to your cupboard. Hopefully, because it will be more instinctive for you to turn by default to your regular storage spaces, habit alone should have you searching there first, but hence not having all the stacked items too close to hand. Not to the extent that you're deliberately curtailing your cooking, but certainly being mindful to use as little as possible. What's instructive is to note which items you always turn to. Do you unconsciously have a favourite mug, pan or preferred chopping knife? Which are the items you find yourself searching the dishwasher for? This exercise will quickly reveal your essential kitchen kit.

• **Step 3: What to keep and what to let go.**
At the end of the ten days, hopefully there's a reduced selection of items in your cupboards. However, don't now jettison all of your baking paraphernalia just because no cupcakes were made this week, but do ask yourself how many times a month you bake. And do you really need four loaf tins, a flan base, a jelly mould and two large cake tins? Do you even have sufficient containers to store such a feast if you did bake up such a storm? Seasonal items require careful thought, too. Do you keep an extra-large roasting tin just for the holiday season? A preserving pan and 20 empty jam jars because you absolutely intend to make fig jam again come the autumn? Consider that Christmas or Thanksgiving dinner – all of your guests probably have their own over-sized roasting tins. So if space is an issue, what might you borrow rather than have to store yourself for a once-a-year occasion? Likewise with the jam-making. Give yourself the next six months to have a go. If it doesn't happen, then it can't be a burning priority. And any other very specific items should be rigorously assessed too – bread makers, juicers, blenders with numerous complicated attachments. Do you use

them at least fortnightly, do you enjoy using them, are they still fit for purpose, and do you have room for them? Use these as your criteria and no doubt a few more items can be let go. And the less stuff you have to store, the less storage you will require, ergo a lighter, brighter space overall. Furthermore, in completing this exercise, perhaps you'll have noticed that some of your dishes are a bit chipped, mismatched or old, so now would also be a good time to upgrade them to neat nesting sets so they take up even less room.

CROCKERY

Unless you regularly host dinner parties for ten or more, then six place settings – with associated cutlery (flatware) – is the standard starter set, allowing a couple to eat all day without needing to run the dishwasher, or to throw a dinner party for two further couples, both sets of parents or four entirely unrelated friends. This is more than sufficient. And then, as you potentially add to your family, or choose to start hosting supper clubs, you can request additional sets for your birthday, making unwanted gifts a thing of the past. Stick to plain white bone china or porcelain, and you'll always be able to add to it without any trouble, even if the precise design of each plate and bowl is a little different (this will only add to the overall textural joy). Also, if anything breaks, it will be easy to replace, with no hoarding of spares required. Over time, if you wish to spruce up a place setting with a few coloured or patterned pieces, then all well and good because you are building from a firm foundation of timeless classics. Most importantly, such elegant settings allow the food to be the centre of attention. And on the surprisingly persistent notion of keeping a formal versus a casual set: the things that you use every day should be the best you can afford, and the things that you love to use the most. Keeping 'best' sets for use only when you have guests comes with the assumption that unless it is a 'special occasion', you do not deserve to eat off them. This is a subtle dig that goes right to the core of your self-esteem. Are you alone not deserving of the best? If you still have two sets so designated, ditch the 'casual' one immediately and start dining like a champ off that fine porcelain every day. It reminds me of the film *Sideways*, starring Paul Giamatti and Thomas Haden Church in which Giamatti plays a brilliantly observed character called Miles Raymond, a struggling writer, junior high school English teacher and wine snob with a much-prized bottle of 1961 Château Cheval Blanc. As the story plays out, both men address various midlife issues, but the pivotal moment for me is when Miles believes he has finally hit rock bottom and decides 'to hell with it' as he drinks his vintage wine from a plastic cup with a burger in a fast-food joint. And he savours every drop with the realisation that every moment can be a 'special occasion', if you choose to let it.

A NOTE ON BOWLS

A standard Western place setting would traditionally include five different pieces: a dinner plate, salad/dessert plate, a bread-and-butter plate and a cup and saucer. An accent plate (midway in size between a dinner and dessert plate) and a rimmed soup bowl were also sometimes added. Yet clearly

'Keeping "best" sets for use only when you have guests comes with the assumption that unless it is a "special occasion", you do not deserve to eat off them. This is a subtle dig that goes right to the core of your self-esteem. Are you alone not deserving of the best?'

most of these pieces are somewhat out of date for everyday contemporary eating. And who still drinks from a cup and saucer? Instead, let's ponder the wonder of the bowl as an essential item of crockery by calling to mind the *oryoki* nested bowls used by Zen monks. *Oryoki* is often translated as 'vessel that contains just enough' and such a set usually consists of between four and six lacquered wooden bowls of varying sizes (to accommodate every possible permutation of food and drink) wrapped up in a cloth, with – in another narrow cloth pouch – a single pair of chopsticks, a spoon and a small spatula-like item called a *setsu*, which is used to clean the bowls. A napkin and a wiping cloth complete the set. The outer cloth also doubles as a placemat upon which the bowls are arranged in a prescribed sequence. It is a lyrical example of the fewest items required to do the job alongside a poetic paean to the usefulness of the bowl. Zen teachers also maintain that partaking of meals with an oryiko set cultivates gratitude, mindfulness and a better understanding of the self. For the non-monk then, the inspiration is clear: a broad-based bowl can happily accommodate everything from cereal to salad, soup to stews, pasta to pudding. And a modern place setting for everyday use would therefore best comprise one medium-sized dinner plate,

two bowls (one small and one large) and a mug. Not to forget that food eaten from a bowl allows for a marvellous intermingling of flavours that tends to feel more wholesome and satisfying than food arranged neatly in isolated portions on a plate.

A NOTE ON GLASSWARE

There is a saying along the lines of life actually being quite simple but it's people who complicate it. I feel this way about glassware. How many households have all manner of glasses, tall, short, fat, thin, some for this drink, others for that, and a few fragile flutes for champagne? And yet, day to day, I guarantee there will be one set of basic tumblers that get reached for most often. How much simpler it would be to have just one stackable glass that felt wonderfully comfortable in the hand, was perfect for both water and wine, hot drinks or cold, that was heat and shatter resistant, so practically indestructible, and inexpensive to replace should the worst occur. Enter the classic Duralex Picardie tumbler, chic and superbly multi-functional, mainstay of many a French bistro, and one of the most affordable design classics around; usually priced from as little as between £1 and £2 each (approximately $2). I also use mine for serving puddings, such as individual portions of chocolate mousse! •

THE HEART OF HEALTH: THE BEST INGREDIENTS

If you wilfully pollute your body, you increase your chances of becoming ill. So if you want your rocket to fly, put rocket fuel in it! But this needn't mean throwing out all the cakes and biscuits and drinking only green juice with a side of raw celery sticks from now on. It's more about loading up on those foodstuffs that naturally work to clean up free radicals and any other nasties we may have absorbed. Especially as there's an increasing amount of research that places the gut on a par with our hearts and brains in terms of importance in wellbeing. According to the German medical researcher Giulia Enders, in her fascinating book *Gut: The Inside Story of Our Body's Most Underrated Organ*, an unhappy gut can lead to an unhappy mind so anyone who suffers from anxiety or depression should take note. As she writes, 'Grumpiness, happiness insecurity, wellbeing and worry do not originate in isolation in the mind'. Instead, Enders believes that science has long focused on the might of the brain at the cost of the influence of other organs. As she says, 'Recent gut research has contributed significantly to a new, cautious questioning of the philosophical proposition "I think, therefore I am".' Essentially, it has uncovered the gut/brain axis, a direct line between our stomachs and our thoughts. So having a 'gut feeling' about something suddenly has a lot more resonance. And when it comes to stress, the condition of your gut also plays a pivotal role; therefore if you are careful about what you eat, you are looking after yourself in many more ways than previously realised. It's also a call to ensure that the dinner table remains a stress-free place in order to improve the digestive health of our tummies. Especially for young children whose gut brain develops in tandem with their head brain. As Enders puts it: 'The earlier in life that mealtime calm is introduced, the better. Stress of any kind activates nerves that inhibit the digestive process, which means we not only extract less energy from our food, but we also take longer to digest it, putting the gut under unnecessary strain.' This goes hand in hand with mindful eating – the act of consciously appreciating what's in front of you, the textures and tastes as well as the very life-giving sustenance of it all. Here are some more things you can do to supercharge your fuel for life.

CLEAN UP YOUR DIET

All of the kitchen clutter-busting and general clearing is because *you cannot create healthy food in a hectic kitchen*. Clearly, then, cleaning up your diet as well as the space in which you prepare and eat food is the number-one thing to do. And bearing all the gut/brain research in mind, while your kitchen might not be the heart of the home, it most certainly is the heart of your health maintenance. Here are your new health rules, and this time I do mean rules, not suggestions.

• **Fill your pantry with real food.** In other words, things that have a limited shelf life or go bad if they're not refrigerated. Aim to consume a rainbow of different-coloured fruits and vegetables, a variety of raw seeds and nuts (i.e. not the ready-salted and roasted ones), olive oil, and no more than once or twice a week some grass-fed meat and oily fish (salmon, herring and mackerel). Often referred to as the Mediterranean diet, it's a way of eating that's also earned a reputation as a depression buster for its certified mood-boosting credentials.

• **Dump the empty calories.** Anything containing refined sugars is to be given a miss, along with hydrogenated fats, overly refined carbohydrates as found in many processed snack foods, high-fructose corn syrup or artificial sweeteners such as aspartame and flavour enhancers like MSG (monosodium glutamate). Use stevia or agave syrup to sweeten food if you have sugar cravings.

• **Trial giving up wheat.** Do it for a week and see if you feel more energetic. This won't necessarily mean you are gluten-intolerant, but it could indicate that your gut struggles to process it. Skip most ready-made gluten-free products, though, as they are often stuffed with other substances that will do you no favours. Opt instead for pasta made with rice or corn, and try buckwheat (a seed with no relation to wheat) or rye bread (which is lower in gluten).

• **Drink plenty of water.** Give your kidneys and liver a hand by drinking as your thirst dictates but aiming for a minimum of 1.5 litres (2½ pints) of pure filtered water a day. Nettle tea is great as a gentle kidney cleanse, and beetroot, eaten oven-roasted or juiced, is also a fabulous overall internal cleanser.

• **Avoid sodium nitrate.** Often used as a preservative for dried fruit and processed meat such as bacon and sausages, and believed to increase the risk of heart disease. Preservative-free options are available, so check labels and buy these instead.

• **Eat more vegetables than fruit.** It's easy to up your consumption of fresh fruit because it's sweet and delicious and rarely needs to be cooked, and while they contain valuable nutrients and fibre, alongside the natural sugars, it's in the vegetable aisle that you need to linger longer. The more colourful the vegetable the better as this is an indication of its phytonutrient content. These are the substances that protect plants from disease, and they can do the same for you. A fun way to approach this, especially with children, is to try to get at least three or four different-coloured options into every meal. Once you're conscious of this as a goal, you'll be shocked at how bland-looking many meals otherwise appear.

• **Get with the antioxidants.** These are foods that protect the body's cells from being attacked by free radicals. Items naturally rich in antioxidants include sour cherries, strawberries, kale, kelp, garlic, ginger, beetroot, pomegranate seeds, grapes, pineapple, walnuts and sunflower seeds.

• **Learn to love your greens.** Dark leafy greens are more nutritious, calorie for calorie, than any other food. Cruciferous veggies in particular – cauliflower, cabbage, broccoli, kale, bok choy, rocket (arugula), collard greens, mustard greens, watercress, radishes, turnips and Brussels sprouts – are thought to lower inflammation in the body, and because of the glucosinolates (sulphur-based compounds) they contain, they have potentially potent cancer-fighting properties.

• **Investigate probiotics and digestive enzymes.** There's no point eating super-healthily if your body isn't in the optimum state to absorb all the nutrients. Probiotics and digestive enzymes will help to top up or replace anything currently missing from your gut, as unfortunately most people's natural gut flora is woefully depleted.

• **Go fluoride-free.** There's much ongoing debate around the necessity of fluoride, so if you're serious about a full chemical purge, opt for fluoride-free toothpaste. If you clean your teeth regularly and aren't eating refined sugar-full products in the first place, then this won't be a problem.

• **Go meat-free on weekdays.** Eating a vegetarian meal a minimum of once or twice a week is the perfect way to boost your vegetable intake. Do it four or five times and you'll likely save money as well as significantly support your wellbeing. Nevertheless, a diet that contains a degree of good-quality grass-fed meat, fish (small, middle-of-the-food-chain species to limit exposure to mercury), organic eggs and a little dairy produce can be perfectly healthy too. After all, even in the blue zones of the world – those areas where the occupants markedly outlive the rest of us – while their diet is 95% plant-based, on average they also regularly consume small portions (2–3 oz) of meat up to five times a month; eat fish three times a week, and add an egg into their meals about three times per week. So, plant-based on weekdays with a roast on Sunday is my recommended way to go.

• **But if following a strictly vegetarian or vegan diet,** it's important to bear in mind the following: soya, as the base of many meals, must be organic and GMO-free to avoid the vast amounts of pesticides commonly used on such crops; the ingredient labels of 'fast' vegetarian/vegan foods need to be read very carefully as some frozen faux meats contain high levels of preservatives, processed oils and salt; some vegan desserts and ice creams too contain above average levels of starch, gums, pectins and sugar to achieve the right consistency;

and finally seitan, a vegan meat substitute, is made from wheat gluten, so no good for anyone who is coeliac or gluten-sensitive. All this aside, one of my absolute favourite ingredients is an ostensibly vegan food: dried yeast flakes, made from inactive yeast. With a cheesy, nutty flavour, it's a rich source of B vitamins and minerals and can be liberally sprinkled on almost anything, although it's especially tasty on roasted cauliflower!

HEALTHY STORE-CUPBOARD ESSENTIALS

These are the foods you'll want to try and get into every meal, because they are bursting with nutrients that will fortify your wellbeing from the inside.

• **Garlic, ginger and onions.** All three actively support healthy immune function and can be thought of as the 'three musketeers' of culinary healing: garlic has antiviral and antibacterial properties; ginger helps to reduce infection and alleviate nausea and vomiting; and onions have properties that help lower blood pressure and cholesterol, reduce phlegm and decrease inflammation in the nose and throat.

• **Healthy oils.** Number one would be a richly flavoursome, high-quality cold-pressed olive oil for drizzling on to everything, from salad leaves to mashed potato; it can be used to cook hot food, too, though it loses a lot of its goodness when heated. Other good oils include rapeseed and hemp. Avoid refined vegetable oils as harmful substances can be formed in them during processing.

• **Red chillies and tomatoes.** Chillies contain a substance called capsaicin that gives them their characteristic sweetness and pungency. This also works as a natural pain reliever, helps clear congestion, boosts immunity and has cardiovascular benefits. Tomatoes are a major source of lycopene, which has been linked to many health benefits, including reducing the risk of heart disease and certain types of cancer. Combine the two with onions, garlic and olive oil in a slow-simmered sauce and you have a highly nutritious super-sauce! Plus, a punnet of cherry tomatoes kept in the door of your fridge makes a great go-to snack when the sweet cravings strike.

'For while a common cold cannot be "cured" as such, it can be curtailed, and this combination of ingredients basically disinfects you on the inside, strengthening the body's ability to repair itself.'

TONICS

At the very first hint of any cold, I mix this concoction and I swear that any virus is more swiftly dispatched. The juice of one lemon, a few generous splashes of apple cider vinegar and a spoonful of Manuka honey in half a mug of hot water with a small pinch of cayenne pepper. For while a common cold cannot be 'cured' as such, it can be curtailed, and this combination of ingredients basically disinfects you on the inside, strengthening the body's ability to repair itself. Contrast this to many over-the-counter cold remedies which serve only to mask your symptoms rather than supporting your body to heal. They may make you more able to temporarily soldier on regardless, but this is seldom a good path to robust health for the long term.

SLOW COOKERS

If you live on your own (and even if you don't), then the self-care benefits of a slow cooker, or an oven that can be set on a timer to start up automatically, must be trumpeted loud and clear. To be greeted by the welcoming aroma of a hotpot or stew as

*'The power of chicken soup to soothe and restore is a
thing of legend, because, in a similar way to a good stew,
all nutrients stay in the pot.'*

you cross your threshold is a pleasure akin to an olfactory hug. It also means that you save time in the evening as there's no meal to prepare, just one to eat. Leftovers can be frozen in individual portions for lunch the next day, and most slow-cooker recipes are insanely easy to prep, usually requiring nothing more than ingredient chopping and mixing. It's a win-win!

SOUP

The power of chicken soup to soothe and restore is a thing of legend, because, in a similar way to a good stew, all nutrients stay in the pot. That said, I've always preferred a thick, hearty vegetable soup made with a base of the aforementioned garlic, ginger and onions as a nourishing pick-me-up. You can use as much garlic and ginger as you like, depending on your taste, then add roughly chopped vegetables such as butternut squash, fennel and carrots for a lovely creamy consistency. Pour in bone broth (or stock made with a good-quality,

low-salt vegetable stock cube) and simmer until they're softened, then blend, swirl a little olive oil on top and feel the warmth of these super-nourishing ingredients with every spoonful. It also freezes well.

GIVE THE DETOXES A MISS

Sweating is the natural way for the body to detoxify itself, and our liver and kidneys are dedicated to cleaning us up on the inside, so support these and they will support you. In this way, every glass of filtered water you drink is a detox, every vegetable you eat is a detox, and every time you walk in nature, you are detoxing. Giving your system a little nudge from time to time with juices and such like can do no harm, but avoid anything more aggressive. Better to slowly reboot your system with the gradual introduction of a healthier lifestyle in a less toxic environment and let your body do what it does best at its own pace. •

THE IMPORTANCE
OF THE
DINING TABLE

As already indicated, a dining table is the pivotal piece of furniture in the *happy inside* home, followed only by your sofa and your bed. Sharing a home is an agreement to be connected; to tell your stories and intertwine your tales. And to gather together around a table – the ultimate symbol of communion – is the only truly authentic way to do this. It also properly prioritises the ritual of eating.

Too often food has become something to be consumed quickly, squeezed into a slot between other 'more important' things. And if we dine out, we often sit impatiently in a restaurant wondering why it takes so long for our meal to arrive, or, worse, we preoccupy ourselves scrolling on our phones, disengaged from both our fellow diners and the surroundings.

Of course sometimes it's simply not possible to linger lovingly over a bowl of homemade soup, and a takeaway sandwich munched in transit must suffice. But whenever you can, take the time to stop,

'To gather together around a table – the ultimate symbol of communion – is the only truly authentic way to properly prioritise the ritual of eating.'

sit and savour what you are eating, for this will nourish your soul as well as your body. Better yet, find someone to eat with. As a family, or with your flatmates or work colleagues, lunch, tea or dinner might well be the only times that you naturally come together without another purpose. Make it into a habit that unites your clan; something that you always do, because you want to hear about each other's day. But at home, this table, your gathering point, does not necessarily have to be in the kitchen, even though the two are intimately related.

Wherever it is sited, the very process of laying a table with plates, mats and glasses signals the considered intention to stop and take a pause of appreciation for what you are about to eat, even if just for a suppertime snack. But it can go further than this. You should also take the time to really notice who you are sharing your table with. At breakfast this can be a particularly powerful start to the day, especially for children. Taking the time to acknowledge the good they may already have done, from 'I noticed

how quickly you got dressed this morning!' to 'Well done for coming downstairs when I first called you' and other such positive affirmations. It's too easy to start the day with 'time travelling' – the what, when and where of plans for the forthcoming day – instead of enjoying a precious moment of togetherness before going your separate ways. Read more about this in the section 'How to "do" mornings' in the following chapter; meanwhile, here are some top tips for choosing and positioning your table.

• **It's all about the surface.** Always make your choice guided by the table top as this is what you will interact with on a daily basis. Any wood or natural stone would always be a top pick; however, marble must be protectively sealed and wood regularly waxed or oiled to protect it from stains and spills. But if you do this, then no additional coverings beyond placemats and coasters will ever be required. There is great joy to be had from dining at a table that has seen much life, though 'life' here refers to wear and loving usage, not ring-marks and grease spots. Don't forget, too, to stand back and take a look at the legs if your table will be positioned where these will be clearly visible, such as at one end of a long room. Some tables are as beautiful below as on top, and some really are not.

● **Shape is important too.** Round or oval tables work best if centred in a space, adjacent to a door or any walkway through to another room, as they encourage optimal energy flow and limit the potential for sharp corners catching you as you walk by. Choose a square or rectangular table only if it is to be placed at the end of a room, in a designated nook, or aligned parallel with a run of kitchen units.

● **Buy as big as possible.** Just as with your sofa, always buy as large a table as can be appropriately accommodated. In other words, one that fills the chosen area with enough space for you to walk, and thus sit,

all the way around it. Do not push them up against a wall as this instantly constricts energy flow. Also do not be tempted by extendable tables that cannot be used unless you turn your entire room around. They are rarely worth the effort. Just buy what fits your space and accept that this is your limit on guest numbers for dinner.

● **But think carefully where to put it.** Although the kitchen often seems the logical place to site a dining table, and if the space is big enough (see above), then this can work, it's worthwhile to consider other options. Certainly a direct passage from kitchen to table is advantageous, but that doesn't mean the table has to be immediately adjacent. In an open-plan space, if chairs and sofas were shunted around, could a table-sized space open up *between* your existing living and cooking zones? Or perhaps a larger shake-up is required with any nearby or comparatively underused rooms commandeered to create the dining space you and your food deserve.

- **Benches can be better than chairs.** Benches are a great alternative to chairs if you have a long rectangular table, as you can generally seat more people on them if guest restriction is an issue. Snuck into a corner, a built-in bench with a comfortably upholstered back-rest can be the best of both worlds – and you have the option to include storage underneath it too. Make it the sort where you either lift up the seat/lid to reveal it, though, or have drawers that pull out for ease of access, rather than fitting it with standard left-/right-hung cupboard doors.

- **Budget options can be beautiful.** Everyone can own a beautiful table. Second-hand and thrift-store wooden tables can be sanded down and brought quite spectacularly back to life – this is the beauty of wood. To note, though, if an old table has been varnished, send it to be acid-dipped to remove this, and then restained or oiled in one go – a relatively quick and usually inexpensive process that ensures a perfect finish.

- **Be mindful of any table coverings.** But if dressing an existing table to disguise a sub-par top, don't drape a layer of plastic over it as the interface between your fingers and your food. Go for a naturally waxed plain linen or cotton cloth instead. Alternatively, have a sheet of glass cut to the same size as the table top and place this over a more decorative cloth to protect it from everyday staining. Likewise with placemats and coasters. Select these with care, as littering a beautiful table with synthetic placemats is something of a crime! Even for children, a cloth mat is preferable. They stop dishes skidding and can easily be washed.

- **Don't forget the candlesticks.** To light a candle as you sit down to eat, is to instantly create an air of intimacy and occasion, whether you're tucking into cheese on toast or a Sunday roast. It pays respect to your meal. Buy 100 per cent beeswax candles and the sweet scent as they burn (along with their other benefits, covered in Chapter 3) will only enhance your meal further. Be sure to light them when you're sitting down on your own too, a small gesture to yourself. Gazing into the flames is also tremendously relaxing and so good for the gut.

- **Demarcate the territory.** Depending on your flooring, it can be a nice touch to add softness under a table. It signals that here is a separate, and special, place to settle. Go for one approximately twice the size of the top as a minimum and stick to flat weaves to prevent chair legs from catching. Likewise, install an enclosed pendant light overhead to softly accent the table from above avoiding the unflattering glare of an exposed bulb. And fit a dimmer switch too, so it can be further adjusted according to meal and mood. •

AN
ENERGISING
ENVIRONMENT

Now that we understand the role of the kitchen as engine not trophy – we have cleared them so that they contain only what is truly required, our cupboards are stocked with the best ingredients and only the most well-thumbed cookbooks are to hand – we can turn our attention to the decoration. And while the function may be simple, the decor definitely need not be. To recall Chapter 2, our spaces of gratitude are an opportunity to 'crank up the pace and avoid predictability'.

Sadly kitchens often fall into the decorative trap of defaulting to basics: plain white units, tiled splash-back confined to behind the sink or hob and possibly a large jolly-coloured standalone fridge-freezer as the one note of individuality. This is often because, having witnessed the complexity of plumbing and electrics that goes on behind the scenes, the decorative will for what's up front gets somewhat lost. And while an enormous amount of professional design effort has been expended on an ever-increasing array of performance appliances on steroids, the focus needs to return to the main structural components of the kitchen rather than the equipment, namely the cabinet fronts, countertop, walls and ceiling. Colour, pattern and texture can, and should, reign supreme (as long as your kitchen is adequately ventilated), to give full expression to this most creative of adult play spaces. Here are some suggestions.

'Sadly kitchens often fall into the decorative trap of defaulting to basics: plain white units, tiled splash-back behind the sink or hob and possibly a large jolly-coloured standalone fridge-freezer as the one note of individuality.'

• **Upgrade your cabinet fronts.** This is one of the quickest ways to give a kitchen a makeover or to bring it into line with your newly devised palette. And, many innovative companies now offer a wonderful selection of colours, finishes and textured reliefs, all available to purchase online (be sure to request colour samples before ordering, though) and for shipping worldwide. Alternatively, good-quality existing doors can easily, and speedily, be professionally resprayed.

• **Always buy integrated appliances.** For a completely seamless look, opt for fitted units and integrated appliances – dishwashers, fridges, freezers, dryers, washing machines. There's no need for any of these to be on show, and it's ridiculously easy to fit a door to conceal them if you've purchased appliances that are designed to be concealed. They are exactly the same as under-counter units (fridges and freezers may sometimes be a little smaller); just make sure any venting grilles at the bottom are properly installed and allow sufficient space behind all units for cables and pipes.

• **Save on cabinet carcasses.** These generally come in absolutely standard sizes, so if you are on a budget, this is where you can make savings especially for any units that will house only basic shelving or corner carousels.

• **Splurge on the countertop.** Spend the most you can afford here, because this is what you will see and touch every day. In this way it should be on a par with your dining table top in terms of quality.

• **Consider Corian®.** I have always used DuPont's solid surfacing material Corian® (made of natural stone or marble dust combined with resin) for my countertops as it can be used to create a completely seamless look that can, not only incorporate the sink, with no visible joins, but also swoop up walls to form fully integrated splashbacks. Available in a vast array of colours and finishes, Corian® is also completely non-porous and therefore absolutely impervious to mould and bacteria.

• **Take a look at Jesmonite®.** This is one of the newer composites to find favour for kitchen countertops. Made from a combination of minerals and a water-based acrylic resin, it's lighter than stone, as well as strong, flexible and durable, and can be pigmented to any colour. It can also be made to mimic any texture, reproducing the effect of stone, metal, wood, leather or fabric.

• **Remember cork and copper.** An underrated material, cork has perhaps become tarred by association with the decade that style forgot, the 1970s. But did you know that it is naturally antimicrobial and water resistant? These properties are of course why it's used to stopper wine bottles, but cork is also hypoallergenic with the ability to repel dust, hair, dirt and dander, making it a great choice in the home for anyone with allergies. Likewise copper has antibacterial properties that make it a good choice for kitchen counters and sinks. And because it comes in sheet form and is easily workable, it can be used to clad existing countertops without having to remove them first. It will weather, discolour and mark with age, but this should be seen as part of its natural charm. If you're after something that will stay more pristine, then copper is probably not for you.

• Limit high-level cupboards. To enhance a sense of openness, wall-hung cupboards should be kept to an absolute minimum. Shallow, boxy open shelving is better for frequently used items such as mugs and glassware, as they can be stored both within and on top of it.

• Embrace the display shelf. Kitchens can tend to lack those ornaments and paintings that we display in other social areas of the home. This is because storage units are often enclosed with doors, and countertops are covered in appliances. But now that you have decluttered your kitchen and jettisoned the toaster and microwave, you might have room for an elegant shelf on which to display some treasures – one of the most striking I have ever seen was a plank of raw-edged, gnarly wood propped on two simple brass brackets. Rotate the objects shown often and enjoy making your kitchen as personal as the rest of your home.

• Strike out with your splash-back! Instead of a solitary patch of tiles behind the sink or hob, be generous with your splash-back and use it to wrap around and along the full length of your units – perhaps alternate rows of patterned or plain tiles, all in coordinating shades. It can be a wonderful feature that lends cohesion and adds interest and textural intrigue to a kitchen.

• Keep rugs out of the main kitchen traffic spots. Despite an encroaching trend for treating the kitchen as an extension of the living room, keep soft floor coverings out of here. They can quickly become unhygienic as well as being terrible trip hazards. Confine them to slower zones and spaces where you might be more likely to contemplate sitting on the floor.

'Remember, lights are the jewellery of the home, so think of pendants as finishing-touch earrings for a room.'

• **Bar stools are banned.** They are, as the British newspaper columnist Katrina Burroughs so perfectly once described them in the *Sunday Times*, nothing more than 'uncomfortable adult highchairs topped with plastic bum cups'. Just stand, or sit down properly supported in a chair.

• **Always fit more double sockets than you ever imagine needing.** And at least two of them should have integrated USB charging ports. These are a brilliant way to free up the main sockets and lose a lot of unnecessary plugs. In recognition of this, some high-end kitchen manufacturers now incorporate wireless charging zones within worktops or offer the option of designated charging drawers. But a new socket will suffice.

• **Layer the lighting.** Be sure to include functional directional lighting, such as adjustable spots or strip lighting mounted on the underside of wall-hung units, to light work surfaces, but combine them with overhead lighting for more ambient illumination. And remember, lights are the jewellery of the home, so think of pendants as finishing-touch earrings for a room.

• **Make it simple to recycle.** There are lots of bins on the market with separate compartments for every kind of waste, but, in my experience in a busy household, it often gets muddled up anyhow. Better to keep a large paper shopping bag tucked in a corner for all your old newspapers, magazines, cartons and cardboard. Then when it's full, the whole lot can either go into your neighbourhood recycling bins or be put out on the kerb for collection, depending on the policy where you live. Use another smaller one for glass bottles (or any other material that your local council requests to be kept separate). Likewise plastic.

I also keep a pretty glass bowl on my countertop for raw food waste (as soon as it's full, the contents get tipped straight into my external composter). Having a closed waste-food container inside made it too easy to forget to empty it until alerted by either a horrible smell or an infestation of fruit flies. Whereas my bowl is emptied daily. Likewise, I recommend a *small* under-counter general dustbin. It might feel like a pain to begin with, but it limits the temptation to throw away things that should be recycled and prevents the undue accumulation of any sort of rancid waste indoors. •

AND

FINALLY

ESCAPE THE LURE
OF THE KITCHEN ISLAND

Here I'm referring to those oversized oases in the middle of a kitchen that commonly have a sink in the centre, bar stools on one side and integrated bookshelves and wine racks. The sort of kitchen installation that's basically a too-high prep table that you can't stretch your legs out beneath. They have become increasingly fashionable as open-plan layouts become the norm, regardless of the fact that a linear arrangement of kitchen units is more efficient and safer (no hot or heavy pans being lifted *across* a space, only along it). The main attraction is supposedly being able to face into the room while cooking, except that this generally isn't relevant as hobs and stoves are usually fitted next to an external wall for ease of venting, so as you cook you would be turned away in any case. Or vice versa during prep if you're able to put the hob in the centre. Additionally, because of the increasingly inclusive, multi-purpose nature of our kitchens, such islands, unless you are supremely disciplined, tend to become magnets for admin, toys and art materials, which have no place in a food prep area. A level of separation must be maintained, and a better use of resources would be to look into the advantages of having a classic U- or L-shaped kitchen layout. And if space is at a premium, then a galley-style layout – parallel runs of units with a minimum of 1.2 metres (4 feet) between them – will nearly always be the most efficient. Besides, it is perfectly possible to maintain the connection, physically and visually, between living, eating and cooking areas without an island. It's called a table, as previously detailed at length.

MAINTAINING EFFICIENCY

If your kitchen is to be the engine of your home, then it must run itself and be supremely functional. In a Zen temple, the cook (*tenzo*) is much revered, and temple kitchens are always polished to perfection. Even in the midst of cooking, it is deemed essential that all drawers or cabinet doors be closed immediately after anything is removed for use. For the monks, to do otherwise is not just to leave the kitchen untidy, but also your heart. While this may seem a bit full-on for a domestic kitchen, the cultivation of a sense of discipline around its use is a good move. Here, then, are some straightforward domestic home hacks to improve efficiency and enhance harmony in this pivotal space.

• **A place for everything.** Now that you have only what you actually need and use in your kitchen, it's essential to store things in a logical order – like with like and putting the most used items at the front. Stack all baking stuff together. Mixing bowls. Measuring jugs. Saucepans in order of size, sieves on top. But, most importantly, once you have determined where everything will go, stick to it! Every item and tool must have its proper place to which it is always returned. Fully utilise the depth of corner units with a carousel insert, and if you have the option, choose deep drawers for saucepans rather than standard shelving, as they make it a lot easier to view the contents at a glance.

• **Wash up as you go along.** During food prep, keep a sink of hot water ready for washing up utensils as you go, or get into the habit of placing used items straight into the dishwasher. Do the same before sitting down to eat, too. It takes seconds to do, and subconsciously you'll be in a more relaxed state to enjoy your meal knowing that the kitchen is already partially cleared.

• **Never leave dirty dishes overnight.** By all means soak heavily soiled dishes to loosen food deposits, but do not leave them overnight – a paste of baking soda and water is superb for quickly getting rid of any really burnt-on bits of food.

- **Keep countertops clear.** Only ingredients that are used every day should be kept on your countertop – olive oil, salt, or tea leaves in a beautiful container – everything else should be inside a cupboard. Use large, shallow trays to group pots of dried herbs or spices, so you can pull the whole lot out in one go when you need to see what you have. An old shoebox is often the perfect size and height.

- **Curate and contain.** Use a similar box or container for any vitamins or supplements. Also spare dishcloths, scrubbers or other such items kept under the sink. Easy-to-pull-out storage makes a cupboard simpler to keep clean as well as facilitating access to things at the back.

- **Ditch the drawers.** Deep drawers for saucepans: good. Small drawers for anything else: bad. They invite just-in-case clutter. Store cutlery and cooking utensils in upright pots instead, and you'll never be tempted to stuff an old ticket stub, odd screw or matchbox in them again. However, if you have an in-built oven, then a

slim drawer underneath this is ideal for keeping flat baking trays, grill racks and/or shallow roasting tins.

- **Invest in quality equipment.** You don't need to spend a fortune to make good meals, and any appliance that takes longer to clean than to use is probably not worth the trouble. But quality knives are an investment that can last a lifetime with the right care and maintenance. And these, along with well-made pots and pans (re-read Chapter 3, if needed, for what *not* to buy), glass storage jars and mixing bowls and a decent basic blender with a glass jug, should see you through a lot of prep.

- **Consider a water softener.** While this is by no means a mandatory requirement, if you live in a hard-water area, as most of us do, then the benefits can be numerous. Although not dangerous, the problem with hard water is the dissolved metals and minerals that invariably get left inside pipes, dishwashers, washing machines and hot-water cylinders, creating scaling that renders them less efficient, and therefore more expensive to run. It also gets left on your clothes, fading and wearing them out more quickly (especially delicates), as well as making glassware, dishes, showers and

'Deep drawers for saucepans: good. Small drawers for anything else: bad. They invite just-in-case clutter. Store cutlery and cooking utensils in upright pots instead, and you'll never be tempted to stuff an old ticket stub, odd screw or matchbox in them again.'

baths harder to clean. Not to forget the effect on your hair and skin. Softener options include magnetic descalers that clamp to your 'in' pipe (with the main advantage of no plumbing or maintenance being required, although evidence that they work is hard to come by), to entire softening systems that fit under a sink or in a garage. With traditional systems, initial costs vary, they can take up valuable cupboard space, they must be professionally installed and regular maintenance is essential, but they quantifiably work (by directly removing calcium and magnesium from your water and replacing it with sodium) and significant savings can be made over the long term with equipment lasting longer and lower energy bills. On the issue of whether hard water is better for you due to various trace minerals in it versus the perceived danger of the added sodium – rubbish. Any benefit would be negligible if not non-existent, especially when you take into account all the other noxious stuff routinely added to our water.

Besides, hard water or soft, filtering your drinking water is essential, as highlighted in Chapter 3, and relying on your water for your nutrients is like claiming vodka is good for you because it's made from fermented grains or vegetables! •

OTHER ZONE THREE ROOMS

HOME OFFICES AND STUDIES

To be able to have, as the English author Virginia Woolf so memorably put it in one of her essays, 'a room of one's own' in which to be creative can pay happiness dividends in many ways. But whether it's for book-keeping or book-writing, in order to do your best work, there should be a sense of decorative liberation. And this stands regardless of its size – private retreat or somewhere more open, an alcove in a corner or a dedicated room with its own lockable door; here you must feel free to craft a profoundly personal and intimate space. Maybe a wallpaper used discreetly in a main living area is here splashed large over an entire wall? Perhaps another wall could be dedicated to a collage of meaningful memorabilia.

In terms of furnishing, it might only require a desk and the use of a wall as a noticeboard. Or perhaps there's room for a sofa and more ample storage? The only 'rules' are that it cannot become a repository for any I'll-sort-this-later stuff, and that you place your desk or main seat so that you can look directly at something inspirational. It could be a window, a mood board, or a single small painting, but something carefully selected that catches the eye. This will help to keep you focused and able to resist other distractions.

In all other respects, you should draw inspiration from the palette components you have already identified for this zone as a whole, but go deeper. We have discussed in Chapter 2 how moving upstairs to the bedrooms might well invite a dilution of colours; for home offices and studies it is the opposite. Here we might well take one or two tone steps towards the dark side in an effort to encourage concentration.

DOWNSTAIRS TOILETS

Don't let the decorative ball drop just because it's the smallest room in the house; it will probably be one of the most visited, certainly by guests. Could you instead use its size to your advantage and reflect the luxury of having an additional toilet in your home by making it feel supercosy, with dark colours and soft drapes? Could it reveal a surprise like that of an unexpectedly vivacious lining in an otherwise sober suit, by being decorated entirely in one of your stronger accent colours or statement finishes? Even an exotic stone could be eminently affordable here. But whatever you do, make it warm. A cold, sterile closet is no place to comfortably do your business! Have heat alongside towels, scented hand wash and books, and have fun. If nothing else, your guests will thank you. •

A QUICK WORD ON ENTERTAINING

This chapter has been primarily focused on the routine, everyday eating partaken by the permanent residents of your home. And yet the home is also a place for friends and extended family to gather, and indeed it is important that they should feel welcome. Hospitality can be seen as an investment in one another. An invitation to enter our homes is an act of openness, a willingness to be seen for who we are without any expectation of criticism of either our food or our decor.

In the *happy inside* home, then, entertaining is always casual and informal. Dinners or suppers are no longer a rite of slaving and servitude as they once were in the past, with formal place settings, the politics of placement and overly prescriptive instruction on which courses to offer first or what cutlery to use. Rather, the best way today to create an atmosphere of communal conviviality is to get everyone involved. Perhaps you buy all the ingredients but attendance involves the anticipation of help with the prep. Or you ask each of your friends to come with a contribution and dine potluck or buffet-style. As we already know, food need not be complicated to be good; it need only be fresh and unadulterated.

In any event, it's still important to gather around the table as this draws everyone together and instils a sense of community. No doubt if we think back to former homes or even student pads, it will be the memories of meals shared or parties hosted that we recall most vividly; the life lived within the spaces we inhabited, not necessarily the decor.

And if it is sunny and we have the room and the opportunity – perhaps an ample porch or deck, a small roof garden or even a local park – then the meal can be moved outside, and blankets substituted for the table top. But wherever we sit, if we are attentive to what we are eating, and to what our friends or family have to teach us, then there is much to be learned. It is a wonderfully sustaining habit to form, one that can be started incredibly modestly with the sharing of a simple pot of perfumed tea and maybe a few homemade biscuits. •

'Revisit those old cookbooks and find a recipe you haven't tried before, buy that unusual vegetable from the corner shop and get set to become happy inside so you really can be *happy inside*.'

SUMMARY

What we put into our bodies underpins our every action and reaction, whether physical or emotional. The deceptively simple act of limiting any incoming pathogens, alongside fuelling, hydrating and regularly moving our bodies, ensures that they run as smoothly as possible. In addition, stability in one's emotional and physical life helps to eliminate stress, anxiety and worry, mental states which can also lead to ill health. Of course genetics play their part, as does luck, to a certain extent, but there's still a lot we can do to take proactive responsibility for our wellbeing.

And it starts with making our cooking and eating spaces as pleasurable as possible. We must want to spend time in them in order to enjoy both the preparation of healthy food and its consumption – after all, eating well is infinitely preferable to medical intervention, being generally devoid of any unwanted side-effects! So don't let the decorative ball drop here, and don't default to white. Lavish this zone with as much care and attention as elsewhere in your home and allow your palette to lead you into more experimental territory as befits the space in which you conjure your daily sustenance.

And what of a ritual to consider? Because a repetitive diet is one of the worst things for your gut health, why not make it a resolution to introduce a new food to your plate and your palate every week? Whether it's just you who takes up the challenge, or the whole household, make it something that you are inspired to do because it is fun, not just because your disease-preventing intestinal bacteria will thank you for something fresh to feast on!

Revisit those old cookbooks and find a recipe you haven't tried before, buy that unusual vegetable from the corner shop (while also remembering to ask the proprietor how to cook it) and get set to become happy inside so you really can be *happy inside*. •

8

RETREAT

'TAKE REST. A FIELD THAT HAS RESTED GIVES BOUNTIFUL CROPS.'

OVID
ROMAN POET
(43 BC–AD 17)

The importance of a good night's sleep cannot be overstated; without it our memory and immune function are impaired, our mood, metabolism and hormones become unsettled, and we cannot be effective or efficient, let alone energetic, in the way we live our lives. As Arianna Huffington, author of *The Sleep Revolution* and founder of Thrive Global, a health and wellness portal, puts it: 'By helping us keep the world in perspective, sleep gives us a chance to refocus on the essence of who we are. And in that place of connection, it is easier for the fears and concerns of the world to drop away.' Thus, the spaces in which we retire to bathe and sleep are grouped together as the fourth and final zone of the *happy inside* home.

IN
PRAISE OF
SLEEP

The art of creating a really supportive place to snooze is much more than ensuring you have fresh sheets and haven't gone all boudoir bonkers with the decor. In fact, probably more so than any other zone in your home, it relies upon a truly holistic approach to achieving its goal – one that may be summarised as follows:

- UNDERSTAND THE PURPOSE OF YOUR BEDROOM

- GET ON BOARD WITH WHAT YOU NEED TO DO BEFORE YOU GET ANYWHERE NEAR IT

- ONLY THEN, CONSIDER THE DECORATION

THE PURPOSE
OF YOUR
BEDROOM

Your bedroom is a room in which you will primarily go to sleep. Yes, other more active things may well occur here too, but its chief purpose is to enable you to rest, recover and, if you are unwell, recuperate. Therefore, the main non-negotiable thing is that this space *is never used for anything else*! In other words, a fervent 'no' to the notion of the study bedroom. No TVs. And no storage of 'hobby stuff' under the bed. Admittedly, this could present a dilemma for studio flats, or student accommodation, but this is in no way unresolvable, and we'll cover it later in the chapter.

This is about setting the intention of the room. That said, one of my favourite and most productive places to write is sitting up in bed, but only during the day, using a laptop (Wi-Fi disabled), and with curtains and windows wide open. My bedroom is a supremely restful room with no distracting elements, hence it helps me to concentrate. Regardless, the founding principles of its design were the desire to create a space for calm, not toil – its integrity would be utterly compromised were I to move in a permanent desk and a fixed computer.

No mobile phones must be left in your bedroom at night either. The temptation to fall into the rabbit hole of a late-night social media ramble is too great; a segue, then, into a quick check of emails, or a scoot around messenger apps, is a short hop away, and all the time you're doing this, the blue light emitted by your phone or tablet – quite apart from any electro-magnetic radiation – is tricking your brain into thinking it's daytime. The result: instead of falling gently towards slumber, you're racing towards a mind crowded with images and anxiety. Purchase a classic wind-up alarm clock rather than setting a phone to wake you; indeed, this is probably one of the best remaining reasons to retain a landline. Then, if ever there were a genuine emergency, you are still fully contactable, with no excuse for a mobile left switched on next to your head. Regardless, once you

'Purchase a classic wind-up alarm clock rather than setting a mobile to wake you; indeed, this is probably one of the best remaining reasons to retain a landline.'

put everything else in this chapter into play, you'll soon be waking naturally at the same time every day, so you won't need an alarm clock. Quite aside from the fact that being wrenched from sleep by artificial noise is probably one of the absolute worst ways to start any day. So here are four things to successfully set the intention of your bedroom.

• **Keep the amount of furniture to an absolute minimum.** All you need is a bed, two bedside tables (or one if you're on your own), adequate lighting (bedside and overhead) and storage for your clothes. Absolutely nothing else – any additional furniture (chairs, ottomans, chaise longues) only invites their use as a dumping ground – unworn clothes should be either hung up or put in a laundry bin, which are the only two places they belong. Plus, your bedroom will feel larger with less in it.

• **Limit the distractions.** Unless you're in the enviable position of having enough space for a dressing room, the ideal is to have clothing storage built in rather than

using free-standing wardrobes – furniture that's impossible to move to clean around helps no one. My wardrobes are a run of six units from the brilliant IKEA Pax system. They were constructed, centred to the wall, then bolted and boxed in, in a straight line opposite the bed. The boxing-in was because they ran just short of the total width and I did not want to leave them floating with a skinny (impossible to vacuum, dusttrap) gap down either side. It also enabled the creation of a shelf above them. Not a shelf for storage, though, rather a space that I use to display a collection of white ceramic vases and pottery. A light is hung there too, and a favourite piece of artwork. This is what I see when I wake up, which brings me smartly to the next point . . .

• **Position your bed with care.** The goal is to have your bed facing something of beauty, which, depending on the size of your bedroom, could be as simple as a picture or painting hung on the wall, a dedicated display, as mentioned above, or, if the architecture of the room permits it,

a window. But *never* place the bed facing the door. According to the principles of feng shui, putting a bed in this position is equivalent to lying in your coffin waiting to be taken away! While that may seem a touch melodramatic, I agree that a bed facing a door could make you feel subconciously anxious (similar to sitting with your back to a door, as discussed in Chapter 4). Best, then, to place your bed so that the door is to the right or left of the bedhead. In my own bedroom, my bed is to the left of the door, and facing the aforementioned wardrobes – those opposite the bed are finished in glossy white, while the pair facing the door have mirrored fronts – all the better for me to see anyone coming in without having to twist my head (another small move that subliminally supports calm). Also, do not put your bedhead up against a window; you need to allow air to freely circulate around the room, not be blocked by furniture, besides, if you have

radiators set under the window, as they so frequently are, it'll make your bed too hot.

• **Ban candles.** Herewith candles are not allowed in a bedroom, or in fact anywhere upstairs, because the chances of you falling asleep with a candle still burning are too high. The speed at which flames can spread is truly terrifying, and to date I keep a small fire extinguisher in my bedside closet! However, because of the power of scent to soothe, a ceramic oil burner big enough for a single standard (non-paraffin wax) tealight is a good investment. These burn out after about an hour and can be used to infuse your room with naturally relaxing fragrances (see Chapter 3), or tea tree and eucalyptus if you have a cold. Nevertheless, to avoid accidents, keep them *at least* an arm's length away from any bedlinen, and always stand them on a hard, uncluttered surface. I put mine in the sink of my en suite. •

ESSENTIAL
PREP FOR
SLEEPING WELL

There is a huge amount of scientifically backed research that details precisely how injurious to body and soul it can be to skimp on sleep, but let's not overlook that it also makes you more irritable, short-tempered, less able to take a joke and, in short, a lot less nice to be with. This section, then, covers the good habits you need to get into *before* you go anywhere near your bedroom, in order to maximise your chances of getting some decent shut-eye. And while you may be familiar with the term 'sleep hygiene', which frankly sounds rather unpleasant, I prefer to think of it as creating *a ritual of readiness for sleep*. Bear in mind, too, that you don't get skipped sleep back, which means we are all in effect staggering around burdened by a metaphorical backpack loaded with the weight of all our lost hours! So the sooner you get with the sleep programme, the better. The key tenets are as follows:

- ACCEPT THAT SLEEP IS ESSENTIAL AND SHOULD BE PRIORITISED

- REJECT THE ALWAYS-ON FALLACY THAT DOES NO ONE ANY FAVOURS

- STIFLE THE ELECTRONIC STIMULATION AND DEVELOP THE DISCIPLINE TO HONOUR THIS

- CREATE A RITUAL OF PRE-SLUMBER SURRENDER

Admittedly, you may accept all of those pointers, but find that what keeps you awake is a whirring brain, what Buddhists refer to as 'the relentless monkey mind'. This is when you find yourself mentally scrolling through the minutiae of your day, conversations you've had, better responses that could have been made, concerns for the next day and a hundred other random thoughts that your brain sees fit to process just as you want to be drifting off. It is the absolute opposite of being in the moment. Instead you are reliving every past moment and even projecting into future moments that haven't yet happened.

And while meditation might well be the most powerful path to quietening the mind, when actively in the grip of stress – specifically that horrible feeling of overwhelm when you can't think straight because *everything* seems urgent – it can be that much harder to do, which can further fuel the stress. So, while developing a daily practice is absolutely to be recommended, at times of particularly sticky anxiety I've found the following pragmatic suggestions to work more immediately.

- **Always keep a pen and notepad next to your bed.** Every time a 'must do' pops into your head, however minor, scribble it down. This is about getting it out of your conscious mind *and* preventing your subconscious from tenaciously holding on to it, playing it over and over in case you forget it. As the popular Buddhist saying goes: 'Worries and tensions are like birds; we cannot stop them from flying near us, but we can certainly stop them making a nest in our mind.' Write it down, *then* forget it. I keep a stack of blank postcards handy for quick note making (they also fit neatly into a handbag, so any additional thoughts can easily be captured when out and about too), but any notepad will do. However, do not use your phone to make notes; the act of committing pen to paper is a better means of shifting thoughts from the mind, quite apart from the fact that your phone should already be switched off and left in another room or downstairs!

- **Prioritise.** On that same pad, every night before you go to bed, highlight the three most important things that need to be accomplished the next day. No more, no less, just three (I've tested adding more, and while sometimes it's possible, three is always achievable, and thus more motivating). These aren't necessarily the most urgent things (as usually determined by external factors like work) but they are the most *important to you*, for a balanced life. And put them in order of priority. Again, it's about discharging the worries and perpetual planning from your subconscious mind. Trust me, this is a small BIG step on the way to undisturbed sleep.

• **Develop a gratitude practice.** According to therapist and author Barry Neil Kaufman, 'Gratitude is one of the sweet shortcuts to finding peace of mind and happiness inside. No matter what is going on outside of us, there is always something to be grateful for.' And as it's often due to a stream of negative thought polluting your mind that you are unable to sleep, developing a practice of gratitude can begin to reset your brain to dwell on the good rather than the bad. You can buy a special journal for this purpose or just use a blank notepad, though it should be separate from your list-making one – that needs to be more throwaway. A gratitude journal is a keeper, something you have treated yourself to and think is beautiful to write in. The idea is to close each day giving thanks for three things that made a positive difference to your day. Small or large, it doesn't matter. But try to be as specific as possible. To quote Tamara Levitt, head of mindfulness for the Calm app: 'Express gratitude for the comfort and conveniences you enjoy, for the everyday facets of life that are easy to overlook. Part of this practice is to be grateful for what we have even when it appears that we have very little. So even if life hits a rough patch, you can still feel grateful for clean socks, fresh air and a beating heart.'

• **Set your sleep schedule.** If you need to wake up between 6.30 and 7.30 a.m., then the optimum time for adults to get to bed is between 10 and 11 p.m. as the average amount of sleep believed to fully restore body and soul has recently been increased from eight to eight and a half hours. The key, though, is that once you determine your sleep schedule, you stick to it (give or take some evenings out!), and that means always going to bed and getting up at the same time, whether on weekdays, at weekends or on holiday. I'm afraid lie-ins are completely counterproductive as our bodies thrive on established routines. And while it can sometimes feel that you have too much to do to go to bed 'early' and so you work late to catch up, it's self-defeating as you inevitably get slower as the evening progresses, your judgement becomes impaired and quality drops. It is always better to get to bed 'on time' and give yourself the chance to properly reboot. You are guaranteed to be more alert and productive the next day and will whisk through tasks twice as quickly.

• **Accept your circadian rhythms.** It is entirely natural for the human body to wake at around 3 a.m. It's a function of the pre-programmed circadian rhythms that govern our sleep and wakefulness cycles. If you're a good sleeper, you probably won't even be aware of this because you'll just drop off again. However, people who think they sleep badly are often those who, on realising that they're awake, fumble for the clock, internally shriek, 'OMG, it's 3 a.m.! I've only got four hours left until I have to get up,' and so jump-start an instant cycle of worry, overthinking and general fretting about not sleeping. How different might it be if you thought instead, 'Yippee! *Another* four hours in bed!' Better yet, do *not* reach for the alarm clock, simply acknowledge that this is a natural phase of your cycle, not some aberrant quirk known only to you, and look forward to the more active

REM (rapid eye movement) dreaming part of your sleep that will come next. And by the way, you may rouse slightly at 4.30 and 6 a.m. too. This is because, in this stage of sleep, each cycle is about 90 minutes long, dipping down into deep dreamland before rising up to peak with a moment poised right on the brink of wakefulness before dropping again for the next round. Those moments on the precipice are just that, moments before the next cycle begins – if you let it. Don't feed such moments with paranoia. Greet them and let them go.

• **Give up coffee after 2 p.m.** However, the above is all shot to pieces if you consume caffeine. Caffeine works by blocking the body's natural chemical processes that serve to regulate those innate circadian rhythms. While overriding sleepiness in the short term, a long-term repercussion is the sabotage of your entire hormonal system at a very basic level. And the effects are longer-lasting that you think: caffeine

has an average half-life of about 5–7 hours, so your 4 p.m. pick-me-up is still having 50 per cent of its initial effect on your body by bedtime (note: decaffeinated does not mean *non*-caffeinated, simply that it contains *less* caffeine, usually only 15–30 per cent of a regular brew). And if you say, 'Oh, but I always drink espresso with dinner and still fall asleep,' I'd counter that you're probably so intensely sleep-deprived that you're falling asleep *despite* the caffeine. Regardless, while your eyes may be closed, you'll never be fully recharging your batteries, merely adding more bricks to that metaphorical backpack. Plus you probably need more caffeine to wake yourself in the morning too. Bad, bad, bad. Make no mistake, caffeine is an addictive stimulant that perks you up, only to leave you physically craving more when it wears off. In my opinion, the whole seductive industry built around coffee is nothing more than a reflection of the increasingly unrealistic demands we put on ourselves. So if you're serious about your health and wellbeing, give it up, or at the very least, aim for no caffeine whatsoever after 2 p.m. But wean yourself off slowly, the equivalent of one half-cup a day.

• **Forget the night-cap too!** Many think that an alcoholic drink before bed helps them to sleep more soundly. Again, categorically untrue. As a sedative, rather than a stimulant, sure it can fast-track you to a state of unconsciousness, but alcohol inhibits restorative REM sleep, a crucial function of which is to boost emotional intelligence. A night deprived of adequate REM sleep will leave you feeling ragged, not restored, in the morning. Thus, in an ideal world, you should have no alcohol within three hours of bedtime. In this sense, the Italians get it right with their habit of *aperitivi*: snacks with a single drink immediately after work. It's a social event as friends and colleagues gather in local bars to offload from the office before going home. The snacks are free, and the whole thing is a mere convivial

prelude to dinner with the family, not an evening out in its own right. Contrast this to the peculiarly British habit of a night spent lining up the pints with a solitary packet of peanuts on the side.

• **Say *adios* to late-night gym sessions, but hello bath-time.** Similarly, you should take no aerobic exercise within approximately four hours of bedtime. It makes your body too hot to sleep. Although, as counter-intuitive as it might seem, taking a bath before bed cools your core, which is proven to be beneficial. Toss a handful of magnesium salts into the water too, and you'll be well away: magnesium is a mineral that not only helps to regulate melatonin – a hormone which affects our sleep/wake cycles – but also supports a balanced central nervous system, so sufficient levels are essential for a relaxed mind and body. The temperature of your bedroom is also crucial. Set your thermostat to no more than 16–18°C (61–65°F).

'The whole seductive industry built up around coffee is nothing more than a reflection of the increasingly unrealistic demands we put on ourselves.'

• **Digital detox.** This is imperative! As touched upon already, your bedroom must be a technologically clean zone. And if you still have a Wi-Fi router, then it *must* be switched off at night too. Likewise all phones and any other electronic devices; and plug them in to recharge well away from your bedroom, preferably on another floor entirely. Needless to say, the nightly digital detox is essential for children and teenagers, too, if not more so. To support their physical and mental development, they need a minimum of 8–10 hours of uninterrupted sleep per night. And the best way to teach them? Model the behaviour you'd like to see by starting and finishing each day device-free yourself.

• **So what can you do before bedtime?** Read! A study conducted by the UK's University of Sussex in 2009 found that reading for just six minutes before bed reduced stress levels by 68 per cent.

• **You can also have a snack.** Sour cherries contain a small amount of melatonin and can be mixed with some natural yoghurt, which is a good source of tryptophan, the amino acid that turns into the happy hormone serotonin before also being converted into melatonin. Sprinkle with a few sunflower seeds, cashews or flaxseeds, and top with a chopped banana and you'll be all set as these contain magnesium and vitamin B6, good levels of which are additionally associated with sound sleep. And if you fancy a bedtime beverage, then non-vegetarians might want to swap the warm oat milk or camomile tea for some bone broth, as this is super-high in glycine, another amino acid that's been found to improve sleep quality.

• **Don't forget the earplugs.** Quiet is often under-rated as we become inured to a low-level hum of continuous noise, especially if you live in an urban area, but as much as you think you might be used to it, it will impact the depth of your sleep so I highly recommend the use of earplugs. Tapered soft foam earplugs are the best, the sort you roll between finger and thumb before popping them in. The feeling of all ambient noise fading into oblivion as they expand to fill your upper ear canal, is blissfully sleep-inducing in itself.

BUT DON'T GET HUNG
UP ON YOUR RITUAL

If you have a beer and skip the bath, or run out of magnesium salts, you will not be automatically condemned to toss and turn all night. Being a bad sleeper is as much in the mind as the body. Go to bed feeling guilty and, for sure, it's all downhill. Just accept you've done what you can, and move on, otherwise the ritual itself will become the block to sound sleep. In the same way, I heartily condemn any sort of digital sleep-tracking device; they serve only to make you unhealthily obsessive about your sleep, which is completely counterproductive.

Most importantly, even if you regularly struggle with your slumber, please resist the temptation to resort to sleeping pills. In acclaimed neuroscientist Matthew Walker's seminal book *Why We Sleep: The New Science of Sleep and Dreams*, he refers to research that suggests a correlation between the use of sleeping pills, whether taken occasionally or frequently, to higher-than-average rates of mortality and cancer. So pretty much everything else is, without question, worth a try first. •

'I heartily condemn any sort of digital sleep-tracking device; they serve only to make you unhealthily obsessive about your sleep, which is completely counterproductive.'

255

'The pleasure of a freshly dressed bed is one of the finer things in life, and yet many stumble here, not sure what can go with what, or whether it's okay to mismatch pillows and duvet cover. The simple answer to this is that anything goes.'

THE ROLE OF THE DECOR

When you're asleep, you can't see what's on your walls, so does it really matter whether you paint them pink or blue, or keep them patterned or plain? Well, yes, actually it does. But not to the extent that there's a prescribed 'bedroom only' decorative palette. Beyond intrinsically stimulating shades such as red, orange or a particularly bright yellow, which would by their very nature undermine your ability to relax, you could probably use anything you like in your bedroom. Here are some further guidelines on what else would work well:

• Consider removing your ceiling! Yes, really. Obviously this depends on the slope and extent of your roofline, and the assumption that your bedroom is on the top floor of a building you own. But I mention it upfront because, if you can, it's easier than you think and the benefits of giving yourself more space above your head can be enormous. And while it might be a bit messy to do, it's not that complex from a construction point of view. Most ceilings are entirely cosmetic – just sheets of plasterboard nailed to the underside of rafters –

so they can easily be removed without affecting the structural integrity of your roof (though you should have someone double-check this beforehand, of course!). Ensure the roof is adequately insulated directly under the eaves, then cover with water-resistant, foil-backed board, replaster, paint with gloss (my personal favourite for superbly light-reflective ceilings), and give yourself the benefit of increased light and height all in one go. It also stops you from storing any clutter up there!

• Have fun with your headboard. As it's behind you, it cannot be considered distracting, so this is the one spot you could really go to town on, whether you tile it, pad it or cover it with a sumptuous button-backed velvet. A headboard treatment that extends behind any bedside tables is great for a sense of cocooning comfort, particularly in smaller rooms where oversize features help focus attention on the bed rather than the dimensions of the room. Above your headboard the whole wall could be a riot, again because it's behind you as you sleep. So why not paste up some mad wallpaper, add a digitally printed meadow or have it hand-painted with butterflies? Combined with your headboard treatment, this will provide the decorative focus for the room, something to engage with *before* sleep. By extension, though, the other walls must remain plain. They can be coloured to coordinate, maybe even be textured, but they must stay free of pattern. It's all about balance.

• **Dressing the bed**. The pleasure of a freshly dressed bed is one of the finer things in life, and yet many stumble here, not sure what can go with what, or whether it's okay to mismatch pillows and duvet cover. The simple answer to this is that anything goes. However, for cohesion – and no surprise here: work within your palette. That said, the colours used for dressing the bed do not have to be identical to those picked for the rest of the room, *so long as they are similar in tone*. For example, pale blue walls could be combined with sheets and coverlets in equally pale shades of rose and pistachio.

Don't forget to layer up in winter with perhaps an additional eiderdown thrown on top, and never underestimate the sheer heaven that is an electric blanket underneath it all, switched on for a few minutes before bedtime. Just always remember to switch it *off* before you get in.

• **Top tip**. A length of coordinating fabric is an easy, inexpensive and instant way to add a touch of texture and colour to a bed. Most fabrics come in 140cm (55 inch) widths as standard, which is more than ample for a purely decorative throw. Purchase a length of about 2.5 metres (8 feet), hem the ends and drape across the bottom of your bed. Don't bother to sew the long side edges, because an exposed selvedge (the machine-bound edges of the cloth) will lend a nice informality to your throw. It's just the cut edges that need to be neatened to avoid fraying. Any thick fabric will work (so it drapes well); just choose a pattern and colourway you love! •

HOW TO 'DO' MORNINGS

Now that we have readied ourselves for sleep in a conducive atmosphere and enjoyed an uninterrupted night, what happens when we wake up? After all, how well we seize the day is dependent not just on how we slept but also on how we choose to start it. So, are we all predetermined to be night owls or morning larks? Not at all. It's purely habit. Habit perpetuated by myth and self-suggestion. In other words, we think we work best at night, so we allow our schedule to slip to accommodate that belief and use caffeine to override any misgivings. But human biological clocks are dictated, like those of many warm-blooded animals, by the passage of the sun. Our bodies naturally produce melatonin, the sleep hormone, in response to falling light levels. We all tend to slump a little in the afternoon and have a 'second wind' in the early evening. Sleep scientists believe this is linked to our evolutionary heritage, in that an energy peak as night falls would be necessary to protect primitive man from nocturnal predators,

'One thing is for sure, there's no point getting up early if you end up pottering about doing nothing of any significance.'

whereas a post-lunch snooze, out of the midday sun, works for animals as well as people. Even post-primitive humans tending the fields and living off the land would have risen with the sun and been tucked up by nightfall. But contemporary life with its artificial light, manufactured stimulants and incessant distractions has us working against the innate cycles of our bodies, and indeed the natural world. A stark example of this is what happens during daylight saving time (DST).

Every year, most parts of North America and Europe currently lose an hour in the spring and gain it back in the autumn. And every year, the incidence of traffic accidents, strokes and hospital admissions due to heart attacks increases in the spring and decreases correspondingly in the autumn. Why? Well, it's because this time shifting, introduced in the early twentieth century to save energy and make better use of daylight, messes with our circadian rhythms and for people with an already weakened nervous system, whether due to illness or fatigue, such a disruption can be too much. So how can we retune ourselves to more proactively accommodate DST, but also make mornings a delight not a dread? Let's tackle DST first.

It does not creep up on us by surprise. We always know the dates in advance, so here's a suggestion: indulge in the autumn, and prep for the spring. And by prep I mean get up five minutes earlier, every other day, for a month beforehand, or if you're really organised, start on New Year's Day and do five minutes a week! Increasing your wake time slowly, instead of shocking your body with a sudden early start, is the best way to ease it in gently and ingrain it as a new habit. If you set your alarm back by much more, even 15 minutes, you may well be able to bounce out of bed fuelled by enthusiasm for the first few days, but inevitably even this small change in waking pattern will conspire to bring about a day when you cannot manage it. Once the pattern is broken, it very quickly becomes harder and harder to get back into the groove. And when I say indulge in the autumn, I do not mean by staying in bed! Rather, could you consider the extra hour as a gift, and use it to do something meaningful? Could you wake at the same time as before, but now keep this precious hour for yourself? Perhaps you've always wanted to start a blog? Or have the time to read more? Or even to take a morning bath; there's something a bit delicious about doing this in the morning; plus you can read in the bath, which is highly acceptable multi-relax-tasking. One thing is for sure, though, there's no point getting up early if you end up pottering about doing nothing of any significance – be clear about what you wish to achieve in the new-found hour *before* you fall asleep (remember that notepad by the side of your bed?). Of course, the reality for many is that this extra hour presents an opportunity to try to offload some bricks from that lost-sleep backpack. Nice try, but it won't help.

Use it instead as a chance to establish a healthier ritual around sleep; the pointers below are a good place to start.

• **Forget the snooze button**. Unless you have a whole 90-minute sleep cycle worth of time ahead of you, get up when your body prompts you, no more than a few minutes after waking in the morning. If you use an alarm clock, the temptation to hit the snooze button is counterproductive as it will then go off mid-cycle or sooner, and you'll be horribly wrenched from sleep instead of naturally rousing yourself.

• **Rehydrate**. All adults need a *minimum* of six standard glasses of fluoride- and chlorine-free water a day to keep the body ticking over – it is integral to the function of every organ. While some of this can be obtained from other beverages or whole fruit, pure filtered water is the equivalent of five-star fuel. Start as you mean to go on and get at least one down the hatch as soon as you wake. Make it easy for yourself by leaving it on your bedside table before you go to sleep.

• **Regularise medications.** If you take supplements or other medication, they will always work better for you if you take them at the same time every day, whether morning or night. Unless they need to be taken with food, pop these down with that first glass of water. Again, have it prepped by your bed the night before and you can do it without thinking. Otherwise, have them ready for taking with your breakfast.

• **Jump-start the neurons.** Open curtains and blinds as soon as you get up, especially if you have blackout screening. A shot of daylight sends a 'wake-up' message to your brain and gives your internal body clock a kickstart. In the winter, it can be helpful to invest in an alarm that mimics the sunrise, rather than sounding a klaxon, as darker mornings make bouncy starts that much harder. The second best way to jump-start your brain? Have a shower; it'll wake you like nothing else. Otherwise, splash your face with cold water. There's no need for a whole face-cleansing routine (assuming you did this before you went to bed), as you'll strip your skin of its essential barrier oils and make it more prone to infection. A light sweep with a gentle toner after splashing will suffice if your skin feels oily.

• **Do a ten-minute meditation.** You could do it just before you go to sleep too, but a morning session really helps to instil a calm frame of mind. There are even some fantastically relaxing body-scan meditations you can do lying down, so you don't even

need to get out of bed (except to collect your phone, which you can do after you've opened your curtains!).

• **Write in your gratitude journal.** We've touched upon closing the day with gratitude, but it's also a lovely way to start your day too. What reasons to be grateful do you already have today? What would make this day especially great? It's another small thing that sets you up with a positive bias from the off. Be sure to make your expectations realistic, though – for example, a wish for seamless train travel rather than the purchase of a winning lottery ticket.

───────────────────

'Never skip breakfast.
It kick-starts your metabolism,
gives you the energy to start
your day with vigour,
and keeps you focused.'

───────────────────

• **Prioritise breakfast.** Never skip breakfast. It kick-starts your metabolism, gives you the energy to start your day with vigour, and keeps you focused. Porridge in particular is a golden charm as it's an excellent source of vitamins and minerals as well as complex carbohydrates that release their energy slowly, thus less reaching for sugary pick-me-ups come 11 a.m. Sprinkle a handful of walnuts and some sunflower seeds on top and this will boost the effect even more. Otherwise, add a mixture of fruit to a blender, plus a banana, some frozen spinach (which turns everything madly green and adds valuable nutrients without adversely affecting taste), a spoonful of a superfood supplement like maca (a Peruvian root that tastes slightly malty or nutty) and some milk of your choice, and you can whizz yourself up a power breakfast in a glass.

• **Leave the phone alone.** This is worth stressing: *do not use the very first part of your day for anything other than readying yourself.* Don't waste early-morning minutes mindlessly checking your social media feeds or attempting to 'get ahead' on emails before you even have breakfast. If you plough straight into external obligations, you are sabotaging the rest of your day. Start as you mean to go on, with a plan for consideration and calm, and the day will, if not follow accordingly, be much more manageable for your having given yourself a self-supporting start.

• **Have a routine.** Notwithstanding the reality of hectic mornings, trying to persuade/order children into their clothes or downstairs in time to eat, it's like they say on an aeroplane: put your own oxygen mask on first. If you're grouchy from too little sleep or suffering from caffeine withdrawal, the odds are stacked against you for a streamlined start. Beyond that, have a routine that everyone buys into and decide together the family rules: for example, dressing before breakfast, or afterwards? Then be consistent. Is everyone actually clear on what time is leaving time? Is there a clock in the hallway that's easily visible? And be your own best helper by determining what can reasonably be done the night before – schoolbags prepped; lunch boxes filled; your handbag ready; oats pre-soaked. If you live alone, then a routine will provide an incredibly sustaining framework of order. If you live with a partner, it's helpful to agree together how best to start your day, right down to who uses the bathroom first and who makes breakfast. Such things are often the cause of petty irritation or argument and yet it never occurs to us that such knowledge isn't transmitted by telepathy! Good communication is the foundation of all good relationships. •

'Have a routine that everyone buys into and decide together the family rules: for example, dressing before breakfast, or afterwards? Then be consistent.'

AND NOW TO BATHING

Over the last decade, in much the same way as kitchens, a huge amount of design energy has been expended on overhauling our bathing spaces in an attempt to make them into stylistic trailblazers in their own right. The trend has been for ever larger, mini spa-esque temples to bathing that invite solitude and reflection as much as getting clean. Showers have become wider and larger, and tubs bigger and deeper, with sometimes the entire room being envisioned as a 'wet room'. Has it all been necessary? Absolutely not.

Such emphasis is on escape, exaggerated by the fact that this is probably the one room in the home that has a lockable door, hence providing a retreat in a literal sense. But this is not the answer. The whole purpose of the *happy inside* home is the creation of an entire space of retreat and replenishment, so you should no longer need to lock yourself in the loo to take a quiet moment for yourself!

Accordingly, I'd like to champion a return to bathrooms for the purpose they were intended: to allow you to rid yourself of the dirt of the day in a clean and private space. This is not to say that I underestimate the power of a contemplative bubble bath or the invigorating refreshment of a power shower. Instead I'm advocating a need for perspective. Bathrooms must not be neglected, but they need not rise above requirements. The most important components of a good bathroom, regardless of size, are listed below. And if you are a renter, then it is *always* good policy to check out the bathroom first when considering a new tenancy. Other rooms can easily be tweaked and redecorated, the bathroom less so without significant financial investment by a landlord and extremely intrusive disruption to yourself, so make sure it absolutely suits your needs before you fall in love with the view from the lounge.

CLEANLINESS IS EVERYTHING
You cannot clean yourself in a dirty space. Neither can you relax. So a bathroom must be spotless and finished in a manner that enables you to keep it that way. This is why carpet is forbidden and easy wipe-down

tiles an automatic go-to. But the ambience must still be homely, not one of clinical precision. The following will help you to achieve that.

- **Work within your palette.** This will ensure a continued sense of flow from your bedroom to your bathroom, whether or not it is en suite or separate. Do not suddenly stray from your palette here because this is such a different space to work with. Even if you decide to use predominantly white, consider what touches from elsewhere could be introduced. A textured wall of colour? Some embossed wall tiles? A burst of pattern on the floor, perhaps? Even curtains! As long as the space is well ventilated (see below), there is absolutely no reason not to have curtains in a bathroom – in mine they are full-length grey velvet.

- **Good ventilation.** Bathrooms are high risk for mould because of the potentially damp atmosphere, and the only way to combat this is to allow fresh air to flow through on a regular basis. It can be tempting to shut the door after a hot bath and leave steam to disperse by itself, but this will only store horrors for later. Once you're towelled and dry, open a window. For the same reason, always use moisture-resistant paint, eggshell or gloss, on bathroom walls. Any sealants and tile grouting also need to be certified as suitable for damp rooms. They may be a little more expensive in the short term, but they will be a lot cheaper than having to gouge the wrong stuff out and redo it when it inevitably fails (this is particularly important inside showers or around the bath as otherwise water can make its way behind tiles and cause all sorts of problems). Wood such as cedar and teak are naturally water resistant, but other types of wood must be properly sealed and varnished to preserve them.

• **Add a touch of luxury.** As well as curtains you *can* have wallpaper in a bathroom as specialist companies exist today that offer waterproofed and coated papers that can be used even right inside a shower cubicle, and there are a huge array of patterns to select from as well. Something unexpected rather than discreet will work best to emphasise the exclusivity of such a treatment, such as a 'living' wall of leafy verdant foliage or oversized blooms for impact. It's also a clever way to give the impression of marble if the real thing is beyond your budget. Application involves special adhesives, though, so this is not a DIY job. Don't forget, too, the pleasure in decanting run-of-the-mill bathing products into beautiful glass jars, or the joy of plump white towels and embellished bath mats. Texture is key here: mix things up a bit with towels in ribbed Egyptian cotton, Turkish flat-weave or Japanese waffle designs, as rigidly matching sets are outdated and boring.

• **Sufficient storage but not too much.** If designing from scratch and boxing in a bath, incorporate a generous ledge on the side nearest the wall for products (or bath toys) to live. (I sit mine in a rectangular white ceramic dish so I can pick them all up in one go when cleaning.) The same can be done behind a sink, especially if you are already building out to accommodate a hidden toilet cistern and the sink and loo

are set against the same wall. Continue the boxing behind both, tile the lot, and you have created for yourself an instant, and highly useful, built-in shelf. But don't fall at the final hurdle and use it for stashing umpteen half-finished bottles of shampoo or free sample sachets of products you'll never use. If you've tried a new cleanser and didn't like it, then do not cave in to the just-in-case impulse; give or throw it away. In the same breath, do not be tempted into buying new before you have finished the old. This makes it unnecessarily hard for you not to be wasteful. The only exception is if you are replacing like with like, in which case it's always handy to have a spare deodorant or face wash on standby. Unless you are a beauty journalist or make-up blogger, channel the mantra: minimise and contain, and aim for a capsule collection of necessities. What is the minimum you need to clean face, body, teeth and hair, to condition and moisturise, and otherwise primp, preen and perfect, alongside any more mundane monthly maintenance needs?

• **Wall-hung sanitary ware.** As indicated in Chapter 2, if you own your home, installing wall-hung items, from the loo and sinks to storage, make the floor easier to clean and enhance the sense of space. In a bathroom, this is essential. A shallow, wall-mounted, mirror-fronted cabinet (with integrated lighting and shaver socket) hung directly above the sink is best for products in daily use. A vanity unit suspended beneath sinks is the ideal for everything else – *never* buy a sink unit that cannot accommodate storage beneath it; they are an absolute travesty of wasted space. And if you rent and your

*'Unless you are a beauty journalist or make-up blogger,
channel the mantra: minimise and contain, and aim for a
capsule collection of necessities in your bathroom.'*

landlord has not provided a wall cabinet, then this is an inexpensive and worthwhile investment that you can take with you when you leave. Any wall fixings are usually small and can easily be made good with a little filler. Your only other requirement might be a small stacking trolley on wheels as a portable home for anything else.

• **Other furniture.** Two towel rails (one for hand towels near the sink, one for larger sheets near the bath), a small bin, two hooks (for dressing gowns or pyjamas) and a small stool are the only other things required in a bathroom. The rails keep towels off the floor, the stool can be used for spares if required, and is also a handy prop for a book while bathing (and to help you poo – see the last item in this list!).

• **If space will allow.** Twin sinks and a separate bath and shower encourage efficiency because a pair of sinks (or one that's wider than average) allows two people to brush their teeth at the same time, and showering and bathing can also happen concurrently if the units are separated. Likewise

if there's only going to be one toilet in your home, it helps to locate it independently, if at all possible.

• **Two types of lighting.** Lighting is mood making. And a bathroom has to accommodate morning rushes and evening slow-downs. The ideal is a central pendant for atmosphere on a dimmer switch combined with dedicated spots over the bath, shower and sink, operated by their own switches. Safety is an important prerequisite, though, as any light fittings *must* be specifically designed for use in a bathroom and be fully enclosed in a water-resistant casing. All switches must comply with regulations, too, and sockets are not allowed within 3 metres (10 feet) of a bath or shower.

• **Consider linoleum or rubber flooring.** Tiles can be wonderful but unless you have also installed underfloor heating, they can be unpleasantly cold to walk on. A good alternative can be linoleum, which, unlike synthetic vinyl, ages well, improves with use and is antibacterial. Studded rubber is another excellent non-slip option.

• **Keep the porcelain white.** Never ever consider any other colour. Ever. White is a classic. And you will have a greater choice of styles and fixtures. Anything else will date. Express your fun and quirky personality elsewhere, or with details that are easy to change, such as towels and accessories.

• **Import a little from the Japanese ritual of onsen.** Like many things in Japan, there is a strict etiquette to how *onsen* – geothermically heated hot spring pools – are used, and one aspect of this makes a lot of sense: thoroughly cleaning yourself in the shower *before* you get into the pool. Entering an *onsen* with soap, dirt or sweat on your body is unacceptable and grounds for ejection. If we transfer this to a home context, think how relaxing it would be to soak in a bath anointed only with essential oils or mineral salts, rather than wallowing in self-sullied water.

• **A last word on poo.** In earlier chapters, we've talked about food and energy, and the importance of the gut and detoxification. Well, it all ends in the bathroom.

While sorting out your food at the top end is the obvious starting point, it is also essential that you poo well to ensure that all waste gets out of your body as efficiently and completely as possible. And it's easier than you think. According to Giulia Enders, the author of *Gut: The Inside Story of Our Body's Most Under-rated Organ* who we met in Chapter 7, it involves a small foot stool. Popping your feet up on the stool and leaning slightly forward puts the end of your intestinal tract in the perfect position for full and easy bowel evacuation. As she puts it, you are in effect squatting on your throne! You might feel a bit silly at first, but try it before you mock. It is a fact that in countries where the squat toilet is commonplace, there is almost no incidence of digestive conditions like diverticulitis (an inflammation of your intenstine lining) and a significantly lower incidence of haemorrhoids. So use a stool and, as beautiful as your bathroom now is, you'll be in and out in seconds. •

CHAPTER EIGHT

A FEW OTHER POINTERS

NEW HOMES

When moving into a new home, always prioritise getting the bedroom ready and do not allow boxes to be piled here. Nor should you think, 'I'll make do on the sofa while I sort everything else out first.' Put your wellbeing at the top of the list, and everything else will take care of itself. Besides, after a hectic day of unpacking, nothing beats the feeling of slipping a freshly bathed body between clean sheets in a clear room.

STUDIO FLATS AND STUDENT ROOMS

All is not lost if this is your base. Think laterally and take inspiration from caravans and boats. It's still all about zoning; and switching things off for the creation of that tech-free space after 9 p.m. Paramount for good sleep in a restricted space is to identify one corner as your dedicated sleep sanctuary – it need be nothing more than a raised nook the size of a double mattress. Raising the bed up on a platform of some sort is the ideal as it physically and symbolically lifts you away from the rest of the space, while also providing valuable storage potential underneath. This is the one exception for the nothing-being-stored-under-the-bed rule, as here it is incorporated deliberately rather than by default. In any event, its contents must be ordered not dumped, and the best design would be a large pull-out drawer on wheels. A final touch would be to enclose the whole bed in some way, whether it be boxed in or lightly curtained off across the front with a length of gauze draped over a taut cable or curtain wire (the sort that's used for net curtains and comes with screw-in hooks and eyes).

LAUNDRY

Do *not* shoehorn washing machines et al. into a bathroom. As indicated already, the path to a serene bathing space entails not overcomplicating its function. A utility room dedicated to washing and the storage of spare towels and bedlinen would be beyond excellent, but if space is at a premium, an additional downstairs loo is a better option; indeed, sometimes it's possible to combine both in the same room. Otherwise conceal integrated washing and drying appliances in the kitchen, use laundry bags hung on hooks instead of baskets (if there's nowhere unobtrusive to put one), and see Chapter 9 for a cheat's guide to linen closets. And if you have a boiler here, a good trick is to box it into a run of wall-hung cupboard units that can then also be used to house seasonal items like blankets and extra duvets that are tricky to store elsewhere. If possible, set the whole lot high above head height and mirror-front the doors as a canny way of sneaking in additional storage, as well as reflecting more light around!

WARDROBES

As we've learned already, increasing the space allocated to anything simply invites the filling of it, and this is especially true of wardrobes. You may well be able to close the doors to hide any over-stuffed horrors within, but a cluttered closet will wheedle its way into your subconscious and undermine sound slumber, as well as making it harder for you to choose what to wear in the morning. Instead, assess what you have based on honesty about who you are today (this means the size you are as well as the life you lead). Admittedly, as I've said in Chapter 1, sometimes you need to hold on to some things until you're really ready to let them go. And that's okay. Hopefully, you will already have made a start on tackling your wardrobe after reading that chapter, but here are a few more targeted tips.

• **Sort clothing by type.** That is, all cardigans, all knitwear, all dresses, etc. This way it won't become unduly overwhelming and you'll be able to clearly assess what you have in each category.

• **Fold, fold, fold those jumpers and T-shirts.** Here, Marie Kondo's advice on drawer management is frankly genius. With each item in a drawer folded and stacked vertically, rather than laid in flat piles, it becomes easy to see what you have too much of, or do not regularly wear, and hence could probably let go. Colour-coordinate those stacks and suddenly your drawers become a thing of great organisational beauty.

• **Ditch the shoeboxes.** Invest in several sets of stackable clear perspex shoe drawers and you can arrange your shoes by type too, and probably get everything slotted into the bottom of a single closet. Cardboard boxes take up a phenomenal amount of space. Reuse some to sort your kitchen, recycle the rest and marvel in being able to clearly see what you own.

• **Accept that the money has gone.** Sometimes we keep things just because they were expensive, even if we don't wear them. See them instead as a source of 'free' money if you then sell them! The money you spent has long gone, but there's still capacity to make some back.

• **One in, one out.** Because we are retraining ourselves to consume mindfully, we will now only be purchasing that which we truly require. In other words, shopping only to replace items that have become worn out or irretrievably damaged. Avoid temptation by limiting online browsing or idly perusing the shops of a Saturday, unless you have a will of steel. What you don't see you can't desire.

• **Clothes need space to breathe too.** Closets should never be so full than everything is squashed up against each other. Fibres need to breathe to stay fresh and in the best condition. And never ever put anything damp back into a wardrobe, whether it's fresh from a dryer or hot off your back – this is a first-class invitation to mould and moths – hang it to air first on a curtain rail in front of a window. •

SUMMARY

To be clear: no amount of fancy decor will make the slightest bit of difference to your ability to sleep soundly if you do not take heed of what you do before you get anywhere near your bedroom. Only once this has been addressed, can this room become one of your most powerful allies in pursuit of wellbeing, happiness and good health.

What, then, could be instilled as your personal ritual of readiness for sleep? For me it begins with the drawing of curtains and the switching off of all overhead lighting in favour of low-wattage side lights or the soothing glow of salt lamps. I also add a few drops of lavender and bergamot to an essential-oil burner as an olfactory wind-down nudge to my brain, and whenever possible, on the dot of 9 p.m. all computers and phones are switched off as well. A bath may be run, a book chosen to be read, and handwritten notes made to clear tomorrow's priority to-dos from my head, but the household is now closed for business. Whatever you choose to do, if you can learn how to start and finish each day in a way that is consistent, calm and full of gratitude, then you have created for yourself the strongest possible foundation for the cultivation of self-discipline, self-acceptance, patience and alert attention – all key qualities for a more intimate engagement with life and true long-term contentment. In short, follow the night, allow it to fall in your home and encourage your body to do the same. •

9

NURTURE

'THE ACHE FOR HOME LIVES IN
ALL OF US, THE SAFE PLACE WHERE
WE CAN GO AS WE ARE AND NOT
BE QUESTIONED.'

MAYA ANGELOU
AMERICAN POET, AUTHOR AND ACTIVIST
(1928-2014)

This final chapter covers the finishing touches that
should be layered over everything that we have discussed
already. These are the details which ensure that your
home works for you on *every* sensory level. For while
we tend to make first impressions based largely on what
we see, it has to be confirmed by our other senses – ever
spotted someone and thought they seemed terribly chic,
only to be subsequently affronted by bad breath or a
squeaky voice? Your opinion is permanently reversed.
It's the same at home. From the sounds you wake up to,
to the scents that surround you, your connection to a
space involves much more than what it looks like.

THE FINISHING
TOUCHES

Scent provides an indelible first impression to any visitor, noise plays a huge part in our daily lives and the everyday touch points of our homes – door handles, taps, cutlery, light switches and sockets – are often overlooked in favour of bigger, more obvious decorative moves, and yet they are equally, if not more, important. But to stress, when referring to scent, I do *not* mean deodorising sprays of any sort, and especially not those designed to plug in and poof out a spritz of synthetic pong at all hours of the day. You quickly become immune to something used so consistently, which can lead to inadvertent fragrance overload, especially for guests. Our goal is that the air inside your home is naturally fresh and clean *before* you add anything to it. And thus, when you do so, it is a deliberate act with a defined objective.

Likewise, in a busy household it can be hard to find a place to be quiet and still. From the incessant sounds of TVs and mobile notifications to the continuous external hum of planes, car alarms or police sirens, it soon adds up to a relentless acoustic burden. Unsurprisingly, the World Health Organi-

zation has determined that noise pollution is the second biggest environmental threat to health after air pollution (excessive noise levels cause elevated stress levels, higher blood pressure, low productivity and poor sleep habits). Regardless, for some people, silence is deafening. And yet, flicking on a radio without thinking is the same as masking undesirable odours with artifical deodorisers. So even if we can't eradicate all external noise, we can begin to select what we will treat our ears to as carefully as we'd pick what we're going to eat.

And then of course there is the art of display: surrounding yourself with carefully selected pictures, art and ephemera is a wonderfully inspiring way to give yourself those all-important emotional boosts. It promotes the mindfulness we first introduced with the idea of decorating in planes or the 'soft fascination' that makes walking in nature so restorative – enough to stimulate but not so much as to be overpowering. Let's then explore the last few ways in which we may completely fulfil the potential of your *happy inside* home. •

COMING TO YOUR SENSES: SCENTS AND SENSUALITY

In Chapter 3 we covered the healthy ways to introduce scents from natural sources, such as herbs and essential oils, to rebalance and harmonise your home, so here we'll look at when and where you might use them.

• **As we follow the night towards sleep.** The evening is an optimum time to introduce a relaxing scent to your space. As mentioned in Chapter 8, lighting an essential-oil burner can easily become part of a ritual of readiness to sleep. Place it either in the hallway, so that the aroma infuses your home from its very heart, or in your bedroom to fill the air with somnolent scent in preparation to wind down.

• **Mornings to encourage focus.** Unless you work from home, the mornings are best left to their own devices on the scent front, bar briefly opening windows to flush out stale overnight air and to quickly freshen and cross-ventilate rooms. However, if you will be staying in situ, scent is a wonderful way to encourage focus and mentally signify the start of a working day. Choose a revitalising scent – think rosemary or black pepper – and again, use an essential-oil burner, always my preferred means of fragrance distribution.

• **During illness.** When you are unwell, the air in your home can rapidly become stagnant. It's not for nothing that Florence Nightingale was hailed as a revolutionary for flinging open the windows in her hospital wards, as the natural tendency is to keep rooms warm and cocoon-like, when this can be counterproductive. Certainly, stay cosy in bed, but do everything possible to maximise air movement and introduce scents such as eucalyptus and tea tree to cleanse and heal. Something headier – frankincense or oregano – can be used later at night when their warmth will be soothing.

• **When entertaining.** Set the scene with scent as an unseen yet vital player in an evening's event, just as you might dab perfume on yourself. Do you wish to evoke a light ambience? Or something more sultry? Scent may be used to achieve either effect, but the key is to do it with subtlety. Entering a room with a candle placed centre stage is to bash guests over the head with your intention. Much more powerful is to place it or a diffuser to one side, perhaps even on an upper landing if you have more than one floor, so that the fragrance floats softly around, adding imperceptible atmosphere rather than anything too overt. •

'Entering a room with a candle placed centre stage is to bash guests over the head with your intention. Much more powerful is to place it to one side, so that the fragrance floats softly around, adding imperceptible atmosphere rather than anything too overt.'

PEACE AND QUIET:
THE SOUND
OF SILENCE

According to Patrick Shen, director of the documentary *In Pursuit of Silence:* 'Noise causes us to be reactive whereas silence inspires proactiveness. In silence we are better equipped to reflect and simply think. Research shows that silence can improve brain function and help cultivate more meaningful and healthier lives. Silence restores us.' So what can be done to engender more of this at home?

• **Investigate Quiet Mark appliances.** In 2012, Poppy Szkiler founded Quiet Mark, an international approval award programme to encourage companies worldwide to prioritise noise reduction when designing everyday appliances and tools, from washing machines and dishwashers, to lawnmowers and electric drills. It also offers consumers a convenient checklist of top-performing equipment that does its work well, but quietly. And she has form in this area: in 1959 her grandfather founded the Noise Abatement Society in the UK, a charitable organisation currently run by her mother.

• **Deliberate listening.** Have you ever paused long enough *before* reaching for a remote control to stop and really listen to what surrounds you? For sure, behind any 'noise' over which you have little control you will hear something else, from the pulsing of blood through your temples to perhaps a clock ticking, distant music, birdsong and other sounds. Perhaps, if you stopped you might actually notice and appreciate the natural soundscape of your home, whatever it might be composed of? The point being, when you choose to add to it, you do so deliberately, consciously and mindfully, not simply to obscure or fill. After all, even if you installed double or triple glazing to block out external noise, you must still take responsibility for the soundtrack of your interior.

• **The power of birdsong.** According to scientists at the University of Surrey, of all the natural sounds bird calls were those most often cited as helping people to recover from stress, allowing them to restore and refocus their attention. So if all else fails, pop on a CD of birdsong, and feel the irritations fade away.

• **And if you're building new.** Then you might want to consider using Rockwool Sound Insulation. Saving more energy than is used to produce it, its high-density stone fibres trap sound waves and dampen vibrations. Another innovation is the Armourcoat Acoustic Plaster System that offers a smooth mineral surface and stands out for being free of VOCs and containing a high percentage of recycled materials. Finally, you could ensure the complete integrity of bedrooms by installing a soundproofing door, while making sure that smoke alarms are always still audible.

TOUCH:
THE IMPORTANCE
OF QUALITY
HARDWARE

Previously our focus has been on the soft materials that we can surround ourselves with, or the reassuring tactility of humble textures for furniture and flooring, but from door handles to knives, if these essential components of the home are too small, uncomfortable, slippery or inadequate, they will be a daily discomfort or annoyance, like a favourite shoe that always chafes. But once you find designs that feel really good in the hand (the equivalent of a squishy inner sole for that shoe), you'll wonder how you ever lived without them.

• **Door knobs and handles.** Such hardware can seem expensive on the face of it, but when you consider the cost over a lifetime of use, as these are extremely unlikely to fail or break, they quickly pay for themselves in the pleasure they bring. Also, in most cases they're straightforward enough to fit yourself, so replacing them can be a gradual upgrade project, one pair at a time, as your budget permits.

• **Light switches and sockets.** Many a lovely room has been ruined with an ugly switch.

And again, considering that you are likely to touch these every single day, it's worth paying a little extra for something more attractive than the basic white plastic options. My personal preference is for a screwless, white powder-coated metal socket or switch, the sort with a slim cover that clips over the top of a screwed-in base plate. It ensures a completely seamless look. They're also great when decorating as you simply flip off the top cover, cut in your paint or wallpaper around the base plate, then clip the cover back on for a perfect edge. They're available in many different colours and finishes, so if you're setting one into a bedhead or against a coloured wall, it can be fun to vary the treatment, perhaps stainless steel or another metal. Custom-colouring is a step too far though (as well as expensive) and not necessarily helpful as a degree of contrast makes it easier to find a switch in the dark.

• **Taps and shower heads.** Some taps can be phenomenally expensive and it's hard to understand why until we consider that the components within them may well be twisted on and off several times a day, and on cheaper models the threads soon wear, causing drips, or stiffness in use. Regardless, sometimes it's definitely a case of designer overcomplication with levers that are impossible to use with soapy fingers. Nevertheless, it makes sense to spend a little more on your kitchen tap, and if you have room under the sink for the necessary kit, then a boiling-water tap means you can ditch your kettle (creating even more space on your countertop!). And mixer taps are always sensible in bathrooms to help prevent being scalded by hot water, though their style is a matter of taste. I like classic cross-head taps, each clearly marked 'hot' or 'cold'!

• **Cutlery.** When it comes to eating, keep cutlery as simple as your crockery, with a set that has a pleasant heft in the hand and feels comfortable to use. Skip fiddly forks, overly teeny teaspoons or anything that seems too light or flimsy. But do ensure that you purchase a set that includes proper deep soup spoons as these make stews, hotpots and soups so much more enjoyable to noisily slurp. •

CURATION AND CONTAINMENT: THE ART OF DISPLAY

If your carefully curated possessions are not well contained and beautifully displayed, they can end up looking more trashy than treasured. Art that's hung without thought can become distracting, and unconsidered collections of anything can be overwhelming. And while it's helpful to designate key spots for display, it's also good to have fun by occasionally placing things in more unconventional places to give you a lift when you least expect it. And remember, when you invite anything new inside, whether painting or pot, use it as a chance to swap other items around, rather than just slotting it in alongside your existing things. It's amazing how different this can make a room feel.

• **Alignment of art.** In Chapter 2, I talked about alignment and the need to determine a consistent hanging line for the tops of the frames of any large artworks. That said, I once visited a home in which about ten different-sized paintings were aligned horizontally using their bottom edges as the guide and the whole collection was positioned such that it sat just above the top of a wide modern sofa. The jiggledly nature of the top of the paintings kept the overall impression loose, while the dead-straight line at the bottom worked perfectly with the homeowner's contemporary aesthetic – it added the necessary level of consistency to balance the differing natures of both the picture frames and the subject matter.

• **Collages of art.** Creating a gallery wall packed with art prompts a pause to admire works as a collection, as well as encouraging the search for links between the pieces. If all the artwork has been collected from the heart, then it's fascinating to see what they can reveal, something not usually perceptible unless they're grouped together. But there's no set way to compose a collage, except to lay everything out on the floor first to ensure they'll all fit together; keep the gaps between all pieces roughly the same and add to each side in turn so the arrangement stays balanced. You might start by taking any two pieces and place these roughly centred to the allocated space such that they 'talk' to each other but are not strictly aligned: one stepped slightly above the other, for example, and with the upper one set slightly higher than eye level. Then simply expand outwards. Let what best fits the spaces created be your guide, but allow for the fact that a few frames may need to be updated as collages work best if no more than four different frame finishes are used in total – for instance, silver, oak, black and white – and any mount colours limited

to no more than two (white as a default, plus one other), remembering, of course, that all shades and materials must always reflect your personal palette! Once you've mapped it all out on the floor, you can see if anything needs to be re-sized or re-framed, and then get hanging. Take your time to measure where the hook needs to be. (Hold the picture by its wire, or hanger, with one finger backwards against the wall, mark the centre point of the top of the frame on the wall, then simply measure the depth below that mark to where you're holding it. This is where the indent of your picture hook needs to be. Note: when holding a picture to measure it's important that you let its full weight naturally pull against the hanging string or wire, otherwise your picture will end up lower than anticipated.) Stick to using simple classic brass picture hooks (unless a picture is very heavy), and don't worry if you need to make adjustments – any holes will likely be hidden. Most of all, don't overthink it. Just start and keep going!

• **Display shelves.** Perfect for open display of a mix of things you love – from postcards, pebbles and driftwood, to beautiful book covers, decorative matchboxes or other ornaments and ephemera. They work best when set within alcoves, whether naturally occurring by virtue of the architecture of a room or created as a recess between two cupboards. But what's particularly good about this form of display is the ease with which it can be updated. If you have a lot of different pieces, rotate them in turn rather than trying to have everything out at once. Besides, things left perpetually the same rapidly become unnoticed.

• **Integrated bookcases.** Like display shelves, built-in bookcases can be the most fabulous way to exhibit your things as they can accommodate so much more than just books. Intersperse your volumes with objects and art to create multi-media mood boards of the things that inspire and sustain you. This could neatly and almost imperceptibly take over an entire wall if it stretched from floor to ceiling and was boxed in all around (being mindful of any existing details like skirtings and picture rails). Paint it the same shade as the surrounding walls and it'll have the effect of being an extension of the wall, rather than an obtrusive piece of furniture.

• **Unexpected placements.** What do you see when you wake up? When you stand in the shower? What's at the bottom of the stairs, or at the top? We probably look at these areas more frequently than many other spaces and yet they are often left bare. Enliven them with anything from a single picture to a small floating display shelf on to which one object of significance has been placed.

• **Collections of things.** Whatever it is that you have an urge to collect, spend a little time considering the allure. Perhaps it's habitual rather than purposeful, or an assumed love indulged by gifts from others. Regardless, coming up with a way to attractively present such objects will not only honour them appropriately, but also provide boundaries to curtail unnecessary additions. For pottery, coloured glass, porcelain, vintage clothing, or anything else that's robustly 3D, grouping them together highlights the extent of a collection. For printed matter, perhaps one shelving system could be dedicated to a library of first editions, or a set of matching albums selected for a football card collection. Keeping such things relatively compact also encourages regular review.

• **A further note on albums.** It can be a thing of great joy to have all your best photographs, magazine cuttings, old theatre programmes or other prized matter carefully catalogued in matching albums, so spend time choosing the album! Will it stand the test of time? Will it be big enough to accommodate all possible sizes of whatever you're collecting? Is the spine capable of withstanding pages heavy with glued-in memorabilia? Of course, you don't need to be an absolute slave to the impulse for co-ordination, but let's not deny the sheer bliss that is a matching set of scrapbooks. Look to the archives of such revered aesthetes as British interior designer David Hicks if you need a little inspiration.

• **Family portraits.** Regardless of any mixed feelings you might have about your heritage, because we all grow from our roots arranging a display of family photos can be a profoundly grounding exercise. Stairs ascending to upper floors are perfect for such a display as there is a natural sense of chronology, and of moving from the public to the private. Groupings here should be dictated by the relationships between those pictured, hence not all in a straight line but something more free-flowing and organic. A good tip, too, is to scan the photos into a computer as you go, so you not only have

a permanent record of them, but it will be a lot easier to get them printed at different sizes to suit chosen frames, to crop images or convert them to black and white as required, especially as you can do all of this online. Most photographs of people look better in monochrome, and if you're mixing in older photos, it'll help to tie them all together. Keep a few in colour, though, to add rhythm and catch the eye.

• **Planters.** The natural benefits of plants was covered in Chapter 3, but it's unlikely that terracotta plastic is one of your palette choices! Always invest in decent planters to conceal such basic containers (regardless, when plants need to be repotted, transfer to real terracotta or natural clay as these are more breathable for the roots). For your decorative planters, aim for coherence of form, such as consistently cylindrical rather than tapered, but vary the finish and surface treatment. Baskets can make great containers too; just remember to add a draining dish. And always buy larger than you need to offset plant growth, otherwise you'll limit their use. And don't forget hanging baskets – a wonderful way to keep windowsills clear and introduce greenery at a higher level, with many variations on macramé! •

FORGOTTEN ROOMS

Libraries, larders and linen closets: there is something deeply comforting about seeing a cupboard full of fresh food, clean towels or rows of books waiting to be read, so much so that you can even buy wallpaper that replicates the look of a wall lined with books. Better, though, if you have the space to hang the paper, to indulge in the real thing. And what of the morning room, a space of yore primarily for the ladies in which tea would be taken and correspondence completed. Such a romantic notion! And yet there's something to take away from all of these for the modern home, and rest assured, you do not need whole rooms to feel the joy. Here is my cheat's guide:

LIBRARIES

Forget at once grandiose visions of an entire room groaning with heavily book-bedecked walls and think instead of where you might be able to sneak in shelving the depth of a paperback. Good spaces for sneaky library-ettes include under built-in seating in bay windows, or in a small downstairs loo, especially if taken wall to wall above an enclosed cistern, which often automatically creates a natural shelf. And if your home is arranged over more than one floor, sometimes there's enough depth in the turn of a landing to accommodate a shallow set of shelves – make them built in and floating rather than free-standing, though, to keep them off the floor.

LINEN CLOSETS

Set within an alcove, or squeezed behind a door swing, a linen closet needs to be just capacious enough to store clean towels and bedsheets because crisply folded stacks of linen are always a glory to behold. Open shelving works well to keep things nicely aired, but be careful if sited deep within a bathroom, as condensation might become an issue. Be inventive, too: one of the prettiest linen cupboards I've ever seen was a vintage glass-fronted bookcase, decorated inside with wallpaper and placed in an ample hallway. It worked because it was a beautiful unit in its own right.

LARDERS

With the rise of big fridges, a walk-in food cupboard has become almost obsolete, but as the desire to know exactly what's in our food grows, so too a continued drive for more home cooking, and no doubt in turn the pleasures of the larder will be revisited. Historically a small room located on an outside, north-facing wall next to the kitchen, a larder might also have been in a well-ventilated basement, but essentially anywhere that could be kept cool with access to fresh air. Today, deluxe kitchen designs often incorporate tall, pull-out, double-sided racked units for the storage of dried and tinned foodstuffs, but a corner cupboard with a rotary shelf will do the job just as well. Store all tins together, all baking ingredients, and so on, so that you can see at a glance what you have to prevent unnecessary multiples or the stockpiling of seldom-used ingredients. If you have room, a feature cabinet – a glorious, lacquered Chinese armoire, for example – could make a striking store-cupboard and a more original talking point than a coloured fridge. Place it against an external wall, certainly away from the oven or any other heat source, and make sure it's vented to let air blow through.

MORNING ROOMS

The original concept here was a room that benefited from the morning sun, providing a pleasant spot for convivial gatherings that did not require the formality of the front room – the equivalent of a coffee in the kitchen today. If you have the space to devote an entire room to nothing more than a writing desk, a pair of chaise longues and a backgammon set, you would indeed be living in the lap of luxury, yet the most important thing would be its aspect. To benefit from the first rays of light, it must face east. But if the renaissance of this romantic idyll is somewhat beyond current capacity, the easiest way to recreate it would be to designate any east-facing spot as the perfect location for a small reading chair. •

DIRECT

DESIGNING FOR

MENTAL HEALTH

Because many of us will likely find ourselves touched in some way by mental-health problems, such as anxiety, dementia or depression, whether directly or by association, it feels appropriate to conclude this chapter with ten pragmatic steps that could be put into play to help support yourself, friends or family, in addition to seeking professional help. All of these are already part and parcel of the *happy inside* way, so grouping them together also serves as a handy summary of key aspects of the philosophy.

1. CLEAR THE CLUTTER

Mess causes stress. When your mind is crowded or confused, the last thing you need is to see this replicated in your surroundings, and yet the two often go hand in hand. But a good throwing-away session can be incredibly therapeutic.

2. KEEP IT WHITE

The exercise of whiting out your walls before beginning decoration serves an additional purpose for someone struggling with mental-health issues. Beyond conveying a feeling of brightness and lightness, it can also be viewed as a metaphor for yourself: a blank canvas to be gradually filled in as you gently rediscover who you want to be.

3. BUT ADD A DOSE OF COLOUR

Colour is energising. Harness this within your white backdrop with a few carefully chosen soft accessories, cushions or throws in a favourite shade, and use them to make your sofa your safe place. They are a reminder that the joy is in there somewhere.

4. NATURAL LIGHT

When someone is feeling locked inside their mind, an ability to look outwards and see that the world is still in motion is reassuring if not essential. Thus clear away fussy window treatments or external planting that might block views, keep glazing clean and make it a given that you will open drapes or roll up blinds to greet the day every morning, whatever the weather – daylight triggers the production of serotonin, the body's natural happy-maker.

5. BRING NATURE INDOORS

If you don't have a garden or a view of one, then bring greenery indoors with house plants. They encourage a sense of perspective and positivity by giving you something to nurture beyond yourself, as well as naturally cleaning indoor air.

6. ENCOURAGE FLOW

For those with dementia, clear lines of sight are incredibly important. Being able to see both a front and a back door (glazed doors being preferable, as then you can also see who's outside), and knowing exactly where the bathroom is, gives a sense of security. And we can all benefit from avoiding pointy corners and trip hazards – aim for

at least a 30 per cent difference in shade between walls and floor to clarify where floors start and walls finish.

7. INTRODUCE POSITIVE IMAGERY

Landscapes or photographs of loved ones can remind you of places and people that you care about. Hang such a picture that uplifts you somewhere you can see it as soon as you come home.

8. GO ANALOGUE

Exercise by walking in nature. Choose paper over the digital for reading. And disconnect from all other unnecessary tech (do you really need to talk to a machine to activate the radio?). Prioritise real connections with people instead.

9. INVEST IN THE BEDROOM

How you finish your days is as important as how you start them and what you do in between. A good mattress and nice sheets will pay dividends in improved sleep, as not getting enough quality rest undermines every bodily and cognitive function.

10. APPEAL TO YOUR SENSES

Finally, choose to surround yourself with textures to thrill, scents to rouse and sounds that soothe. Even if you live alone, make it a habit to lay the table. Honour thyself by exercising, cooking and eating well, and keep the faith that, day by day, you will begin to feel better. •

ACCEPTANCE

'WHEN I LET GO OF WHAT I AM,
I BECOME WHAT I MIGHT BE.
WHEN I LET GO OF WHAT I HAVE,
I RECEIVE WHAT I NEED.'

LAO-TZU
ANCIENT CHINESE PHILOSOPHER (BORN 601 BC)
AUTHOR OF THE TAO TE CHING

With room to breathe and room to think, we can live a more meaningful life. And we now know that this type of 'room' is not necessarily physical space; rather, it is the absence of all that is extraneous alongside the sweet feeling of liberation that comes with realising that you have enough, and that you are enough, just as you are. To put it another way, that you can become spacious in yourself as your home becomes your place to be fearless, completely at ease and absolutely splendid in your imperfections and obsessions.

But, as we journey along this path, we must also commit to not waiting for everything to be 'perfect' before we enjoy it – not delaying simple suppers with friends or chats over tea because the house is too messy, or not quite how we want it yet. Don't be too precious: that rug with the frayed edges, the drawing sticky-taped to the wall, the sun-faded edges of velvet curtains – these are the signs that a home is authentic, and they are to be embraced.

And, this concluding chapter is called 'acceptance' because we must also let go of any expectation that our home will ever be complete. Change is inevitable and the more flexible you can be to adapt to it, the healthier you will become – as the tastes and passions of each member of your household change, so too must your home evolve. Ultimately, the effort of the endeavour is worth more than the final product as the *happy inside* habits are intended to sustain the whole self – mind, body and spirit.

Some of you will have come to this with a clear understanding already of what fires your soul; for others this will be the catalyst towards attaining that insight. It's all good. The important thing is to keep going. However, to move forwards we must also leave things behind.

We must have a desire to wake up and listen to those internal narratives that push us where we do not want to go. But, bearing honest witness to our journey and thereby owning our personal stories is the only way to be truly 'at home' with ourselves, and thus able to further enrich our lives with the creation of a space that fulfils our real needs and expresses our true character.

My deepest hope, though, is that the repercussions of this journey will ripple out far beyond your personal threshold. That as you become more balanced and contented, instead of reacting in times of stress, you are able to approach life with a more considered and thoughtful outlook. We can only ever gain mastery over ourselves as individuals, but the impact of that can be far-reaching. And it is my sincere opinion that taking charge of the space in which you live is a very good place to start. Right here and now you have within your grasp everything that you need. So onwards and upwards, my friends; it is the only way to go! I'll leave you then with a few life lessons I've compiled over the years, some based on my own experience, others gleaned from those I respect and admire. I hope they resonate with you too. •

'We can only ever gain mastery over ourselves as individuals, but the impact of that can be far-reaching. And it is my sincere opinion that taking charge of the space in which you live is a very good place to start.'

MY RULES FOR LIFE

TO DO ANYTHING WELL, YOU MUST FIRST CARE. PASSIONATELY.
AND BE ENTHUSIASTIC.

BE HUNGRY. STAY HUNGRY.

BE PROACTIVE.

DO MORE THAN YOUR JOB DESCRIPTION.

IN FACT, CREATE YOUR OWN JOB.

UNDERSTAND THAT RECEIVING CRITICISM IS THE QUICKEST WAY TO
IMPROVE. AND THAT SOMETIMES BEING FIRED, OR NOT GETTING
WHAT YOU WANT, IS ABSOLUTELY THE BEST THING THAT
COULD EVER HAPPEN TO YOU.

BE A TEAM PLAYER.

GIVE CREDIT WHERE CREDIT IS DUE;
'WE' IS ALWAYS STRONGER THAN 'I'.

BUT IF SOMETHING GOES WRONG,
TAKE RESPONSIBILITY; STAND UP AND BE COUNTED.

LOVE YOUR LIFE OUTSIDE WORK – IT'S THE ONLY WAY TO STAY SANE,
AND THIS IS MORE IMPORTANT THE HIGHER UP YOU GO.

KNOW YOUR PHYSICAL LIMITS, BUT NEVER STOP DREAMING.
NEVER MOCK ANOTHER PERSON'S DREAMS.

YOUR MIND IS YOUR MOST POWERFUL ALLY;
DO NOT POLLUTE IT WITH NEGATIVITY.

KEEP AWAY FROM TOXIC PEOPLE. YOU OWE THEM NOTHING.

IF YOU BELIEVE YOU CAN DO SOMETHING,
YOU'VE ALREADY DONE THE HARD PART.

BE CURIOUS. STAY CURIOUS.

RULES ARE OVERRATED BUT RESPECT IS EVERYTHING.

WHAT YOU DO EVERY DAY MATTERS MORE
THAN WHAT YOU DO ONCE IN A WHILE.

PRACTICE MAKES PERMANENT.

PLAY FOR WIN/WIN SCENARIOS.

DON'T ASK PERMISSION TO SUCCEED, JUST GET ON WITH IT.

IF SOMETHING HASN'T BEEN DONE BEFORE,
IT DOESN'T MEAN IT'S NOT POSSIBLE.

BE PREPARED TO WORK HARD, OVER AND ABOVE EXPECTATIONS.
HOWEVER, NO ONE WRITES 'I WISH I SPENT
MORE TIME AT THE OFFICE' ON THEIR TOMBSTONE.

NEVER CHEAT.

DON'T GOSSIP.

HAVE A MORAL CODE.

HOLD ON TO YOUR INTEGRITY AT ALL COSTS.

ENJOY THE RIDE.

THE AIM IS TO SCREECH TO A HALT WHEN YOU FINALLY GET TO THOSE
PEARLY GATES AND SAY, 'WOW, WHAT A RIDE!'
NOT 'OOPS, I FORGOT SOMETHING.'

ACKNOWLEDGEMENTS

There is a saying that it takes a village to raise a child, well it takes a similarly connected team to create a book, and I'm grateful that mine were among the best, and such a pleasure to work with. For sure, the words are all mine, but it took a supremely gifted designer, Alex Hunting, to lay them out in a way that makes them easy to read, and digestible in chunks. It took a wonderful illustrator, Nicola Rew, to create images that convey the joy of the *happy inside* journey; and a very talented photographer, Emma Harris, to capture the right fragments of my home in explanation of the palette. To you all, I am enormously indebted. And of course, none of this would have come to pass, were it not for a great publishing director, whose personal enthusiasm for my philosophy got it off the ground in the first place, and whose professionalism and patience kept us all on track – thank you Lizzy Gray! Not to forget the dedicated editing and diligent proofreading which subsequently ensured my manuscript was the best it could be: thank you accordingly to Celia Palazzo, Kate Parker and Tamsin English for caring so much about everything from hyphens to headlines. Also, my family and friends who so stoically put up with me droning on about every aspect of this project for the many months from first draft to final cover – without your unwavering support, it could not be what it is. Likewise, a big hug to Elizabeth Cairns for her warmth and positivity when I needed it most. Sophie Robinson for introducing her to me in the first place, alongside her podcast partner in crime, Kate Watson-Smythe, for being early cheerleaders for this endeavour. A hearty shout out to my original core team and colleagues at *ELLE Decoration*, the launch pad and practice ground for so much of my thinking. You're all doing brilliantly on new paths now, and you all contributed to this book in so many ways, whether you realise it or not. Finally, a heartfelt double dose of gratitude to my agent, Sophie Laurimore, who believed in this book and understood what I wanted it to be from the very start. In short, it's amazing to have finally got it out there, but it was all the better along the way for every single one of you.